FRED CORCORAN

THE MAN WHO SOLD
THE WORLD ON GOLF

JUDY CORCORAN

Published by Gray Productions
New York, New York

Published by Gray Productions
212-315-2449
JudyCorc@aol.com
www.FredCorcoran.com

This book is available at www.FredCorcoran.com.

ISBN 978-0-578-04907-6

Cover and book design by Judy Corcoran
Cover illustration by Frank Becerra, 1977
Printed in January 2010

To Fred, my father, who I wish I had known now
rather than when I was a teenager.

And to Dennis Clawson who, with a love of
history, ancestry and me, encouraged me
every step of the way.

Judy

A SPECIAL THANKS TO MOLLY KAWACHI, Jane Aderhold, Dave Anderson, Frank Becerra, Jr., Susan Belair, Carol Corcoran, Freddie Corcoran, Jane Costa, Lisa Cribari, Stephen Cribari, Michael Dann, Martin Davis, Jeanne Fico, John Garrity, Peter Gogolak, Liz Khan, Tom Kochan, Renée Martin, Bob Mead, Peggy Mead, Bill Morely, Bill O'Hara, Dermod Sullivan, Burch Riber, J. Richard Ryan, Rick Schwab, Nick Seitz, Tom Stanton, Peter Thall, Jean Ufer, Ken Venturi, and the other Tiger.

AND A HUGE THANK YOU TO GREG WALKER, who came along to find my missing hyphens, eject my extra commas, and help me "play the course" specific to editing golf-related copy.

INTRODUCTION

FRED CORCORAN SOLD THE WORLD ON GOLF. HE WAS A MAN WITH A PASSION for the game, an encyclopedic mind, an ear for a punch line, an eye for a headline, and a keen sense of marketing long before the business schools named the tools. As one of golf's first businessmen, he was inducted into the World Golf Hall of Fame in 1975, some thirty years after he first proposed it.

Fred's story about the business of golf and his devotion to it spans sixty years, from around 1913 when golf was in its infancy in this country until 1977, when he left it in the hands of the corporations. This book is the story of how Fred, "not single-handedly, mind you," as he would say, put golf on the map and turned it from a minor curiosity to a major business that today delivers billions of dollars in endorsements, tournaments and associations.

I don't know how old I was when I realized my father was famous. "He's famous in golf and sports," I'd tell my friends when they'd ask why there was a limousine parked in our driveway or why we were flying to Hawaii just for the weekend. I knew something was up when I was about ten and we skipped school for two weeks to go meet the King of Morocco.

As a child, I just thought everyone had a fake uncle named Sam, whose last name was Snead, and one named Ted, whose last name was Williams. But I really knew my father was important when we went to Disneyland in 1960, and we were met by a woman in a uniform who looked like a stewardess. She took us around the park and cut in the front of the lines, letting us go on the rides without a wait. It seemed General Dynamics had just put in their Nautilus submarine ride and my father knew someone at General Dynamics. Actually, he always knew somebody everywhere we went.

"Get me anyone," Fred once said to a telephone operator. I heard him tell the story a million times, and his love affair with the telephone was real and documented.

"AT&T should erect a monument to Fred Corcoran. He's trained more telephone operators than Ma Bell," Bing Crosby wrote in Fred's book *Unplayable Lies*. Bing, the famous "White Christmas" crooner, and Fred went back to 1937, when Bing had a little golf tournament and Fred worked for the PGA Tour.

While Fred started out as an impoverished caddie, he found many measures of success, earning an international reputation as "Mr. Golf." By the time I was born in the early 1950s, he was at the height of his career, having made a lot of money with some high-profile clients. It was then that I think he embarked on his true calling in life. "He goes around the world and teaches other countries how to put on golf tournaments," I would tell the kids. Fred liked to say that his claim to fame was having three-putted in forty-eight countries. But it was actually a lot more than that.

Early on, Fred befriended the press, who had enormous respect for him as an agent, publicity man, and storyteller. Unique to Fred, he was a sportswriter's best source, always able to come up with a fresh angle, historic comparison, or hypothetical argument for deadline-driven writers. But Fred also had some heart-wrenching breaks and an Irish temper, all part of a legendary life story that generated some entertaining moments and many original ideas, while it laid the foundation for the business of golf.

In his words, Fred "committed autobiography" in 1963, some fourteen years before he passed away. He wrote *Unplayable Lies* with Bud Harvey, a delightful golf writer with a rich vocabulary, who also played the piano and sang in a barbershop quartet. I remember vividly the summer he spent at our house, taking notes that my mother typed as my father told his stories into a tape recorder that only I could thread properly.

Over the years, a few people suggested I re-write or re-publish *Unplayable Lies,* which is now out of print. After reading it again, I longed for a sense of chronology, which wasn't how Fred wrote it. When Fred told stories, he jumped around. A story about Ted Williams would remind him of one about Walter Hagen, which would remind him of Tony Lema, and so on.

So I set out to tell Fred's story as it happened, and through the process, I saw more clearly just how much he accomplished and what a rock star of golf he was. While working on the new book, following his career year by year, I kept thinking that once I finished one year, I'd a catch a break. But then that next year was just as full of stories, people and events as the one I had just finished writing about. He just kept going and going.

Along with using *Unplayable Lies*, I spent many hours reading other golf books, downloading newspaper and magazine articles, looking at photos on eBay, watching videos, interviewing people who knew Fred, and sorting through my mother's scrapbooks and Fred's letters to her. From all this, I connected a dot or two, added some context, and wrote some dialogue, but I tried to remain true to his original story, which was interesting, impactful and important to golf—and me.

Judy Corcoran

Photo Gallery

Most of these photos appeared in *Unplayable Lies*.
Others are in the family's collection.
Credit is given where credit is known.

Jack Sharkey, Lefty Gomez, Fred and Craig Wood in 1943

Fred in his American Red Cross uniform

Julian P. Graham photograph

Fred Corcoran with Bob Hope and Jimmy Demaret (sitting)

Craig Wood, Stan "The Man" Musial, and Fred

Fred and Babe Didrikson Zaharias, signing a deal

Jimmy Demaret, Bing Crosby and Nancy Allison in 1944

"I can beat Ruth anywhere, anytime," Ty Cobb, 1939

Bob Hope and Bing Crosby challenge each other in 1941

Walter Hagen and Fred — "Don't hurry, never worry."

Hagen (standing, far left) as Captain, Ed Dudley, Henry Picard, Gene Sarazen, Sam Snead, Horton Smith, Fred Corcoran as manager, Byron Nelson (sitting, far left), Tony Manero, Ralph Guldahl, Denny Shute, Johnny Revolta. The 1937 Ryder Cup Team in Southport, England—the first U.S. team to win on foreign soil

Bob Harlow and Fred at Pinehurst, 1941

Horton Smith, Bob Jones and Fred at the Masters in 1937

Joe Louis and Fred

Sam, receiving his winnings in nickels,
courtesy of Fred, in 1937

Peggy and Judy Corcoran with Dick Mayer,
1957 U.S. Open champion

Toney Penna, Fred, Byron Nelson and Jimmy Demaret

Walter Winchell, who invented the gossip column,
Fred and Alice Bauer in 1950

Fred and Nancy's wedding, April 1, 1951, L-R: Dana Corcoran,
Nancy, Fred, John Corcoran, Wanda Allison (Nancy's mother),
Moe Berg, Peggy Brophy, Joe Walsh and Lee Eastman

Bill, Fred, Sam and John Corcoran

Ted Williams in 1950,
after his first 18 holes of golf

Bill Mark photograph

Bob Drum (left) and Charlie Bartlett (right) present Fred with
U.S. Golf Writer's Award in 1960

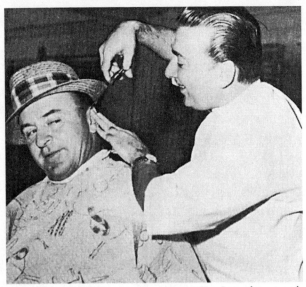

Jim Leo photograph

Sam Snead getting a hair cut at the Boca Raton Club
in 1964, while the Beatles appeared on *The Ed Sullivan Show*

Wide World photograph

Jim Thorpe, considered the greatest athlete of the first half
of the 20th century, Fred, and Ted Williams

Bill Mark photograph

With Ben Hogan — the "Greatest"

Bill Mark photograph

With Winnie and Arnold Palmer in 1960

Bill Mark photograph

With great friend, Gene Sarazen, the Country Squire

With Red Smith of *The New York Times,* toasting to
Champagne Tony Lema at an impromptu Corcoran party

The Corcoran Brothers — Joe, Billy, John and Fred

Fred—bringing golf to Japan in 1957

Lord Calvert Whiskey's
Man of Distinction from
Cosmopolitan magazine
in 1951

Judy Corcoran, Fred and Uncle Sam in 1963

Fred with Humphrey Bogart

Sam Snead with Valerie and Ben Hogan
on the way to the Canada Cup in 1956

Fred with Ed Sullivan and Roberto De Vicenzo

Wide World photograph

Fred with Edward, the Duke of Windsor, and Tony Lema

With New York Giants Kicker Peter Gogolak

Tony Lema, right after he won the British Open in 1964,
saying, "You didn't think I could do it."

With Seve Ballesteros at the World Cup in 1976

Nancy and Fred at his induction to the
World Golf Hall of Fame in Pinehurst, 1975

World Cup Photos:
Jack and Arnie in Hawaii, 1964
David Graham and Bruce Devlin in Australia, 1970
Jack Nicklaus and Lee Trevino in Florida, 1971
Manuel Pinero and Seve Ballesteros in California, 1976

Johnny Miller, Howard Clark (IGA) and Jack Nicklaus
at the 1973 World Cup in Marbella, Spain

South Africans Harold Henning and Gary Player with
Howard Clark at the 1965 World Cup in Madrid

Johnny Miller, being swarmed by crowd,
at the 1975 World Cup in Bangkok, Thailand

Fred getting to the course in Bangkok

Jack Nicklaus putts out as
the Duke of Windsor looks
on at the Canada Cup in
Paris, 1963

Tony Jacklin tees off for
England at the 1970
World Cup

Mr. Golf with the International Golf Association's
World Cup and International Trophy

"What doth it profit a man if he gain the whole world—and three-putt the 18th green?"

Fred Corcoran
Unplayable Lies

CHAPTER 1

LIKE MANY WHO PLANTED THE SEEDS OF MODERN GOLF IN AMERICA, Fred Corcoran started as a caddie. Born to a poor Irish family near Boston, with six boys spaced two years apart, Fred got swept up in the excitement around the historic 1913 match where Francis Ouimet, a 17-year-old school boy from down the street, beat the established British golfers, Harry Vardon and Ted Ray. They were the Woods and Mickelson or the Palmer and Nicklaus of their day, and much has been written about this match. In fact, Disney made a movie about it: *The Greatest Game Ever Played*.

As you can imagine, the match was big news that year in Belmont, Massachusetts, especially since Ouimet's caddie was ten-year-old Eddie Lowery, one of the local kids. Fred was only eight that year, too young to caddie, but he was already waiting around the yard.

As the story goes, Ouimet's mother gave an interview to the local press, saying that caddying had opened all the right doors for her son Francis, and that caddying was an admirable alternative to hanging around pool rooms. When Winifred, Fred's mother, read that, she jumped on the idea.

"Look what caddying did for that Ouimet boy," she said, as she struggled to get breakfast ready for her brood of young boys. "You could do worse than to try it yourself."

The Corcorans had recently moved from Cambridge to Arlington, Massachusetts, and lived in a shabby house adjacent to the Belmont Country Club. Like many Irish families right after the turn of the century, they struggled to get by.

Seeing signs posted saying, "No Irish Need Apply," Fred's father Sam had all but given up looking for honest work, using this discrimination to his advantage. "I won't work for anyone who won't have me," he added, displaying pride that was lost on all but the young boys.

Sam never let the world trap him into regular employment. There were a couple of times when he signed up for a starting time on a payroll, but never reached the first tee. He finally said to hell with it.

Sam's real name was Michael, but it, like the few paychecks he did manage to earn, got lost somewhere on the way home. He would come home with stories, and he often arrived with excuses, and occasionally, he toted a bottle of Scotch, but bringing home the groceries was not his thing. On a good day, Fred and his brothers ate corn flakes, whether it was for breakfast or dinner. Lunch was often not in the running.

Sam was often called a "seanachie." In Ireland, in the days of old, a seanachie was a strolling historic storyteller. The legends and lore of the Irish people were handed down from generation to generation by the seanachies who drifted around the country, paying their way with tales. They had a very special status in Ireland. There was always a bite to eat and a warm spot by the fire for them. Like Sam, Fred had a gift for telling a story. But not only could Fred deliver an entertaining tale with excitement and humor, he also had a knack for finding the angle that noted some irony or uniqueness that made the tale even more memorable.

By the spring of 1914, Fred's mother pointed her sons in the direction of the Belmont golf course. She urged Frank, the oldest, to become a caddie, but Frank was not much of a trailblazer, so she turned to Fred. By now, he had reached the exalted age of nine, and he was eager and ready to set his feet down on the fairway. At one time, there were five Corcoran caddies in the pen at Belmont—Frank, Fred, George, Joe and John. Billy, the youngest, was still at home, studying the rules and waiting for his muscles to arrive. But on very hot days, Fred put him to work as well, selling sodas on the golf course while Fred told stories as he passed out the bottles or made change.

Fred became a regular at the course, slinging bags that were as tall as he over his shoulder, chumming up to the best players at the club, and studying the game every chance he got. Not being a shy guy, Fred quickly sought out Ouimet and introduced himself, offering his caddie and ball-shagging services. Soon, he was caddying for Ouimet, who was the first player ever to give Fred a dollar.

"I went to get him change," Fred said, "but Ouimet smiled and said, 'You keep it all. You're a fine caddie.'"

Most people agree that tournament golf in America began with Francis Ouimet and that 1913 match. In a thrilling finish, Ouimet became the first American-born winner of the United States Open Championship. But Ouimet's victory at The Country Club did more than just thrust him into the national spotlight. It brought golf out from behind the privileged walls, away from its British ancestry and Scottish dunes, and put it on American soil with a sense of ownership. Up until this time, only the very wealthy in America played golf. There were no professional golfers and most caddies were taught not to swing a club. That's why Ouimet's victory struck such a chord with the young boys who lived near the courses around Boston. The victory gave them a local hero. If Francis Ouimet could play golf and become a celebrity, so could any one of them.

Fred took the course like a bug in a grass rug and quickly became a first-rate caddie, able to judge distance within a few feet and to explain the finer points of the course. His first big assignment came in 1916 at the age of 11. That year, the USGA Women's Amateur Championship was played at Belmont and he caddied for Alexa Stirling, who won it.

That was also the year that Annie Oakley, the famous buckskin gunslinger, gave an exhibition of sharpshooting at Belmont and asked Fred to help set the traps for her. After shattering a few clay plates, Fred had an idea. "How about I toss golf balls into the air and you shoot them instead of clay plates."

"I bet I can do it," Annie Oakley said. "Start tossing 'em, son, as high as you can!"

With that, Fred took a golf ball in his right hand and stepped back for the wind up before letting it rip through the air. Boom! It went as it exploded with a direct hit. He threw another, which Annie Oakley hit, and another, until he thought his arm would fall off. Then she upped the ante, turning her back to Fred until he counted and called, "Now!" Then she whirled around and blasted ball after ball, sending debris in all directions.

By that summer, Fred was totally immersed in the game of golf. When Mike Brady, the Oakley Country Club professional, made the news by scoring two holes-in-one on the same round, Fred felt the importance of this feat and used the back-to-back aces as an excuse to visit the Brady home to congratulate him in person. But when Fred offered his best, Brady just shook his head sadly.

"I should have had three," he mourned. He held up his thumb and forefinger, showing a gap of about two inches and said, "I missed the third one by that much."

"That's golf for you. It's an 'umblin' game," Fred often said, mimicking the way the Scots talked about golf. From a young age, Fred understood the game of golf completely. He saw how it frustrated, how it thrilled, and how it compelled people to play against the course and against themselves, never seeing their accomplishments and focusing on the shots they missed. He saw golf clearly, for its pain and its pleasure, and he loved every minute of it.

"I've listened to the wailing and lamentations of more golfers than any man living," Fred would later say. "I have a shoulder that is perpetually damp and aches in bad weather from amateurs and professionals, men and women, who have cried on it while they described how that second putt hung trembling on the lip of the cup. I have what has been described as the worst case of three-putt ear ever seen at the Mayo Clinic.

"And I have yet to meet anyone who came to me and said, 'I putted like a champion out there today.' Champions who, after setting records for eighteen holes, still mourn, 'Yeah, but I missed two putts I should have holed.' And I have yet to hear of a perfect round of golf. By the way, the only medal I ever won in my life was for being runner-up in the New England Indoor Putting Championship, and if I hadn't three-putted that last hole from twelve feet…but where was I?"

The Corcoran boys lost their mother in the flu epidemic of 1918, after she had nursed three of them through it. But by that summer, while the older boys were marching off to army training camps, Fred was on the job where he was promoted to caddie master, becoming the youngest caddie master in America at the age of 12. With the pay small and the hours long, Fred used to check in at Belmont at five o'clock in the morning, and many a day, he didn't carry a bag until five in the afternoon. There was no salary, but the job functioned as a virtual franchise or concession. He got five cents a round from the boys who carried the bags.

One evening, Fred came upon a curious incident. As he was taking his time closing up, he noticed Harry Hall, one of the members, searching along the stone wall that bordered the third hole. For the next three days, Fred watched him tramping back and forth through the rough. Finally, Fred asked what he was doing.

"I'm looking for my golf ball," Hall said, "and I'll give five dollars to the boy who recovers the ball I've lost."

This struck Fred as rather strange, but sensing an opportunity, he called all the boys together and told them there was money in it if they found a ball that was lost along the wall. He didn't tell them how much was in it. He knew to leave some things to the imagination.

The caddies combed the ground and ended up with a basket load of lost balls—and a few they had brought along. When Mr. Hall came in, he burrowed into the basket like a gopher and came up with a badly battered old ball.

"Aha!" he exclaimed. "Here it is." He handed Fred the five dollars and, after taking a cut for himself, Fred spread the wealth among the other boys. But the episode stuck in his mind for a long time, until two years later, when he spotted Harry Hall on the course and tracked him down. Hall recognized Fred immediately.

"You know," Fred said, "something has been bothering me all this time, Mr. Hall."

"What's that, Fred?" he asked.

"Remember that golf ball you lost along the stone wall? I've often wondered why it was worth five dollars to you."

Hall chuckled. "Well, I'll tell you," he said. "I'm in the paint business, and everyone was looking for a golf ball paint that wouldn't chip in play or soak off in water. I had played 226 holes with that ball when I lost it and the paint hadn't faded or peeled. With that ball as evidence, I was able to land a tremendous contract for golf ball paint. Finding it was worth a lot of money to me."

Fred learned an important lesson that day: For many things, there is no fixed value. An object or a service is worth exactly what someone is willing to pay. All you have to do is find the right person, the one who wants it. After that, everything is subject to negotiation. And Fred also learned that people love golf balls, especially championship balls—those responsible for a hole-in-one or those that sunk after a long putt on the 18th green to win a tournament. People will pick a golf ball as a souvenir over a baseball or football because it fits so nicely in your pocket or sits so majestically on your desk.

But not all of Fred's lessons were that easy to learn. While he scuffled with the other boys on a pretty regular basis, he occasionally stood up before the adults. One was Bert Nicholls, the professional at Belmont. Nicholls would never permit a caddie on the golf course with a club in his hand, reminding the caddies of the societal difference between them and members.

Well, one day Fred was idly swinging a driver in the caddie yard, the way kids will, and Bert shot out of the shop as if he were fired from a cannon. "Put that down," he shouted, "and don't let me ever see you with a club in your hand again."

"I was only swinging it," Fred protested. "Don't get your feathers all ruffled."

With a quick shot across the face, Nicholls snapped. "I don't even want to see you pick up a club except to hand it to a member," warned Nicholls in his Scottish brogue. "The next thing you know, you'll be teaching the members and then looking for my job. Remember one thing…you're here to serve the members, and not to play golf."

It was a rough lesson, but Bert did Fred a great service. He was the pro who taught Fred not to play golf and to seek his success on the golf course as a non-player.

About this time Fred learned another valuable lesson: The man you meet on the golf course or in the stadium often bears only a physical resemblance to the same name you meet in a business office. This fact was driven home by a wealthy automobile agent, one of the club members, who promised Fred that all he had to do was report to his office and pick up his passport to the world of golden opportunity. But when Fred showed up at his office one morning, the man turned out to be just a voice growling behind a paneled wall. A secretary crisply dispatched Fred to an automobile parts stockroom far across the city where he put in ten hours a day, six days a week, for seven dollars a week until a state inspector fined the man as a violator of the child-labor laws.

Then, instead of expressing concern for young Fred, his benefactor not only fired him, but accused him of lying about his age. Actually, the question of age never had come up. But Fred remembered walking off down Boylston Street, puzzling over the inconsistency of a man who offered two different profiles to the world. He was glad to return to golf.

After his mother's death, the burden of holding the family together fell heavily on Sam and the older boys. There was little time for school or anything else not directly related to the pressing problem of economic survival. Looking to make money wherever they could, the Corcoran boys would hike to Fenway Park on days when the Red Sox played and sell peanuts in the stands.

It was at one of these games that Fred first saw one of his heroes and future good friend, Ty Cobb. Despite his reputation for being ornery and mean, Fred thought Cobb was the greatest baseball player who ever pulled on a pair of spikes, and when he first saw him play at Fenway Park in 1919, he was ecstatic. But the Tigers lost the ball game to Boston on a controversial decision that made Cobb boiling mad and sent him storming off the field into the Detroit dressing room.

Fred and some of the kids followed him and climbed on to a water pipe, where they could peek through the steamy window into the Tigers' dressing room. They watched as Cobb stomped angrily through the door, and when he looked up and spotted the kids, he reached around and picked up a bar of soap and hurled it, as if he was throwing it from left field to home plate. It shattered the window pane and narrowly missed Fred's head. "I scrambled quickly to recover the prize and carried it home as a souvenir," Fred said. "It was a bar of Lifebuoy."

In addition to selling peanuts, Fred worked at a variety of slavish jobs by day and hustled Postal Telegraph wires by night. He carried his share of telegrams from the War Department that year. Many of these deliveries required a streetcar ride and Fred was supposed to obtain this ten-cent round-trip fare from the recipient of the wire. But when one of those telegrams began, "The War Department regrets…," he didn't have the heart to ask for trolley money. He just quietly disappeared.

On one of these trips, he met a beautiful young Irish girl. She lived in the neighborhood where many of these families lived so he was in and out quite often. He finally got up the nerve to ask her to go out with him one evening and much to his surprise she agreed. On the day of their date, however, she sent her sister to find him and tell him that she was too sick to go out that evening.

Late that afternoon, Fred passed a field filled with some yellow flowers growing wildly about. Since he now had nothing to do that night, he picked a few and made his way up to the young lady's house, thinking he'd present them to her in person and wish her a speedy recovery. But as he approached her house, he noticed all sorts of activity. Through the glare of the lights in the living room, Fred could see people laughing and dancing. As he got closer he could hear music playing and people having a good time. Then he saw his girl, looking very healthy and sitting on some guy's lap!

Fred threw down the flowers in disgust and swore off women forever. He concluded that women were dishonest and not to be trusted. Without their mother, none of the Corcoran boys had much use for women. The tender, loving care that women provided was gone from their home and their lives.

These times were difficult for Fred and his brothers. Sam was often down at the local pub, acting like one of the boys. Maybe that's why Fred was always grateful for the fatherly advice he received from James A. Stillman, the New York financier and donor of Harvard's Stillman

Infirmary. As the guest of a member, Mr. Stillman was practicing his putting on the new 13th green in violation of a strict club rule. Not wanting to anger the member's guest himself, the club manager instructed Fred to put a halt to it.

Fred walked slowly to the edge of the green and stood silently while Mr. Stillman putted a dozen balls. He then stepped up to him and addressed him.

"Excuse me, sir, but I need to point out that practice is not permitted on a playing green," he said, using an official tone.

Stillman must have been impressed by the fact that Fred courteously refrained from interrupting him in the middle of his stroke because he came over and patted Fred on the head and said, "Young man, if you show this much tact as you go through life, you'll be a great success."

CHAPTER 2

THE UNITED STATES GOLF ASSOCIATION WAS OFFICIALLY FORMED IN 1894 to become American golf's governing body and to administer the national amateur championship along with the rules of golf. The Professional Golfers' Association came on to the scene in 1916 but stumbled at the gate due to World War I. But by 1919 it was up and running, and while the USGA dealt mainly with the amateurs and the golf clubs in America, the PGA looked after the interests of the rising number of professional golfers. Both organizations worked together to bring the players and the United States Open Championship to Brae Burn Country Club, near Boston, in 1919.

Fred had applied as a caddie for the tournament, but with a reputation already preceding him, he was picked for the better job as a runner to shuttle scorecards to the press room. But as soon as he arrived, he was promoted to his first important assignment in golf. He had been picked for the plum job of handling the scorekeeping duties for the USGA's U.S. Open Championship. He would be paid five dollars for his work, and he knew that if he did a good job, they might want him for other tournaments. And, he had an idea.

In those years there was really no such thing as a tournament scoreboard, as we know it today. At best there was only a score sheet, usually one of those advertising gimmicks distributed by the equipment manufacturers, which was tacked to the wall of the pro shop or caddie shack. It offered its information grudgingly as it existed mainly as a privy document, intended only for the information of the players and the tournament officials. The cold numbers told something of the progress of the match or tournament, but the sheet offered no clue to the drama unfolding on the course.

On the first morning of the tournament, Fred stopped at the corner store on the way to the course where he picked up some crayons and then went to the butcher's for a roll of paper. Once at the course, he set up shop against the south wall of the clubhouse. Carefully unrolling his butcher paper, he tacked it up to the wall. Then with a black crayon, he wrote the names of the players in big letters, so everyone could see them.

"What are you doing there, Fred," one of the members asked.

"I'm going to post the scores as they happen so everyone here will know who's winning each hole."

"But how will you know what's happening out on the course?" the gentleman asked.

"My brothers are going to run back and forth and tell me the score and I'll write it here for everyone to see." Fred pulled another paper from his back pocket and showed it to the man. "See, I'm going to put the pars in blue and the birdies in red and the bogies green so you can see how the match is going, hole by hole."

By then, a crowd had gathered and the men asked Fred all sorts of questions. "Is this the first time this has been done?" one man asked. "I'm a reporter for the Boston paper and I don't think this has ever been done before," another answered.

Fred saw his brothers, John and George, walking toward him and he waved to them to hurry up. "Now look it," he said in what sounded like a command for their utmost attention. "Here's what you need to do."

He sent them out to the course with his instructions to watch the play and run back with the score. On his scoreboard, Fred began adding footnotes, reporting the dramatic highlights, and as a result, raised the neglected art of scorekeeping to a new level and produced the world's first leaderboard. But he also noted something more significant. The sportswriters stayed by his side, and whenever John or George reported back, Fred would describe what had just transpired and tell the writers stories about the players, about the course, about the game.

Old Sam, by the way, also had a knack for knowing what was necessary and valued, which he obviously passed down to Fred. Sam probably printed the first football scorecard or program in America. This was back around 1908, before the players wore identifying numerals on their jerseys. Sam had the printer line up the names of the players in their corresponding positions and sold these scorecards at Harvard Stadium the day Jim Thorpe and the Carlisle Indians played the Crimson.

Apples don't fall far from trees, and while Sam may have been a seanachie, Fred was a master storyteller. He could remember a golf match, hole by hole, and then entertain an audience for hours. Fred may have written his way into major league golf with colored crayons and a fresh philosophy of the scoreboard in his head, but it was his nose for news and publicity that set him apart. He soon befriended the sportswriters, who hungered for stories and often feasted on Fred's ability to turn the ordinary into the noteworthy.

It rained all week at the tournament, but even so, the 1919 U.S. Open was a magical event. It was the first time Fred saw Walter Hagen play. Hagen, who had won the U.S. Open five years before, was 27 years old and already a sports-page celebrity. In fact, he was well on his way to becoming a legend and the first professional in any sport to earn a million dollars.

Hagen entered golf at a time when the amateurs were held in higher esteem than the professionals, who were often treated as "hired help" and asked to enter the clubhouse through the service doors. On one occasion, Hagen refused to claim his trophy because he hadn't been allowed inside the clubhouse before the tournament.

"Walter Hagen was unquestionably the most colorful person I ever met in golf," Fred would later say. "And I use that term 'color' in an indefinable way. What is this mysterious and magic quality that brings spectators swarming to the ticket window? What is it that makes someone stand out in a crowd? Why, give me one golfer with color and 144 others, and you'll find him surrounded by fans lining every fairway and green, while the rest play to an empty lot. Not all winners have color but your true champions do.

"True champions are magnificently considerate of people, and this is where you separate the champions from the mob," Fred added. "The champions don't have to step on your corn to prove they exist. Thoughtfulness and consideration is as much a part of their natural makeup as the lightning reflexes and air-conditioned nervous systems that make them champions.

"Hagen never, to my knowledge or in my presence, lost his temper or his urbane graciousness. He had that magic about him. It was there in the way he lit a cigarette, the way he walked and talked, the way he dressed. As they say in the theater, Hagen was always 'on stage,' yet there was nothing stagey about him. What he did, he did as naturally and as easily as he breathed. He was debonair and exciting, and he had a way about him. Hagen always walked with his head in the air as if he was, subconsciously, looking over the heads of ordinary mortals," Fred said frequently about his friend.

There is no doubt that Hagen helped raise the image of the golf professional, even though he had a bit of a prankster in him. Hagen liked to mess with the minds of his opponents. He was known to take a perfectly pressed tuxedo and throw it against the wall a few times and splash whiskey and perfume on it, and then arrive at a match, looking like he had stayed out all night.

During this particular U.S. Open match, Hagen came up to the last hole of regulation play needing a pretty good putt to tie Mike Brady, who was already in the clubhouse, crying over the putts he had missed. Impeccable as always in his traditional white silk shirt and silk tie, Hagen lazily drew his putter and surveyed the putt. Then he looked up with a smile and called, "Where's Mike?"

"Brady had finished two holes before and had gone into the men's locker room," Fred told a group of reporters that night. "And all of a sudden, Hagen's calling out, 'Where's Mike? Where's Mike?' and he's looking around, putting his hand above his eyes, as if to improve his vision. And then he says, 'Tell Mike to get out here. I want to give him something to think about for the next twenty-four hours.' And then he stroked home the tying putt. It was unbelievable!" Fred exclaimed.

The play-off round actually wasn't much of a golfing exhibition. Neither Hagen nor Brady played well. But the turning point came at the 17th hole where Hagen took command with a typical Hagen combination of brains and skill. He put his tee shot into a peat pocket where it lay virtually buried. Then, as now, there was a penalty for playing the wrong ball, so equity permitted the lifting and cleaning of the ball for purpose of identification. Hagen asked the officials to dig out his buried ball in order to identify it. Naturally, when it was dropped again, the lie was improved considerably. Hagen then put his next shot on the green, holed out in four, and went on to win—a patented Hagen finish.

CHAPTER 3

QUICKLY ENSCONCED IN A WORLD OF GOLF AND GOLFERS, FRED MET many who became friends and a few who would become life-long friends. In 1922, Fred introduced himself to a young golfer who would become one of his best friends and favorite people in the world— Gene Sarazen. Like Fred, Gene arose out of the caddie pens in Rye, New York, and at 20 years old, was just starting out on a Hall of Fame career filled with major wins, course records, and major accomplishments, including the invention of the sand wedge.

Sarazen had just won the U.S. Open Championship and was scheduled to team with Francis Ouimet against Walter Hagen and Joe Kirkwood, the Australian pro, in a match that would dedicate the new Charles River Country Club. Tickets were issued by invitation only, and Fred was determined to be there. He went to the downtown office of Barton K. Stephenson, the president of the new club, to ask if he might purchase an admission ticket.

Stephenson gave Fred a pretty thorough grilling, demanding to know who he was, where he came from, and why it was so important that he attend this exclusive and private match. Fred quickly spun a tale of Ouimet and Hagen, adding that he had only heard of Gene Sarazen and badly wanted to see him play. Finally and grudgingly, Stephenson conceded to sell Fred a ticket. He drew one out of a desk drawer. "That'll be two dollars, young man," he said.

Fred paid his two dollars—which was all he had—and then hiked from the Boston financial district all the way out to the Charles River Country Club, a two-hour marathon. He arrived late, but Sarazen was considerably later, reaching the club a full hour behind schedule.

Kirkwood, who staged a trick-shot demonstration to keep the gallery from becoming restless, wasn't amused, especially when a cheer announced Sarazen's arrival.

Sarazen, a jaunty figure, stepped from his car with bold, flashing eyes and a general to-hell-with-you look for all the proper Bostonians he had kept waiting. He swept into the locker room and emerged a short while later, a young dandy clothed in white shirt, bow tie, and white plus-fours, black hose and black and white shoes. To top it off, he had a cigar cocked in his mouth at a rakish angle. There was something about him that day that endeared him to Fred. He told himself: Here's a guy who's going places. And he did. He went right out and set a course record that stood for years.

A year later, Sarazen and Hagen played an epic match in the 1923 PGA Championship at the Pelham Country Club, and it was considered for years as the "match of the century." Hagen had won the championship in 1921 and Sarazen had won it in 1922, so this, in Fred's mind, was a huge deal. Fred felt the attraction of a head-to-head battle of champions, and even though the course was some four hours away by car, Fred hitched his way there, just to witness this final round.

"The match, which rolled along through 37 well-played holes, reached its dramatic peak on the 38th hole, when Sarazen pulled his tee shot and it appeared to go out of bounds," Fred recalled.

"All Hagen had to do was play his ball safely to the green and hole out. But then, Sarazen's ball was found lying in the tall grass, well within the boundary stakes.

"Seeing the ball up close, Walter got really steamed, and I had never seen him like this, pacing back and forth, swearing under his breath. He was usually calm and happy. Well, Walter insisted that Gene's ball had gone out of bounds and suspected that it was tossed back in play by an outside agency, which could have been one of many things," Fred explained. "Maybe one of Gene's fans who lined the course kicked the ball back in bounds. It was, after all, his home turf at a club near Portchester, where he had been raised. He probably had a lot of well-meaning friends in the gallery."

"Sarazen, unfazed by Hagen's outrage, hit a magnificent gambling second shot that carried across a dangerous elbow to the green, within a foot or two of the hole. Hagen stared at Sarazen in dismay and shook his head in disbelief. Then, obviously shaken, he proceeded to put his second shot in a trap, short of the green, and that was the match."

Fred also met Bobby Jones around this time. Jones, who was the same age as Sarazen, was attending Harvard graduate school and the team practiced at Belmont. Fred, who was by then the Massachusetts Golf Association's golf secretary, quickly introduced himself.

"Jones would arrive in the afternoons, carrying a crimson stocking that bulged with practice balls. Then he'd go to the farthest end of the 13th hole and start hitting spoon shots to the green. I was always mesmerized by his accuracy," Fred said. Jones would go on to win the U.S. Open that year.

As the summer stretched into the fall, Fred was drawn away from golf one day in late September when an emergency long-distance call came in for Bill Shriner, the shoe manufacturer. He tracked down Shriner far out on the course and returned with him to the clubhouse, where Shriner called his Chicago office and engaged in a long, muffled conversation.

Fred passed Shriner in the locker room just as he hung up. With a disappointed look on his face, Shriner turned to Fred and said, "I don't know why people can't be honest. Here I have a man working for me in Chicago who I thought I could trust, but they took stock this morning and found his books short. And he's carrying a lot of empty shoe boxes on the shelves that should have shoes in them."

Fred shrugged with an I-know-what-you-mean look. "Can I get you anything? Some water or some whiskey?" he offered.

Shriner turned and looked at Fred. "How would you like to go to work for me?" he asked.

Needing more money than golf during the coming winter in New England could provide, Fred considered his offer, even though the only security he'd ever known had come from the feel of turf under his feet. But two weeks later, Fred stepped off a train at Grand Central Station in New York on his way to work in Shriner's store. A cab took him for a delightful spin through Central Park before depositing him on the sidewalk in front of 350 Madison Avenue. After paying the driver, he looked up and found himself gazing at Grand Central, a block away. Fred never again trusted a New York cab driver.

For two years Fred shuttled around the college campuses as a "shoe dog" for Shriner, returning between semesters to the Manhattan store where he met some interesting people, including Jack Dempsey (size 10-C), Clark Gable (six pairs of patent-leather pumps at a time), and Robert Moses (a tender corn on his right little toe). Fred quickly learned never to sell a man a pair of shoes that were too tight, because he would have to take them back—which meant Fred, not Bill Shriner, had to take them back. And after wearing returned shoes that pinched, pricked and rubbed, Fred honed his sales skills knowing that telling the truth and getting his facts straight was paramount. He also learned how to close a deal and keep the customers coming back for more.

Fred returned to Boston in 1926 to open a Shriner store on Washington Street and that completed the circle for him as a shoe hound. But a few months later at the age of 20, Fred was asked to succeed the ill and retiring Dan Horan as the Massachusetts State Golf Handicapper. He hung up his shoehorn permanently and walked away from the world of profit-and-loss statements (wearing Shriner shoes, of course) and back to the wonderful world of golf. He never looked back over his shoulder.

Chapter 4

Except for this brief detour through the shoe business, Fred devoted his life to golf. From 1923 to 1925, he served the Belmont Country Club as golf secretary and now, in 1927, he stepped into a position as both golf secretary and golf handicapper at the Massachusetts Golf Association (MGA) where he would spend the next ten years. In the winters, Fred escaped to Pinehurst, North Carolina, as an Assistant Golf Secretary in the office of Donald Ross, that grand old Scot and shrewd architect of some of the world's best golf courses.

In the ten years that Fred served as MGA secretary, he was fortunate enough to handle the scoreboard duties for every USGA championship, some thirty-five of them. Just to be part of the pageantry of golf meant the world to him, but more importantly, it was in these years that he began filling his mental file with pictures of people and places that would become his business inventory, so to speak. He fell in step with the gang from the sports department early in the game and won his varsity letter as a legman for the golf writers. They learned to rely on him. Part of his success later in life was that he could remember the details and was quick to point out a story or inaccuracy. "If Corcoran says so," ended many an argument for decades to come.

In 1931, Arthur Sampson, a distinguished high school and college football coach, turned his hand to sportswriting and was sent to cover the 1931 USGA Amateur Championship at the Beverly Country Club in Chicago. It was an important sports story because Francis Ouimet was playing and trying to make a comeback. Samson was told, "Stick to Corcoran like plaster. Don't let him out of your sight and you won't get scooped, because he'll be where the news is." Sampson took the advice literally. He became Fred's roommate and, as luck would have it, he hit the jackpot. Ouimet came back after seventeen years to win his second amateur championship and Fred had the inside scoop.

With Fred on their team, sportswriters put golf on the front page. Whether it was a quote about the rivalry between Hagen and Sarazen, or Hagen's thoughts on practicing, Fred had a story for their next edition, even in the off-season, with no golf tournament within 500 miles. Fred's desire for an audience and the press' need for a lead led to a respectful relationship and a heck of a good time. They began to seek each other out.

He told reporters that Walter Hagen never showed any great enthusiasm for the marathon practice sessions that would become part of the working day for the modern tournament pros. Fred commented, "I remember standing with him at the Colonial Club in Fort Worth, watching the players hammering away on the range. We watched the pros for several minutes while they hit a steady barrage of flawless iron shots. Then Hagen let out a loud sigh."

"What a shame to waste those great shots on the practice tee," Hagen said to Fred. "What are they doing out there anyway? Those guys already know how to hit a golf ball. They don't have to practice that. I'd be afraid to stand out there and work at my game like that. I'd be afraid of finding out what I was doing wrong."

They turned back to the club and Hagen talked on. "You know, I used to go out to the practice tee and hit four or five balls—just to relax and get the feel of it. I always planned to make any adjustments on the course. I always figured to make a couple of mistakes on the first few holes. But mistakes don't hurt you at this stage. It's those mistakes you make on the last few holes that kill you. I always plan to have my game under control by then. That," he said, jerking his head back toward the firing line, "is nothing but corporal punishment."

While Fred was still with the MGA and on scoreboard duty at the USGA, he was also busy promoting the game he loved in any way that landed golf on the pages of the newspapers and introduced it to new audiences. Because golf was still a gentleman's game and golfers dressed like gentlemen, Fred decided to play up this angle at the 1929 U.S. Open at Winged Foot, by holding a Best-Dressed Golfer Contest with a formal judging panel and all.

"But to tell the truth, the winner was picked in advance," Fred said. "It was to be Johnny Farrell, the defending champion, who was living that week in an apartment across the street from the 15th hole. Well, back and forth he ran that day. Between the club and his apartment, he changed his clothes six times. He won the Haberdashery Handicap, but scored an 86 and failed to qualify, which was more tragic than humorous. The previous year he had beaten Bobby Jones, no less, in a play-off for the title."

Fred learned at that point not to mix his promotions of the game with a serious tournament. Championship golf was sacred and even though the prize money was not a lot, the title of "Champion" was what mattered. And Fred knew how to spot a champion.

"There's a thoughtfulness and consideration which seems to be the mark of the real champion," Fred said. "You usually can recognize the bush leaguers in life because they're always pushing, pushing, pushing for every advantage. On the other hand, the real champion with the natural instinct for decency comes equipped with a wonderful humility. The major leaguer, whether it's in sports or in our workaday world, has a way of saying 'we' instead of 'I.' He has the good sense to recognize thoughtfulness in others, and the good taste to respond to it."

In 1929, Fred and his colored crayons arrived in Pebble Beach for the 1929 U.S. Amateur. With Bobby Jones as defending champion, it was a big tournament, and Fred was in the USGA room making up the scoreboard when the USGA committee called Johnny Dawson and Johnny Goodman to appear before them. Dawson was regarded by many as second only to Jones in American amateur golf. But he was employed as a traveling representative by the A.G. Spalding Company, and the USGA committee had come to the conclusion that he wasn't truly an amateur. They told him he couldn't compete in the Amateur Championship.

Goodman's case was a little different. He was a young fellow who worked for a sporting goods firm in Omaha, earning about $25 a week. He had paid his own way to the championship, and after pondering his circumstances, the amateur status committee decided to let him play.

That morning, Goodman and Jones were drawn to meet in the opening round of match play. The Nebraskan, who actually had ridden freights to California for the tournament, knocked out Jones on the last hole, providing golf's greatest upset to date and robbing the tournament of its star at the start of the week. By noon the next day, most of the gallery had checked out of the Lodge and the rest of the championship was played before a handful of local Peninsula residents. That's why the PGA finally changed its own championship from match play to medal. Too often the headliners were beaten in the early rounds by some unknown and the rest would cry from loneliness.

Goodman was eliminated in the afternoon round by Lawson Little, who was then a 17-year-old schoolboy, who lost the next day to Francis Ouimet. Little went on to win two British Amateur Championships, the U.S. Open and two U.S. Amateur titles, and wound up in golf's Hall of Fame. Goodman? He was the last amateur to win the Open championship, which he did in 1933. Then he became a public-links professional in San Francisco and disappeared from the picture. "It was too bad, too; he had toppled the king," Fred said.

"There's a footnote to the Pebble Beach yarn," Fred continued. "A year later, in 1930 at Merion, I sat in on the draw and I remember Goodman was a seeded player. One of the committeemen proposed to set it up so Jones and Goodman would meet in a 36-hole match, but it didn't jell. Goodman dropped out in one of the early 18-hole rounds. Jones, of course, went on to win it as part of his Grand Slam, winning the United States and British Open championships and the U.S. and British Amateur championships—all four in one year."

"I recall it most vividly, not because of any spectacular display of golf by Jones, but because of my own embarrassment," Fred said. "It was blistering hot—110 degrees—and my fancy red and blue scoreboard crayons just melted in my hands."

The episode at Pebble Beach turned a spotlight on another issue: the elimination of headliners through match play. Fred realized the importance of a gallery to a golf match, so he later proposed and eventually helped persuade the PGA to change the format of its own championship from match to medal play. Too often, the headliners were beaten in the early rounds by what the well-known pros called "some diddy-bump," leaving the marshals with no crowd to manage.

"I always regretted, however, the passing of the PGA match-play championship," Fred went on record saying. "Match play has a special dramatic quality that you don't find in a medal-play tournament. The spectacle of a man-to-man duel has more emotional impact than an impersonal contest between a current champion and a norm called par. There are very few match-play tournaments left, apart from the Walker and Ryder Cup matches. We could use a few more."

Chapter 5

Based in Boston, Fred conducted his business on the golf course, in the locker room, and at whatever bar or men's club was popular at the time. He developed a sense for being where the action was, and in those days, the action was at the bar. Fred was a man's man, who loved all sports and those around it.

In the early 1930s, there was not yet a PGA tour, and most of the money in golf came from playing exhibitions sponsored by the equipment manufacturers. Fred set up many of these exhibitions while expanding his network of friends and friendly press.

How Fred met Jack Sharkey, the professional boxer, is uncertain, but an educated guess puts them both in a saloon in Boston around 1932. Sharkey had defeated Max Schmeling in early 1932, at Madison Square Garden Bowl in Long Island City, New York, in their rematch to win the World Heavyweight Boxing Championship in a very controversial split decision.

A week later, Fred was with Gene Sarazen who had come to Boston to play an exhibition match with Francis Ouimet and he called Jack Sharkey. "I've got Gene Sarazen with me. You know he holds two titles right now," he baited Sharkey. "He holds both the U.S. and British Open championships titles, and I thought it might make a good publicity picture to bring you two together. Can we stop by?"

Gene had an endorsement tie-in with the Packard Motor Car Company, and they had given him a brand new Packard to drive during his time in Boston. So the two of them climbed in the car and drove out to Chestnut Hill to visit Sharkey, who as the new heavyweight champion, had just built a $160,000 mansion behind a wall overlooking the Boston College campus. Sharkey greeted them warmly and took them inside the house before showing them around the property.

"Here," Fred said to Jack, pulling a couple of tickets to the golf match out of his pocket. "Why don't you come and watch the match?" Sharkey examined the tickets and mumbled something about his schedule but carefully tucked the tickets into his jacket pocket. Then Fred said, "Jack, would you like to see Gene's new white Packard?"

Jack stared coolly at Fred, and then turned and looked at Gene before returning his gaze to Fred and answered, "No, but how would you like to see my two new Cadillacs?" Sharkey won the match, two Cadillacs to one Packard.

Gene was thoughtful as they drove away. Then it came out. "Listen," Gene said, "what's the idea of giving that guy Sharkey two tickets? I didn't see him passing out any free tickets for the Schmeling fight last week. I had to buy mine." They both had a good laugh as they drove back to Boston.

Sarazen went on to win the 1933 PGA that next year, adding yet another title to his list. And in 1934, he called Fred, rather excited. "There's someone I want you to meet," he said. "It's a gal from Texas."

Fred cut him off. "I've got too many women chasing me right now, Gene, but thanks anyway."

"No, I don't mean like that, Fred. It's 'the Babe' I want you to meet, not 'a babe.' It's Babe Didrikson, the star of the 1932 Olympic Games in track and Field. She's playing golf now and wants to play some matches with me."

"Can she beat you?"

"Not right now…I hope," he said, "but she does want to play men. And she's good enough to beat a lot of them. She's as strong as on ox."

They agreed to meet at the Woodland Golf Club a few weeks later, and Fred was waiting for them when they pulled up. A call to a friend at the Associated Press (AP) had uncovered some photos of Babe throwing a javelin, clearing a hurdle, shooting a basketball, swimming a lap, and cueing an 8-ball, so he was surprised when she, whose given name was Mildred, stepped out of the Gene's car wearing the rather long skirt that was very much the style. All he could think was what a handicap that skirt must be for athlete.

"You must be Fred," the lean 22-year-old woman said as she walked up the steps to the clubhouse with the swinging stride of a sprinter and extended her hand to shake. Fred was taken aback by the strength of her grip but didn't let her know it.

"Let's go into the dining room and get a drink," Fred said.

"What, no ladies allowed in the bar?" she asked. "It figures!"

Fred advised them on some staged matches and a short tour, as this was where the money was in golf these days, not in tournament purses. "And you'll need your wife to travel with you, Gene. It wouldn't look right for you and Babe to travel alone together."

"Mary Sarazen's a great girl," Babe added. "She's been on a trip with us already. There's no problem there."

Fred nodded in relief and then inquired about Babe's amateur status. "Playing for money won't help get your amateur status back," he warned.

"We'll cross that bridge when we come to it," she said with a noticeable Texas accent. "Right now, I want to get rich and get better at golf, in that order. I've been challenging men informally and now I want to do it for money. And with a few lessons and a little practice, I can win tournaments. Right now, I want to beat men in driving contests. Why I bet I can outdrive every man and woman in this clubhouse, except maybe Gene, here, and maybe you, Fred, but I haven't seen you play yet."

"Oh, you could probably beat me," Fred said. "You almost broke my right hand when we shook."

They all ordered steaks for lunch and afterwards, Babe excused herself to go to the ladies' room.

"What's on your mind, Fred," Gene asked when they were alone.

After a bit of hesitation, Fred let it out. "Do you think she's too manly to compete against women?"

"Well, she isn't a sissy girl, that's for sure," Gene said. "And she's determined to be a champ. I played with her last week, and after we played 18 holes, she went out and hit balls for four more hours. Why, her hands were sore and bloody afterwards. I couldn't believe it. And just wait until you see her hit. Why, to watch her throw a javelin is exciting but to see her hit a golf ball 250 yards is amazing."

Fred's green eyes lit up. "I can see the headlines now: GAL BEATS MAN AT GOLF."

"No, no," Sarazen said. "MAN BEATEN BY THE BABE." Fred and Gene both loved to write headlines and bounce them off each other. "Or better, THE BABE BEATS MAN."

"No, you can't call her 'The Babe' because everyone will confuse her with Babe Ruth," Fred said. "No, she has to be Babe, just Babe. How about, BABE BESTS BIG MAN. Of course, we'd need to set her up with a big man for that header."

Fred swished the ice cubes in his drink, his brain racing a mile a minute. "I do see a great curiosity factor with her," he said. "I mean, here's this gal from Texas, who's already won the Olympics and she plays golf, tennis, billiards, basketball and who knows what else."

"The harmonica," Babe added, coming back to the table and obviously overhearing the tail end of the conversation. "Yes, I play the harmonica, too, and I play it well! Golf is the only thing that has given me any trouble. That's why I'm determined to master it. All of the other sports have come pretty easily to me, without much effort, but golf… golf's the devil."

With that, they finished lunch and headed to the car, where Fred hitched a ride toward Marshfield, on Boston's South Shore. Fred was never known to have a car and in later years, give up driving completely, thus relying on others for local transportation. But this was all part of his charm. Players and writers alike loved to have Fred in the car because he would entertain the whole way, telling stories and staging pranks that made the time pass quickly. Usually, Fred knew someone along the way or at the other end that would make the trip even more memorable.

He climbed into the back seat of Gene's Packard and the three of them headed south. En route, they passed a football field where a high school team was practicing.

"Pull in here," Babe said suddenly. "I'd like to stop a minute and have some fun."

Gene parked the car nearby and the three of them strolled out on the field where some thirty or forty helmeted kids were going at it. Babe called to one of the boys.

"Here, son," she drawled. "Let's have that ball." The youth eyed her curiously, but flipped the ball which she caught neatly with her left hand and transferred to her right, her fingers settling comfortably along the lacing. She called to another kid about 25 yards downfield and fired a bullet pass that settled in his arms. Then she kicked off her shoes and called for the ball again. Barefooted, she boomed out a spiraling punt despite the restrictions of her long skirt. She called for another one but before she kicked it, she bent down and ripped open the side hem of skirt about eighteen inches.

"Don't worry," she said to Fred, who was watching her closely. "I can sew, too." Then she let loose with another long punt.

The kids and the coaches gathered about in wonderment that turned to awe and delight when the threesome identified themselves.

"This," Fred said, swinging his arms reverently toward Babe, "is Babe Didrikson, the top woman athlete in the world and soon to be the greatest woman golfer you'll ever meet."

Babe took over, as if there were a mic and a spotlight on her. And then she turned on her charm, along with a thick, sugar-pie Texas drawl for the crowd of young boys. "Hi y'all, come a 'lil closah, herah," she said, motioning to them to surround her. "I becha'll heard 'bout Wal-tah Hagen and Bob-ba Jones, but today y'all is lookin' at tha verah best golfa of 'em all, Mistah Gene Sarazen an our good friend, Mistah Fred Co-co-run."

Thus began Fred's foray into women's golf and another life-long relationship, albeit with an all-too-short life.

If there was a dollar to be made in sports in Boston during the late 1920s and early 1930s, there was usually a Corcoran somewhere in the neighborhood. For seven years, Fred worked as a goal referee for the Boston Bruins hockey club, and he and his brother John handled the ticket sales for the club in their spare time. They were hired for the job by Art Ross, the manager—and almost un-hired immediately by Mr. C. F. Adams, the owner.

Times were tough in post-depression Boston and Mr. Adams called Fred into his office and said, "Young man, I'm a member of the Boston Unemployment Commission. I can't say I approve of the idea of you and your brother John holding two jobs while men are walking the streets looking for work." He stared at him bleakly.

Fred thought fast. "Mr. Adams," he replied. "Aren't you the president of the Boston Braves?" Adams stared and Fred talked on, hoping to make his point before the game broke up. "And you're president of the First National Stores, I think." The First National was the leading food chain in New England. Adams narrowed his eyes. "And you're president of the Boston Bruins?" Fred added before concluding, "Aren't you holding down more than one job?"

There was a brief pause that seemed to last for years. Then C. F. Adams coughed and leaned forward across his desk. "All right," he said. "But young man, you'll be held strictly accountable for any shortages in ticket money. Is that clear?"

In the next seven years, between 1929 and 1936, John and Fred handled about $3.5 million in cash—and never came up short at any time. They had a most pleasant association for many years with Mr. Adams, who often recalled their original tête-à-tête with a smile.

One afternoon towards the end of his 10-year tenure with the Massachusetts Golf Association, Fred had another idea. He was riding to Braves Field with a sportswriter for a Boston paper to watch the Braves play. In those days, the stadium was on the banks of the Charles River and was called the "airport," a sports-page metaphor used to explain its roominess. It took a lot of people wheeling through the turnstiles to give the place a lived-in look.

In those days, too, they played a ball game in one hour and fifty minutes. Pitchers would throw three warm-up lobs and indicate they were ready. The batters used to hit that first pitch as often as not, and it would be one-two-three and you're out. The players scampered on and off the field. There was none of the mysterious and time-consuming brainstorming that bores the majority of fans today. Ball games used to start at three p.m. and everyone was on his way home by five.

On their way back downtown on the subway car, Fred said to the writer, "I can't understand why the major leagues don't play twilight baseball. It stays light enough to play until eight-thirty. Why don't they start their games at six? They could still finish by nightfall, and the working man could get out to the ball park."

"Oh, they couldn't do that," the writer said. "Ball players, you know, only eat two meals a day and they always have dinner at six o'clock."

Fred looked at him incredulously. "Look," he argued, "I saw about nine hundred people out there at Braves Field today. Now I'm going over to North Cambridge to see the North Cambridge Twilight League team play and there will be 15,000 bodies packed into Russell Field. What about those players? They have to eat too, don't they?"

The writer shrugged, seeing no point in debating the issue. But Fred didn't stop there. With golf played at a much faster speed in those days, he went on to introduce Twilight Golf, forming the Boston Twilight League. Even as an idea borrowed from the Twilight Baseball League, it was an instantaneous and enduring success. It brought people to the clubs to play and to dine in the few precious hours before the sun went down.

Chapter 6

With professional golf still in its infancy, Fred was entering his prime. Around the age of 30, he was handling some very important tournament scoreboards, befriending the leading pros, setting up matches, and improving the systems necessary for tournament golf to grow. As part of his duties at the Massachusetts Golf Association, he developed an elaborate handicap system which nearly every state golf body in the U.S. and Canada either copied or adopted. But above all, Fred made it a point to be at the center of things.

"If anyone ever calls on me to deliver a commencement address to the graduating class," Fred told a group of reporters, "my message to the youth of the world would be summed up in one simple phrase: Be where the action is. No man has ever met his destiny crying over a lonely beer at the kitchen table, and you'll never hear opportunity knocking above the sounds of a tranquil forest. You've got to be where the people are, talking to them, listening to them, and even arguing with them."

Fred was at the center of the action near his scoreboard for the 1936 USGA Amateur Championship in Garden City when Richard Tufts easily found him. Tufts was one of the game's true gentlemen, whose own climb to prominence and influence in the austere hierarchy of the United States Golf Association wasn't made any easier by the fact that he carried a taint of commercialism as proprietor of Pinehurst, the nation's leading golf resort.

"Fred," Tufts said, "I was wondering if you could do us the honor of running our scoreboard for the PGA Championship in Pinehurst this November?"

Fred hesitated only long enough for Tufts to finish his sentence. This was a jump for Fred from a USGA event to a PGA event and it would certainly put him in the center of the real action. Working the scoreboard hardly began to pay for the trip to Pinehurst, but Fred welcomed the opportunity to return to that delightful place. "Yes, of course!"

So there he was that November, creating another Corcoran color spectacular on the big board near "Maniac Hill" during the 1936 Professional Golfers' Association Championship when George Jacobus, president of the PGA, came out of the clubhouse calling for him.

"Fred," he beckoned, "come inside for a minute." Fred put down his crayons and walked across the platform that had been erected for the scoreboard. The board, now perched behind the 18th green, reached forty feet across and stretched twenty feet high. Fred needed a ladder to reach the platform from the ground and another to reach the top of the scoreboard once on the platform.

Filled with excitement, Fred followed Jacobus into the locker room where he, Ed Dudley, and the other members of the PGA tournament committee were holding a special meeting. Fred wasn't aware of the details then, but a rift had developed within the PGA over the management of the tournament program. Horton Smith, who was chairman of the tournament committee, had been replaced by Dudley. And in a matching action, Bob Harlow, who was tournament manager, had been released. The PGA thought Harlow had too many irons in fire.

Horton Smith was one of the great golfers of his day with a most exquisite putting touch. He won the first Masters tournament in 1934, repeated in 1936, and appeared destined for a glittering career in tournament golf. "Horton, however, was unbending in his approach to life, unwavering in his allegiance to the letter of the rules, and untiring in his political machinations," Fred later said.

Bob Harlow, at age 57, had been Walter Hagen's manager during Hagen's heyday and also attended to the business affairs of Paul Runyan, Horton Smith and Ed Dudley. In addition, he did double duty as the PGA tournament manager, so he practically controlled the show and was a force to reckon with. To his credit, he erected the framework for the PGA tour and would be best remembered for breathing life and form into the PGA tournament schedule when it consisted of nothing more than a few scattered fragments of tournaments. He would also go on to create and publish *Golf World* magazine, but now the new PGA tournament committee had just ousted him.

Horton Smith and Bob Harlow were very close friends, and it was this hand-in-glove association at the heart of the split. The rank-and-file pros felt the tournament program was being operated by and for a small clique.

"Fred," Jacobus said, coming directly to the point, "would you be interested in taking over the job of tournament manager for the PGA?" That was like asking a fish if he'd mind a job tending the pond. Over George's shoulder, Fred could see Bob Harlow peering around the corner of the lockers, but he didn't immediately think anything of it. That was one of the drawbacks about managing professional golf. You were always negotiating in locker rooms, with locker boys running by carrying shoes and towels and people staring over your shoulder or lurking in the showers. Now Fred was being offered a job right under the eyes of his predecessor.

Starry-eyed and innocent, Fred had no inkling that he was walking into a line of fire and facing a powerful alliance dedicated to his destruction. A cabal was forming that was going to provide him with enough headaches to keep the aspirin factories busy around the clock. But he accepted Jacobus' offer and went back to his current scoreboard duties.

A few days later, Fred returned to Boston to pack. He moved his brother John into his chair at the MGA. Later, John would move Billy, the youngest of the Corcoran brothers, into that job, thus continuing a Corcoran dynasty with the MGA that would last some forty years.

Two weeks later, Jacobus called Fred to Florida for a meeting where he confirmed the offer of $5,000 a year and $5 a day for expenses as tournament manager. Meanwhile, Fred had received two letters from Bob Harlow, inviting him to go to work for Harlow as his assistant in charge of handling a tournament program, for $4,000 and $5 a day for expenses. Fred told Jacobus about this correspondence because it puzzled him.

"Bob Harlow has no authority to offer you anything," Jacobus snapped. "We have terminated his services."

Convinced this wasn't his problem, Fred signed a one-year agreement to manage the PGA tournament affairs and took off directly for California and the Los Angeles Open, first stop on the winter tour. If he had the idea he was embarking on a carefree transcontinental junket, the minefield he entered of cliques, conflicting loyalties, strong personalities, and demanding sponsors set him straight quickly.

The tournament was played at Griffith Park and Horton Smith collared Fred as he arrived and called him into the Park's restaurant. Fred thought he was on friendly terms with Horton, but Horton went after him like a prosecuting attorney, digging at him with questions about his background and qualifications for the job. At one point, Fred felt as if he should to go back to the gate and buy a ticket just to watch the tournament.

"Listen, Horton, I came to California to do the job I was hired for," Fred said, in a discussion that was a little too loud and animated for the comfort of the others in the restaurant. "And I'm going to do it in the best way I know how."

"You don't know anything about the way the PGA works," Horton shouted. "Do you know who pays you salary?" Not yet having received a check, Fred waited for Horton to tell him the new facts of life. "Why it's paid out of a $25,000 fund pumped into the PGA Tournament Bureau by the golf equipment manufacturers. And you know the company I represent and the companies that Lawson Little and Harry Cooper and Johnny Thompson represent make big contributions to that fund, so while you may think you're working for George Jacobus, you'll be answering to us." He poked his finger on Fred's shoulder when he said "you" and on his own chest when he said "us." And he didn't stop there.

"The manufacturers carry a big stick, and they might just have something to say about how the PGA tour is handled, especially if it's not handled the way they want it." The threat was oblique, but it was clear enough to send Fred sprinting to the nearest telephone to call Jacobus and relay the conversation with Smith.

"Don't pay any attention to him," Jacobus assured him. "He's no longer a member of the tournament committee and has nothing to say about the way its affairs are conducted." George also let it be known that the PGA now was on very cordial terms with its banker. Money was rolling in from royalties on PGA golf ball sales, and the association was in robust financial condition. "Some members, in fact, are in a mood to issue a declaration of independence from the equipment manufacturers," he said.

But Fred's hazing was only just beginning. Even as he talked to Jacobus, a group was circulating a petition calling for Fred's dismissal and planning a campaign with more sophisticated weapons for later. This move to oust Corcoran had some support among the pros, spearheaded by the "equipment players," who were different from the "exhibition players."

The real headliners—like Walter Hagen, Tommy Armour, the Scottish-American champion, and Gene Sarazen—didn't play the tournament circuit. In those days, the solid money was made in exhibitions. Hagen and Sarazen, at that time, were off on world tours, carrying the gospel of golf to the high society. Tony Manero, the reigning U.S. Open Champion, had stayed in Florida to comb the coconut palms for exhibition fees. And the great Texas tournament stars—Nelson, Hogan, Mangrum and Demaret—were still standing in the wings.

The equipment group represented the key journeymen and top attractions on the tournament trail and when Smith herded them into line behind Bob Harlow, things looked bleak for Fred. But the equipment makers got wind of the plot and passed down word to their players to withdraw their names from the petition to oust Fred. After that, the only names left on the sheet belonged to some diddy-bumps and a guy named Joe. And oddly, the overwhelming majority of them didn't even belong to the PGA, which in those days required a five-year apprenticeship as a condition of membership.

And Fred had some friends, too. Henry Picard was the first to come to his defense. Henry was a pro from Plymouth, down on the South Shore, and he knew Fred from the Massachusetts Golf Association. "Fred, I don't care what they say. You just do a good job and you'll be okay with me. And that goes for the rest of the boys on this tour."

"Thanks, Henry, I can't tell you what your vote of confidence means to me," Fred told him. "I'll never forget this." And when Fred said he'd never forget something, he never did. His word was his business currency. A handshake was his contract.

Somehow, Fred survived the Los Angeles Open and headed for Oakland and the second stop on the tour. He barely had time to unpack his bags at the Hotel Leamington when he was summoned to a players' meeting in the hotel, called by Horton Smith. Showing surprisingly poor judgment, Horton had also invited the Bay Area golf writers. Or perhaps it was just a measure of the temper behind the move to gun Corcoran down. Someone was prepared to risk pulling down the whole tournament structure to get rid of him.

In any event, Smith took the floor and made a strong plea for the reinstatement of Harlow. "Harlow knows the game, he knows the players, and he's done a great job building the tour. How do you expect to top him? How can you do it better?"

Fred, again feeling like he was on trial, started to defend himself before quickly switching to the offense. "Look," he said. "I have signed a one-year contract to serve as the PGA's Tournament Manager and I propose to do just that, to the best of my ability," he added. "And to do this, I will need the cooperation of all the tournament players, not just some of you.

"I didn't go looking for this job," he explained. "I'm an innocent bystander in a feud that started long before I got to the first tee. You men have to work this out among yourselves. I was brought in at the end and hired to run the tournaments and that's all I want to do. You can fight this out forever if you want. Just leave me out of it!"

"Yeah, well, you took Harlow's job," someone shouted.

"I didn't take any man's job from him," Fred shouted back. "This job was vacant when it was offered to me, and I was one of ten men who were considered for it. Any one of these ten men could be standing here now, trying to defend himself. All I ask for is fair play."

Fred then told them about receiving the two letters from Bob Harlow after the locker room discussion at Pinehurst. He described them as "letters of agreement."

At this point, Smith left the room, raced upstairs, and returned a few minutes later with copies of the letters. When Fred saw them in his hand, his growing suspicion that he was being boxed was confirmed.

Horton took the floor. "These so-called 'letters of agreement,'" he said, "are just letters asking Corcoran to go to work for Harlow. Let me read them to you."

When he finished, Harry Hayward, the veteran golf writer for the *San Francisco Examiner*, got to his feet. "If Harlow was going to hire him to run the tour," he asked, "then what the hell's wrong with the PGA hiring him to do the same thing?"

This was a good question and Horton realized that he had come up short on his putt. Hayward went on from there. "You've given us enough ammunition today to blow a hole in the PGA tour," he said. "You made a serious mistake when you invited the press here. But I, for one, am going to bury this story, and do you know why? Not out of consideration for all of you. You jerks don't deserve any consideration. You're behaving like a bunch of kids. But there are a lot of sponsors, up and down the line, that have a lot at stake. They deserve some consideration. They're putting up a lot of money and expect golf tournaments, not public debates. Meanwhile, I'd suggest you get your house in order."

To the great credit of the men who covered the golf beat, they treated Fred fairly right from the beginning.

Chapter 7

Something else happened at the 1937 Oakland tournament that signaled the dawn of a new era in American golf—and took the pressure off Fred by focusing interest elsewhere. A rangy and picturesque boy from the Back Creek Mountains of Virginia rolled in to win the tournament. It was the greatest thing that could have happened to golf—and to Fred. Sam Snead suddenly exploded all over the sports pages.

The night before the first morning of the tournament, Fred had foolishly promised to deliver a dozen touring professionals to the Lake Merritt Club for a breakfast with the local businessmen. It was all part of promoting the 1937 Oakland Open, and at 6:30 in the morning in the lobby of the hotel, Corcoran and Snead glided into each other's lives. Snead was a boney youngster who didn't think anything of getting up at six a.m. Fred didn't think very much of it either, especially after telling stories all night the night before. "I always gave Snead the honor of being the most interesting person I ever met at 6:30 in the morning," Fred teased.

"Are you a golf professional?" Fred asked the young man who was waiting near the door in the lobby of the hotel, looking a little lost.

"Yes, sir. Ah'm Snead," he drawled, "Sam Snead and I heard there was a free breakfast. This is only my second week on the tour and I'm not quite sure where I'm supposed to go." Sam had a slow smile that lighted up his sharp, tanned face.

It was Fred's second week on the PGA tour, too, and he should have known better than to guarantee anything to anyone. He didn't remember seeing Sam among the dozen pros who solemnly swore they would attend the breakfast, but he was pleased to see someone had shown up.

Fred had no idea whether this kid could play golf, but a quick glance gave Fred a hunch he could. Sam was tall, slender and athletic. He had been an all-star in basketball, football and baseball in high school and probably could have gone on to play any of these sports in college. But he had broken his arm playing football in his senior year and had taken to swinging a golf club to help it mend.

Sam and Fred quickly sized each other up and decided to get along. That was the start of a personal and professional relationship that would survive intact for nearly a half century.

"Well, Sam," Fred said after watching the minute hand rack up fifteen points, "it looks like it's just you and me. Let's go."

"Mr. Corcoran," he said, "I'd like for you to tell 'em I'm from the Greenbrier Hotel in White Sulphur Springs, West Virginia, if you don't mind. They pay me $45 a month to represent 'em."

Fred put his hand on Sam's shoulder as if they had been friends for years. "I'll tell them anything you want me to."

Fred flagged a cab and together they headed off to the Lake Merritt Club where 500 of the local citizens had assembled to stare sleepily at an unknown face who claimed he was a professional golfer, and whose name they'd recall was Stan Speed, or something like that.

The weather cleared later that morning, and after the first round that day, the scoreboard marker had narrowed it down to "Sam Sneed." And as Snead took the lead and held it, the writers badgered Fred for background information that he couldn't supply. "Let me go find him," he said, before taking off, being one of the few who actually knew what Snead looked like.

Three days later, every golf fan in the United States had the correct spelling of Sam Snead's name. Playing in his second PGA tournament, Sam won it with a score of 270. He also picked up a check for $1,200, which was more money than Sam had ever seen gathered together in one place.

Fred waited for Sam as he walked off the 18th green and steered him to the pressroom where the writers asked him to stand on a banquet table while they fired questions at him. The room was blue with cigarette and cigar smoke and Sam didn't like that. He was grumpy and uncomfortable and he wanted no part of this inquisition. When a photographer, kneeling on the floor, fired a flash in Snead's eyes, Sam had enough. Like a tomcat on a mountain side, he jumped off the table, over the head of the photographer and bolted from the room. The photo that nearly blinded him was the famous picture that turned up the next day in *The New York Times*.

"Sam," Fred called when he appeared in the lobby of the hotel early the next morning. "Come here, I want to show you something," he said, pulling out the newspaper that was wedged under his arm. "Look! You got your picture in the paper."

Sam leaned in to get a better look at the photo. "Why, that's me alright," he said, turning the pages of the paper to see the front page. "How'd they get my picture? This is *The New York Times* and I ain't never been to New York."

Fred, of course, told the story to everyone he met, and the sportswriters had a field day with this comment. Snead was on his way to becoming a true character, with Fred as the promoter of many an attributable line or "Sneadism."

A few days later Fred received a wire from the Miami News Bureau. "How good is this Snead?" they asked. He wired back: "He's the best swinger of a golf club I've ever seen." The *Los Angeles Times* the next morning carried a story datelined Miami, with a headline that read: "Snead Picked to Win U.S. Open."

"Who picked me to win the Open?" Snead complained to Fred. "I didn't say I was going to win it. I don't want them laughing at me if I don't."

"So maybe you should win it," Fred told him, half in jest. "It would make a great story."

They were close—Sam finished second to Ralph Guldahl's record 281. And little did anyone know, at the time, that Sam's not winning the Open would become the story to haunt him for the rest of his life. By the time Sam Snead would retire from golf some thirty years later, he would win 82 PGA Tour events with seven major titles. The U.S. Open, however, would never be one of them, even though he finished second four times.

Sam's hillbilly background provided the golf writers with a wonderful canvas for some pretty wild portraits. And Fred pled guilty to furnishing them with some of their colors. Sam was never the country bumpkin he was painted to be, but somehow he always seemed to come off the printed page looking like one with his twang, his innocence and his mail-order clothes. He came down out of the mountains of West Virginia, but he was a quick study and had a keen, shrewd mind. He discovered the pockets of that hillbilly costume were lined with gold and he wore it with relish. And Sam himself enjoyed his role. His own fertile imagination kept pace and he contributed a few gems to the growing file of Sneadisms.

The golf caravan drifted south for the Bing Crosby Open at Rancho Santa Fe, where Fred stumbled onto another battleground. The

California section of the PGA had issued an executive order closing the Crosby tournament to all but PGA members. This, of course, would bar a number of prominent players who were not PGA members, including Lawson Little, a great attraction, especially in his native California.

Fred, dressed in his trademark tie and jacket, was standing behind the 18th green during practice play when Bing Crosby came up to him. "Look," he said, "I don't want any unpleasantness, and I don't want to join a union over this, but what does it all mean? Why can't I have anyone I want play in my tournament?"

The players themselves had confirmed that it was an open tournament, so there Fred was, in the middle again. He agreed with Bing that he had a valid point. So they put in a call to Jacobus who, in turn, got the PGA national office to overrule the California section. Fred escaped this battle without a scratch and with a new Hollywood pal.

But as soon as that storm blew over, another one appeared. And this was real, with black storm clouds—a deluge, in fact. For three days it rained so hard and so persistently that nobody even left the Carlsbad Hotel. On Saturday night Bing came down to the hotel and found Fred, sitting at the bar, holding court with a group of players and press.

Bing pulled Fred away from the group and they took a seat at the quiet end of the bar. "How many players do we have on hand?" he asked.

"Oh, I'd say there are about a hundred," Fred answered.

Bing pulled out a check from the pocket inside the jacket he was wearing. "Fred," he said, "the bridges are washed out. Even if it stopped raining right now, we wouldn't get twenty people down here. I know you boys have a long hop to Houston ahead of you. Here's the check for the full purse—$3,000. Do what you think is fair."

It was a typical Crosby gesture. "Why, that's more than generous, Bing. But I have a contract to play a golf tournament at Rancho Santa Fe and I propose we play it. And if there's any chance the weather will break, I think we should try and move this clambake out to the course tomorrow and see who wins, even if it goes only a few holes." Fred said.

That night the rain stopped, and in the morning, the sun broke through. Even though the course was soggy, they played an 18-hole tournament for $3,000 and Sam Snead won it. He had an amazing 68 on a course that had been reduced to a bog, and through the generosity of Bing Crosby, everyone left happy. Fred suggested they rename the tournament the Bing Crosby Pro Am.

CHAPTER 8

SAM SNEAD WAS NOW THE GOLDEN BOY OF GOLF AND EVERYONE WAS asking about him. No Hollywood script writer could have invented Sam Snead; he was the real deal and he made wonderful copy. He had the flavor and tang of authenticity, plus the magic that promoters dream about, that extra quality that brings people to the ticket window waving their money. Sponsors all along the line were wiring and phoning. They wanted assurance that Snead would play their tournaments. And Fred promised to deliver their new sensation to Augusta. But first, they had to get there.

Sam and Fred were in Greensboro, North Carolina, and Sam had received a wire from Bobby Jones inviting him to play in a special match a few days before the start of the Masters. But after a two-day postponement at Greensboro, the only possible way for him to get to Augusta in time was by airplane.

"We'll fly together," Fred told Sam. "I'll call the airline." But the only flight he could find was in a single-engine charter plane, so he booked it to take the two of them to Georgia.

When they arrived at the plane, Fred had second thoughts. The pilot was wearing a Yankees cap, not a good sign for a life-long Red Sox fan, and blue jeans, something Fred detested. Blue jeans were for ruffians, not for pilots! "Do you know how to get to Augusta?" Fred asked.

"Of course I know how to get there," the pilot said, tossing a cigarette butt to the ground and pulling a Shell Oil road map out of his back pocket to prove it. Fred rolled his eyes and distracted Sam, pushing him in the other direction. Sam had never flown in an airplane before and was assessing the situation on his own.

"I ain't going," Sam said stubbornly, pulling away from Fred and backing away from the plane. "I made a promise to my mother that I would never fly. I'm not getting in that tuna can."

"Sam," Fred said, "if your mother knew you were going to play with Bob Jones she'd say, 'Sam, get in that plane and get down there to Augusta. You can't leave Mr. Jones waiting on the first tee.'" Reluctantly, Sam permitted himself to be strapped into the plane, but he didn't enjoy one minute of that ride. And his pain only increased when he learned the charter would cost him $87.

Right after they took off, Fred's knuckles went white when he looked up at the pilot. Behind the curtain that separated them, on the floor, he saw the Shell road map, stretched out and held open by the pilot's feet. He flew the whole time following the roads below. But the duo got to Augusta in time for Sam's golfing date with Jones where he scored a 68 on the Augusta National course the first time he ever set foot on it, beating the Old Master himself by a couple of strokes.

The Masters champ that year was another new face on the tour—a young man from Texas named Byron Nelson, who made up six strokes on Ralph Guldahl on the final stretch to win his first major title.

Then it was on to Houston. But the next day, Sam went to Fred with a disturbing piece of news. "Fred," he said, fidgeting nervously, "if it's alright, I'd like to pass up this here Houston tournament."

Fred froze like a setter. "You what?"

Sam stared off in the direction of Montana. "You see," he drawled, "I've got a chance to pick up some money playing exhibitions. I had a call from Joe Kirkwood."

"Kirkwood!" Fred shouted, his anger rising and manifesting itself on his lower lip, which he bit when he was angry. Just when he had stopped feeling skittish, just as he stopped checking under his bed every night like an old maid, just when he had stopped thinking everyone was out to get him, one of Bob Harlow's boys surfaced to threaten his peace of mind. He smelled a rat somewhere in the distance, like a back-alley deal meant to embarrass him by snatching away the top gate attraction of the tour. Fred called George Jacobus and relayed the alarming news.

There was silence at the other end of the line, and then George replied, "Why don't you sign Snead to an agreement?"

"Is that ethical?" Fred asked.

"Why not?" Jacobus countered.

Fred had no defense against this kind of reasoning, so he promptly drafted an agreement which Sam readily signed, stating that Fred was

Sam's sole representative in exhibitions and other matters. This piece of paper marked the start of a business relationship with Sam that continued over many years. As his representative, Fred helped fill with cash a few of those tomato cans that Sam supposedly buried in his back yard. Fred picked up a dollar or two along the way on percentage, but he said more than once, that he happily would have waived any part of the action for the privilege and pleasure of knowing Sam.

Houston, incidentally, was a great tournament—a financial and artistic success. Fred had done the legwork up front and had in his pocket the PGA check for $3,000 to guarantee the purse. This was the custom in those days when sponsors were few and wary, and the gate was as undependable as the weather. But the Houston tournament paid off the nut, including the purse, and produced a substantial surplus for the Red Cross. Fred was able to return the uncashed PGA check to the Chicago office.

The 1937 Houston Open was a landmark moment in PGA tournament history. It was the last time the PGA had to guarantee the purse. From that point forward Fred was able to convince the sponsors, usually the local Chambers of Commerce or other civic-minded groups, that it was their responsibility for covering the prize money.

"Think of what this tournament will do for your town," Fred would tell them. "I'm bringing in 100 touring professionals who need hotel rooms and cars to go back and forth to the tournament. And they need to eat and they like to go out at night and see the town. Some of them have wives or girlfriends along and they want to have a good time, too. Why, I bet each man will spend about $100 during the week. That's $10,000 extra these players are spending in your town. And all I'm asking you for is a $3,000 purse. You'll make money on the tournament."

Fred would go on. "And think of the goodwill you'll create, especially if you give some money to charity, and the good publicity you'll get. All over the papers, people will read about what a great time everyone had in Houston or Los Angeles or wherever we are. They'll want to come here to play golf on the same course the Open or the Championship was played on. They'll buy golf clubs and golf balls and golf clothes. And if you make extra money, you can give some to charity, and everyone will feel good."

Fred had learned how to close a deal back in the days when he sold shoes, and as a salesman, he was charming. But what he said was also true, and his arithmetic was simple and convincing. Never again did the PGA office have to mail Fred a guarantee check. And never again, on

Fred's watch, did a tournament sponsor fail to meet its obligation.

Fred noticed something else interesting around this time. When a tournament was connected with a charity, such as the Crosby Pro-Am was, everyone was happier. He saw the power a tournament had to raise money for the charity, but also, to get everyone talking about it. Plus, charities came with volunteers, and golf tournaments needed a lot of hands on deck. Teaming with a charity brought free labor to the course and the charity itself brought more spectators to the tournament. Local businesses were more willing to get on board or donate items and many expenses became tax-deductible. Golf became the first sport to raise money for hospitals, youth programs, the Red Cross and health issues.

Chapter 9

Fred was quick to parade his new client around Boston, where he set up a few exhibition matches for Sam. And with a new sense of his own celebrity, Sam hit the links the next morning with a large crowd waiting. In those matches, Sam played for the gate, which those days, usually ran one dollar per person.

When Fred stopped by Sam's hotel room to pick him up for dinner that evening, he found him sitting on the floor, counting those one dollar bills and stacking them in neat piles of ten, like they were playing cards.

"You know, Sam," Fred reminded him gently, "there are certain expenses that come off the top of the gate. For instance, there's the guy who made all the arrangements for this match. He usually gets ten percent." Fred's brother John had gone to some expense in helping to arrange these matches.

Snead paused in his calculations and just glared at Fred. "Whad'ya mean?" he blustered. "For what?" He tapped himself on the chest as he emphasized, "I was the guy out there playing, not you or your brother John."

"Well, yes, that's true, Sam. But how many people do you think watched you play? How big was your gallery?" Sam didn't answer.

"Why I'd say there were 1,200 people there today. Am I right?" Fred asked.

Finally, grumbling away like a summer storm rolling across the West Virginia hills and reaching an understanding of sorts, Sam counted out 123 dollar bills.

Sam's legendary thrift is pretty well documented but Fred played it up, feeding stories to the press that keep Snead's name on the page while endearing him to the public. One evening in Chicago, Sam joined Fred and some others for an evening at the Chez Paree, which had a minimum charge of $3.50 per person. This minor detail was missed by Sam, who thoroughly enjoyed a Coca-Cola which he shrewdly nursed through the revels. When he got his check for $7.00 he grumbled and fidgeted. "I only had one Coke," he complained.

Fred explained the economics of the minimum charge and Sam's face darkened. Then he reached for the menu, scanned it quickly, and ordered a $6.00 bottle of wine which he tucked under his arm and strode out. The next day, Fred found Sam in the locker room, offering the bottle of wine to the highest bidder, determined to recoup his losses. Fred always said, "If Walter Hagen was known as the first man to make a million dollars in golf and spend it, Sam Snead was the first to make a million— and save two million."

The PGA Tour in those days was like a traveling circus and Fred was unofficial Master of Ceremonies, the go-to guy, the advance man, and the guy who made it all happen. But he was also in the unenviable position as judge and jury, interpreting and enforcing the rules. For every ruling he made, someone was happy and someone wasn't. It was a hell of a position to be in, he would say often. And he, like everyone else, had his likes and dislikes.

But skirmishing within the PGA finally died away. Nearly all the players were satisfied now that Fred was in there working for them, and most of them were tired of the bickering and feuding. And Fred drew powerful support from an unexpected source about this time—one of the leading manufacturers of golf equipment pledged the full support of all his leading players under contract.

So when the call came in July of 1937 to journey to England to manage the 1937 Ryder Cup team, Fred jumped at the opportunity. With Snead as a player, Walter Hagen as the captain, that famous team included the top players in America—Ed Dudley, Ralph Guldahl, Gene Sarazen, Henry Picard, Byron Nelson, Tony Manero, Denny Shute and Johnny Revolta.

Several wives came along on that junket, and since Sam and Fred were both single then, they traveled together from Manhattan on a steamship of the same name. Sam had never been on a ship before, which gave Fred many mischievous opportunities.

"When is this boat going to stop?" Sam asked Fred several times the first day.

"Sam, this isn't a Greyhound bus with rest stops along the way," Fred said.

"You mean we're going to just keep going like this for five days?"

Fred didn't have the heart to tell him the truth. "I'll check with the captain," he finally said that day after lunch, only to return an hour later with this report. "There's an island up ahead in the middle of the ocean. I told him you wanted to stop so he said he would steer that way and tie up for a while. Maybe they'll have a driving range there, and you can give a quick exhibition," he added just for fun.

As the day wore on, Sam gave up on Fred and began pestering the captain for more information about this island. The captain thought Sam was referring to "Ireland" and said we didn't put in there. It all got rather muddled and Sam began losing confidence in Fred right then.

But the next day, he still had enough faith in Fred to make possible an unpardonable hoax. Sam got seasick and took to his bunk in misery. Fred went down to the stateroom to cheer him up, bringing along a man from Boston named Gordon who he had met on deck. At Fred's insistence, Gordon introduced himself as "Doctor" Gordon and he proceeded to take Sam's pulse and thump his chest.

"The only thing for you to do, Sam," said Gordon weightily, "is to get up and dress, and go up to the salon and dance. Dancing is the best cure for seasickness."

Poor Sam dragged himself off his bed of pain, dressed, and went up to dance. He was a pretty fair dancer, too. Even though he looked a little green, he quickly became the dancing star of the voyage. And every time he withdrew to his stateroom, "Doctor" Gordon would pop in and rally him for another set on the dance floor. When Sam learned Gordon was a quack, he didn't speak to Fred for the rest of the evening.

All along, Walter Hagen planned on meeting Fred in London. He was off on a world exhibition tour and had told Fred that he would reach London in time to meet them, which only gave Fred one more thing to worry about. But true to his word, Hagen was standing on the station platform looking fresh and debonair when the boat train arrived from Plymouth at two a.m.

While the luggage was being sorted and the hatboxes were being loaded aboard taxis, Hagen drew Fred aside.

"You'll have to help me identify these wives," he said. "Some I know, but most of them I've never met." Fred confessed that he didn't know many of them either. Hagen thought for a moment and then sprang into action. As the wives stepped off the train he gave each one a little hug and called her "Sugar." From that point on, Fred, too, called many an un-named beauty "Sugar."

Until Hagen and Gene Sarazen came along, American golf existed in a vacuum. American golfers stood with their backs to the Atlantic and either didn't know or didn't care that the game had any roots. But on this trip, Hagen and Sarazen turned their faces to the wellspring of golf. Walter was never happier than when, as a player or a captain, he was leading an American team of professionals over to Britain. He believed every American professional worthy of the name owed it to himself and to the game to play in at least one British Open championship. Or The Open, as he called it.

Sam Snead, along with the other American Ryder Cuppers, played in the 1937 British Open at Carnoustie, following the matches that year. But he didn't play well and he didn't go back, and no amount of money could convince him otherwise.

Soon, Sam and Fred headed to the White Sulphur Springs Open in Sam's home state of West Virginia. The winner's take was $700 from a $3,000 purse, and on the heels of the huge $12,500 purse from the tournament at Belmont, Fred's old course, Sam expressed some concern. He and Fred got into a friendly argument over the worth of the prize, the size of the purse, and the value of a nickel.

"Seven hundred dollars isn't a lot for the winner," Sam told Fred the night before the start of the tournament.

"What do you mean?" Fred argued. "Think of what you can buy with $700." Snead just shrugged and dangled the change in his pocket, but Fred had an idea. Fred considered any idea a valuable one if it was original and worthy of generating positive publicity.

Unbeknownst to Snead, Fred made arrangements the day before the final round that if Sam won, he would be paid in nickels. It took a bushel basket filled with 14,000 nickels to deliver the $700 prize, which Sam carried off proudly, smiling from ear to ear, lending more legend to the tale that Snead still had the first nickel he ever won.

This same characteristic was reflected in Sam's attitude toward bar bills and dinner checks. Sam never polished any bars with his elbows, but had an occasional cocktail. Even so, you'd never find him doing handsprings on a tabletop at three a.m. or giving a party in a hotel room late at night. Some of the high-living players on the tour resented this resolve. Maybe they envied his success and strength of character without ever balancing the two factors in the equation. And human nature being the miserable thing it is, they sniped at him frequently. In turn, this contributed to a growing legend of frugality which had just enough substance to it to fuel the rumor mill.

Actually, Sam was a slow-motion check snatcher. It wasn't that he was ungenerous. He was simply a product of a hardscrabble life in the hills where he caddied barefoot because shoes were something you saved for school and church. Consequently, he never acquired the habit of throwing his money around.

Fred told the story about the time he and Sam were sitting around in Miami, having a drink with some New York sportswriters who were traveling with the Giants football team. Later, Fred said, "You know, Sam, you missed a fine opportunity to make a favorable impression on the writers."

"What are you talking about?" he asked.

"I'm not suggesting you can buy friends, or even buy a good press," he told him, "but for ten bucks you can be a big leaguer to these guys. Pick up a check now and then. You can afford it."

Sam nodded. "I will," he promised, "I will."

The next day, they fell in with Bill Cunningham, Gerry Moore and Burt Whitman, Boston sportswriters covering the spring-training camp of the Red Sox. They all had lunch together and, again, it was a modest tab. Fred waited for Sam to make his move but his reach again didn't go anywhere near the check. So Fred paid and again teased Sam.

Sam listened without saying a word, and then he nodded earnestly. "Okay, Fred, I'll pay it next time. I swear."

"You will?" Fred asked. "But when? I told you about this before."

Sam looked chastened. "I thought you meant when you aren't around!" And that was the day Fred learned what business managers are for.

In addition to feeding the press and the feeding of stories to the press, Fred was always looking for show. Chicago's Wrigley Field opened that year with what would become a legendary scoreboard placed in center field, over 400 feet from home plate. There was much written about its distance from home plate. People wondered if any baseball player would ever hit the sign with a baseball. Immediately, Fred had an idea.

"Sam, can you come to Chicago next Tuesday," Fred said in an excited voice, as he told Sam about the scoreboard. "As a stunt, I've arranged for you to hit the scoreboard with a drive from home plate. I'm betting you can hit it with your eyes closed and that no batter will ever hit it with a baseball."

"I don't have to close my eyes, do I?" Sam laughed as he agreed, delighted to have the publicity and the good time that Fred promised.

Sam was also one of the most natural athletes Fred had ever seen. Sam could kick the top of a seven-foot doorway from a dead stand-still even as he got older, but like many men, he was obsessed with his balding head. He was always trying hair-growth treatments and donned a hat at an early age that came off only on rare occasions.

On one trip, Fred roomed next door to Sam and puzzled by a thumping sound he had heard coming from his room, he pulled Johnny Bulla, Sam's roommate, aside the next morning.

"What was going on in your room last night?" Fred demanded an answer from Bulla.

"I know it's silly," said Johnny, "but Sam's walking on his hands to make his hair grow. Something about the blood rushing to the scalp and stimulating the follicles." Fred just shook his own head of thick, dark hair.

On the way to the Los Angeles Open in 1938, Fred got a call from Babe Didrikson, who was also on her way to Los Angeles. "Can you get me some exhibition matches when I get to town?" she asked. She had improved her game considerably over the years since they had met, and she had worked hard on enhancing her femininity, softening her hard edges to make herself more appealing as a woman golfer.

"I wish I could put you in the tournament," Fred said.

"Can you do that?" she exclaimed. "Oh, Fred, that would be terrific." She started to go on but Fred interrupted her.

"Wait a second before you get all excited," he said, trying to cover himself and calm her down. "I said I wish I could put you in. It's not the right time. You've got to turn pro first."

"Yeah, and I'm still trying to turn amateur," she laughed. "Well, can you find me a match with the biggest man in town?"

Fred's mental Rolodex started churning, sparking an idea that would change her life. "I've got just the right guy in mind," he chuckled to himself at his sheer brilliance. "He's a big guy, must weigh about 240 pounds. His name is George Zaharias and he's a wrestler."

"The bigger the better," Babe said, agreeing to play the day before the start of the tournament. Now all Fred had to do was to convince George to play against a woman.

The handsome, black-haired Zaharias was against the match at first but the moment he laid eyes on Babe, he was taken by her. By the end of the round, they were posing for photographers, his big arms around her in various wrestling holds. She shot an 82 that day and George beat her by one stroke. Their courtship started immediately and in less than a year, they were wed.

CHAPTER 10

THE LATE 1930S AND THE YEARS LEADING UP TO THE OUTBREAK OF World War II saw important changes in professional golf. As with any passage of time, and especially in sports, there was a changing of the guard. Taking center stage with Sam Snead were two young men from Texas, Ben Hogan and Byron Nelson, along with the colorful Jimmy Demaret right on their heels. These new giants of the game became the new Big Four, replacing the equipment foursome which was fading on the fairways. Ralph Guldahl was still playing and in fact had won two Open championships, but he lacked gate appeal.

At the same time, tournament golf was booming, thanks in part to some of the ways Fred promoted the game. For instance, when the tour went to North Carolina on the same weekend as the Duke-North Carolina football game, Fred suspended play on that day and arranged for his pros to stage a "Closest to the Pin" contest at halftime during the game. The pros lined up on the opposite goal lines and simultaneously chipped to the 50-yard line. The crowd, generally unfamiliar with golf, loved it.

But several factors contributed to this growth as well. For one thing, all the equipment manufacturers scrambled onto the tournament bandwagon, taking off the caps of their fountain pens and signing players the way United Artists signed movie stars. Spalding had enjoyed a virtual monopoly in this field, and now, Wilson and MacGregor entered the bidding. Wilson was the first company to sign a woman professional when L.B. Icely contracted with Betty Hicks and sent her off on a world exhibition tour with Gene Sarazen.

With every manufacturer carrying a stable of pros who were booked out on free exhibitions and clinics, the old fee exhibition circuit withered on the vine. Now the money lay in tournament play, and the tour was beginning to lengthen into a full-time, year-round schedule.

Also, the economy and the spirit of the American people were both prospering after climbing out of the Great Depression. Americans were jingling spending money in their pockets for the first time in a decade and they were starved for a little taste of high living. People were breaking down the gates to get into any sports spectacle, and sponsors with leather-bound checkbooks appeared on the scene.

Elmer Ward was the president of the Palm Beach Company, makers of summer-weight men's clothing. As a former New England amateur champion, he also knew his way around a golf course. He had met Fred a few times, who more than once had suggested that Elmer put on a golf tournament. And when they met at a restaurant in New York in 1937, Fred had an idea for something a little different.

Elmer brought Steve Hannagan, the publicity genius who invented Miami Beach, to the meeting. Hannagan didn't think much of golf tournaments, but after Fred outlined a scheme for a round-robin type of contest, using twelve to sixteen players, he fell in with the idea enthusiastically.

The Palm Beach Round Robin kicked off in 1938 with a field of fifteen players who would play seven rounds in five threesomes for a total of 126 holes. They had to call in the mathematicians from MIT to work out the complicated scoring system for the traveling matches, but the format remained unchanged from 1938 to 1946. A player earned or lost points on each hole, in a match-play style, based on his score versus his two opponents for that round. The groups were shuffled after every round so that each player played one round against every other player. The player with the most points after seven rounds won.

The tournament proved a tremendous success until the PGA ordered it off the slate in 1955 because it didn't give employment to enough pros. Through Elmer Ward, the tournament, then called the Goodall Palm Beach Round Robin, had raised a total of $600,000 for charities. And Sam Snead won it five times, including the first and last time it was played.

Sponsors started to come in all shapes and sizes and previous conditions of rectitude. In 1938 an amiable golf enthusiast of mysterious resources underwrote a 108-hole tournament at the Fenway Golf Club, outside New York City. He had a peculiar aversion to photographers, and every time a camera began to focus, the sponsor would position himself behind a large person or tree. In fact, he even declined to make the prize presentation and Fred wound up handing Sam Snead his $5,000 first-prize check in an automobile parking lot in the pouring rain. A few years later in 1942, the men in blue came for the sponsor and took him away to the Federal pokey. It seemed he was in the printing business, with bogus whiskey labels as his mainstay.

Then there was that prominent southern gentleman from Charleston, South Carolina, who had some real or fancied grievance against the gentlemen who ran the Augusta National Golf Club. He wanted to run a tournament in direct competition with the Masters. "Money is no object," he said when he invited Fred to his home to discuss it. "I'm prepared to pay whatever it takes to bust the Masters off the map."

The man aroused Fred's curiosity and Fred had the foresight to take Ed Dudley with him. Ed, in addition to being the Chairman of the PGA Tournament Committee, was also the touring professional from Augusta National, where the Masters was held.

"Would you look at this place," Fred said as they pulled up to a set of enormous white-iron gates, attended by a black man wearing white gloves, who sent a young boy up to the house to announce their arrival. "This looks just like Tara from *Gone with the Wind*," he said as they drove for about a half mile on a long, wide, gravel driveway that was flanked by trees.

After hearing the man out, Fred and Ed went back to the car drove off, and as soon as they turned the corner, Fred turned to Dudley and said, "Let's find a phone booth."

"What for?" Dudley asked.

"I want to call him back and tell him we can't schedule his tournament," Fred said. "The Masters is a fixture. There isn't anything we can do with or for him, and we may as well let him know now."

"Well," said Ed, "why don't we just turn around and go back there and tell him?"

"Ed," Fred said, "did you notice those great big dogs this fellow keeps? They looked very hungry."

Dudley nodded and began digging in his pocket. "You're right," he said. "Here's the nickel. I'll stop at that gas station up ahead."

Fred phoned and reported back to Ed. "That gentleman had a varied and rich vocabulary, one with many four-lettered words that didn't spell g-o-l-f."

Part of Fred's job on the tour was to keep everyone happy, which no doubt was an impossible job. He had to listen to the complaints of the players, both the established stars and young rabbits, the club members and the tournament committee, the sponsors, the wives, the caddies, and all who traveled with the tour's ever-growing caravan.

The selection of the 1939 American Ryder Cup team had narrowed down to a bitter debate over filling the last place. The choice was between Gene Sarazen and Clayton Heafner, then a rookie with only the Carolinas Open under his belt. The final decision was being made by the selection committee at that moment, during the Hershey Open in Pennsylvania. As Fred sat on the veranda of the clubhouse with Gene and Mary Sarazen, they talked about the matches which were scheduled for the Ponte Vedra Inn in Florida. "A rotten choice," grumbled Gene who rarely bothered to conceal his opinions on any subject. "Nobody will come out to see us except the sea gulls."

Inside, the debate raged over the final appointment to the team. Fred campaigned in his own way for Gene's selection, but he had no official role in the process. And as they sat there on the porch, waiting to hear, a voice interrupted the music that played from Mary's portable radio.

"We interrupt this program to bring you a bulletin from our newsroom," the deep voice said as they heard the sound of teletypes clicking. The voice continued, "We've just been told that Hitler's troops have crossed the border into Poland."

"Well," Sarazen said, "you won't have to worry about the Ryder Cup matches any more. The war is on." Sarazen got up from the table and went to the men's room, while Fred went off to find out that Heafner had been awarded the tenth spot on the Ryder Cup team.

But Gene was right and the match was never to be. The next day's headlines proclaimed the start of World War II, and three days later, a cable arrived from Commander R.C.T. Roe, secretary of the British PGA, informing the PGA with regret that Britain would not be able to field a team for the 1939 matches. But Sarazen wouldn't let it drop. He was furious at not being named, even though there would be no match that year, and complained to Fred for weeks.

Fred didn't feel the impact of Europe's war on the PGA tournament program right away. In 1939, it was still somebody else's war. The only visible effect it had on the United States was to advance the throttle one more notch in its defense effort. This acted like a shot of adrenalin in the arm an economy already revving up pretty well.

For Fred, it was on to another pre-tournament publicity event, one that he called a "Bombing Party," at the Los Angeles Coliseum, just a few days past New Year's in 1940. With a makeshift tee at the east end of the football stadium, Jimmy "Siege Gun" Thompson drove the ball into the stands on the west end, some 265 yards away. Ben Hogan was the only other player to hit the stands with his 255-yard effort. Hogan predicted that a bigger man than him might be able to drive the ball 350 yards some day, a statement that made most people laugh. Byron Nelson won the accuracy contest with three shots through the goalposts, and with extra cash in hand, Hogan and Nelson hit the town that evening.

Then came George May, the man who put professional golf on the gold standard. Fred was standing where the action was, the back of the 18th green at Winged Foot during the 1940 USGA Amateur Championship when one of the amateur players employed by May found Fred.

"Mr. Corcoran," he said, "I have a friend who will put up more money for one tournament than you play for on the whole circuit." Nothing held Fred attention like that kind of talk. He listened intently and agreed to meet May that evening at the Commodore Hotel in New York. It was there that they drew up the terms of the first All-American Tournament at May's home club, Tam O'Shanter Golf Club near Chicago, with its fantastic prize schedule.

Unquestionably, George May, a genius of a kind, contributed more than any other individual to making blatant capitalists out of the professional golfers. He must have laid out more than one million dollars in prize money before he soured on the pros and pulled out of the sponsors' guild. The final irony is that before his death there were signs posted all over his golf course reading, "No PGA Pros Allowed."

May was the man who wanted to eliminate caddies, and in the later years at Tam, he succeeded. Everybody who played the course had to rent an electric cart. He was an efficiency expert. That was his business. And he had it all figured out that the more players he could send around his course between dawn and dusk, the more green fees the club would earn—plus the cart fees. It was as simple as that. He also had a rule that every member had to spend a minimum amount of money each month at the club, something many clubs later adopted.

Fred and May differed on their approaches to the business of golf. May focused on the gate, seeing golf as entertainment. The more spectators who came to his facility to watch an event, the more money he collected in admission and concession sales. In contrast, Fred saw tournaments as a way to gain exposure for athletes, manufacturers, charities and the town. This way of thinking was more in line with Wilson and Spalding, who regularly hired golf professionals to travel and put on clinics. Fred felt that sponsoring a tour that was already financially solvent was a better way for all. But by focusing on the tournaments, the sponsors risked losing control of the players, so many of them continued to support individual players, along with funding Fred's salary. This set up two groups that would come to terms later on.

"George gave a lot to golf, but he also got a lot out of it," Fred said. "He came up with the notion of numbering the players in his tournament, an idea that resulted in the first sit-down strike in the history of tournament golf! Actually, the idea had its origin a year earlier at Phoenix when I threw it out as a rainy-day space filler for the local sportswriters. I proposed giving each player a number that would identify him with a big moment in his career. The story headline read, 'By Their Numbers Ye Shall Know Them.' For example, I gave Sarazen the number 2 to represent his double-eagle deuce on the 15th at the 1935 Masters tournament. Hagen would wear Number 11 for the eleven major championships he had won. Johnny Revolta would be Number 7 for the fact that he once seven-putted a green. And so on."

May picked it up and decided to number his players on the second day of the tournament. It nearly caused a riot. Tommy Armour walked off the course, saying, "I wore a number in the first World War and I'll be damned if I'll ever wear one on the golf course!" The others just declined to tee off.

"May finally backed off and compromised by pinning the numbers on the caddies, which I thought was a good idea," Fred said. "The forgotten man in golf is the poor fan who pays his way onto the course for the dubious privilege of being pushed around and scolded, only to guess who is on each tee. I think the fan is entitled to this much consideration by the pros who tend to forget that Santa Claus doesn't just leave that purse money under the sponsors' Christmas tree."

Fred was the king of rainy-day conversations. As the skies let loose, a group always headed to the clubhouse to wait out the storm. Fred would hold court as breakfast turned into lunch and lunch into dinner, and the writers, who were a thirsty bunch, all needed a story. At one event, Fred fed writers sixteen different stories in one day. And if there was nothing happening, Fred would pose questions that would get everyone talking. He was forever pitting players from different generations against each other, asking, Who's the best?" Could Snead take down Francis Ouimet? Or matching boxer against baseball player on the course. Could Jack Dempsey beat Ty Cobb on the course? What about Ty Cobb versus Babe Ruth? The debates raged on long into the nights, and often made the headline in the morning papers.

"The wonderful thing about making sports comparisons," Fred said, "is that everyone is entitled to an opinion, and no honest difference of opinion ever gets resolved. The debate just flows on endlessly, like the Hudson River. You pick your private winners and go through life with them. The debating trophy goes to the guy who survives the other debaters."

It was a rainy day when Fred called Gene Sarazen for a debate. Fred, still on the road, always traveled with twenty nickels in his pocket and was known to make a bee-line across a room when he saw a phone booth. Before he left his hotel room each morning, he would get change for one dollar and then he'd leave the hotel operator a long list of places he might be if anyone called looking for him. That was, if he didn't call them first.

"You know I should have been on that team," Sarazen said, as the conversation rolled on. He was still miffed about not being named to the 1939 Ryder Cup, even after a few months had passed.

"But Gene, there isn't going to be a team this year," Fred counseled.

"That doesn't matter. I should have been named to it!"

He and Fred were going at it for a few minutes when Fred had an idea. "How about you pick a team of ten players, and I'll call Hagen and have him get the other team together, the one that was picked, and we'll organize a charity match. The 1939 U.S. Ryder Cup team, led by Walter Hagen, versus the All-American Team, led by Gene Sarazen." Fred hung up and went back to the hotel desk for more nickels.

In 1940, the PGA accepted the offer by Russell Gnau, a Detroit sportsman, to sponsor this Red Cross "Challenge" series at Oakland Hills Country Club in Bloomfield, Michigan. The match put the ten original players from the 1939 Ryder Cup team as Hagen's Ryder Cuppers against Sarazen's All-American Team, which included Ben Hogan, Tommy Amour, Jimmy Demaret and Craig Wood. The event raised $10,000 for the Red Cross even though Hagen's team beat Sarazen's team seven to five. The match was repeated for the next three years, played also at the Detroit Country Club and Plum Hallow, and raised $90,000 in total. A.J. Ditman, a Red Cross representative, called it "one of the greatest golf matches for charity of all time," saying it did more to stimulate interest in American golf than any other match he'd ever seen.

Chapter 11

1940 WAS A RELAXED YEAR FOR GOLF, EVEN ON THE CUSP OF THE WAR. Fred and the PGA had proved that golf tournaments, when properly organized and energetically promoted, were money-makers, and sponsors were standing in line for dates. Fred was in the position of bargaining from strength, but he still wanted to grow the game. He was always hearing about oddball promotions in golf with someone trying to break a marathon record of holes played in one day or someone else playing a round with a whisk broom. This was strange because the game has been governed from time immemorial by rather stuffy people. Any kind of an offbeat promotion seemed especially bizarre against this classical tradition.

So when John Cavanaugh, the hat manufacturer, tracked Fred down at Augusta during the Masters, Fred threw his own hat into the promotional ring, coming up with an idea that made the national news.

"I want you to put on a charity exhibition for me at my home club in Norwalk, Connecticut," Cavanaugh said, "for the benefit of the local hospital."

"Exhibition golf is pretty dead right now," Fred said.

"Oh," Cavanaugh responded in a way that made Fred realize how important this was to him. "It's for a very good place called the Maternity Hostel, and I was so hoping you could do something."

"Well, let me think about it," Fred said, buying Cavanaugh a drink at the bar in the clubhouse. "The problem is that a golf match today doesn't make any noise above the regular chatter. I could get you a Hagen and a Sarazen and others, but why would it make the news? There's got to be something different or new about it."

"Could you guys quiet down?" someone next to Fred called to a group at the other end of the bar. "There are golfers putting right outside the door here." Fred looked around and noticed two gentlemen shouting at the other near the door leading out to the 18th green.

Most people can't explain how they come up with original ideas but many know exactly when the ideas come to them. Fred's came to him that night as he was undressing for bed. He would put together a celebrity foursome outside of golf, maybe with a great baseball player or boxer, and pair each with a name pro like Sarazen or Hagen. That would grab a headline. But it didn't stop there. He needed a gimmick as well, and that idea came to him as he recalled the conversation at the bar earlier that day with the guy complaining about the noise. Fred's idea was to take the game out of the library atmosphere and put it in the stadium. Instead of requiring the gallery to tiptoe around and speak in hushed whispers, he decided to create a hullabaloo match, complete with bells and whistles, boos and music.

Fred's first call was to Sarazen and once he explained the idea, Gene, being one who never really got the stuffy atmosphere that surrounded golf, was quick to sign on. The next call went to Ty Cobb. Fred had met Cobb in 1937 when he played as an amateur in the San Francisco and Oakland opens and he and Fred became good friends. Cobb was a pretty fair golfer and had entered golf in a big way, playing in whatever tournaments he could. And he was certainly one who thrived in a stadium atmosphere.

"You want to do what?" Cobb said as Fred explained the idea.

"We'll encourage the crowds to whoop it up, heckle you, just as you're putting and driving. I'll get a band to follow you and play music. It will be a spectacle."

"I'd love that. You know how that revs me up. I've never understood why people are so quiet in golf, like whacking a golf ball somehow requires more concentration that hitting a fast ball. But I'm not sure I'll be back east for a while. I'd tell you to call Ruth, but you know how his game stinks these days."

Fred did call Babe Ruth. They had met in 1937 when he joined Babe Didrikson, who referred to herself as "Little Babe" and to him as "Big Babe," in a charity match. Sylvia Annenberg, a regional women's champion, joined the Babes and John Montague, the infamous and mysterious trick-shot, rounded out the foursome at Fresh Meadow in New York.

John Montague was an excellent golfer who was famous for betting on anything, playing with rakes and shovels, driving 300 yards, drinking abnormal quantities of liquor, and reportedly knocking a bird off a telephone line with a golf shot. He traveled in Hollywood's circle, befriending Bing Crosby and Johnny "Tarzan" Weissmuller, before an unauthorized photo revealed he was actually LaVerne Moore, a former minor-league pitcher who had been wanted for years for armed robbery. He stood trial, was acquitted, and was now looking to make some money on the East Coast. On the day of the match, 12,000 spectators showed up and dangerously crowded the foursome, causing officials to call the match before completion, with the "Babes" ahead.

Ruth, now retired from baseball and missing it greatly, turned all his athletic energy to golf. "If it wasn't for golf, I think I'd die," he told friends. He estimated that he played more than 300 rounds of golf that year and had become a regular on the celebrity-golf circuit. And his game didn't stink. He was a respectable golfer, maybe even a little better than Cobb. So when Fred called, Babe joined the party, loving the idea.

With his two headliners in tow, Fred next called Gene Tunney, the heavyweight boxing champ from 1926-1928, who had twice defeated Jack Dempsey, and then he called the colorful and fun Jimmy Demaret. The happy-go-lucky foursome would match baseball great Ruth with Demaret versus boxing great Tunney and Sarazen.

Next Fred added the music. "I've just heard back from Fred Waring and he's on board with his Pennsylvanians, but we'll need a truck or something," Fred told Cavanaugh, "to transport the band around the course.

"Okay, a truck. How many will be in the band?" Cavanaugh was filled with questions.

"I'm not sure, but count on six. And we'll need an announcer," Fred continued. "I'll want him to do a play-by-play over a loud speaker, like he's calling a baseball game. But I want him to really rattle the cage and get the crowd to whoop it up. Maybe add some sound effects. Bells and whistles. That sort of thing."

"Colonel Stoopnagle, the radio guy lives near here," Cavanaugh said. "I could ask him." Stoopnagle was part of a well-known radio comedy team who were credited with being radio's first satirists.

"Great idea," Fred said. "Get me his number and I'll put it all together."

A few weeks later at Shorehaven Golf Club, the foursome teed off to the strains of "Take Me Out to the Ball Game," played by Fred Waring and his combo, who had arrived from New York with trumpets, drums and saxophones, and officiated by Colonel Stoopnagle of radio fame. While part of the band marched from hole to hole in a lively beat, others rode with Stoopnagle in a sound truck.

"And on this first hole," Stoopnagle announced, "we have Gene, the mean and lean, Sarazen who plans to use a putter from the tee. What? Oh…no? He's not using a putter, he using a wedge. What? Hey can you get your facts straight. What club is he using? Someone tell me. Gene! Gene! What club are you driving with?"

The gallery ate it up, and on it went, with silly and absurd comments about each shot and each player and each hole.

"Play on," Sarazen encouraged the band. "I can't wait to get my swing synchronized to that swing music!"

At one point in the proceedings, as Ruth lined up a putt, the gallery, out of tournament habit, was politely silent. Ruth turned to them and said, "How about a little noise around here? How do you expect me to putt in all this silence?" He looked around and took a practice swing, using his golf club as a baseball bat, which evoked cheers and hoots from the crowd.

With a paid gallery of 6,000, it was a wild affair and a widely successful one—especially from the publicity point of view. *Time*, *Life* and *Newsweek* magazines and one radio network sent reporters to cover it. So did the wire services, which resulted in photos of the match in hundreds of newspapers across the country. What's more, Demaret had a 70 and Sarazen a 71, proving that all this tippy-toe jazz and finger-on-the-lips business is unnecessary. A good golfer should be able to concentrate in a factory.

The next day, Fred received a long-distance call from Harold Pierce, the president of the USGA. "I hear you had quite a bit of excitement up there in Norwalk the other day," he started. "Tell me about it."

"It was quite a match," Fred said cautiously, picking up on the tone of Pierce's voice as he went on to relay the events of the day, adding his own color and commentary and pointing out the match's promotional value and the publicity gained.

When he was done, the USGA president chuckled lightly. "It sounds like a lot of fun," he said finally, "but I hope you never do it again."

Fred heard it as an order, not a request.

Fred packed up and moved on to Canterbury Golf Club near Cleveland where he watched as Hagen took his last shot at the Open Championship only to lose to Lawson Little. A small dinner had been arranged for Bob Jones at a nearby country club and Grantland Rice, one of golf's most respected writers, thought it would be a nice gesture to have Hagen there. So Fred went into the locker room to invite him and, of course, Walter said he'd be delighted to attend.

"Hagen was an immaculate dresser," Fred recalled. "In fact, I once asked him what he did about laundry when he was traveling around. He told me he had clothing depots set up around the country where he could always replenish his wardrobe while soiled garments were being cleaned and shipped along in his wake."

"That evening he dressed carefully in a beautiful blue whipcord suit. Unfortunately, the route from the locker room to the parking lot led through the club grill and bar where Walter decided we should stop for 'just one drinkie.' Well, the bar was crowded with the tournament mob and there was the inevitable boor who bellied up to Hagen, recalling their meeting at Memphis five years before—when the clown had waved at him from the gallery. There's always one of them around."

"Walter!" he cornered Hagen. "I saw you win at Midlothian in 1914. They should build a shrine to your memory at Midlothian!"

"At that point, of course, somebody had to jostle the jerk, causing him to spill his drink—a Cuba Libre—all over Walter's whipcord suit. A lesser man would have been tempted to wedge the drunk in the window casement right then and there. But not Hagen. Apparently unconcerned, he turned to the bartender and said, 'My friend seems to have lost his drinkie and we'll have to get him another.'"

"Then Hagen fastidiously drew out a clean handkerchief and mopped a twist of lime from his shoulder. After a few minutes of patient conversation with the slob, he excused himself and returned to the locker room where he peeled off the soiled blue whipcord and carefully dressed all over again in a freshly pressed white whipcord suit."

That same year, Fred met Monsignor Robert Barry, a low handicap golfer himself, who was having lunch at the famed Thompson's Spa, across the street from the *Boston Globe*. He said, "Tell me, how is Walter Hagen?"

"Well, Father, Walter was in good spirits and feeling well when I saw him last, which was a few weeks ago," Fred said.

"You know," said the priest, "when I was going to the monastery, I would drive a couple of hundred miles on a weekend just to watch him play. There was something about the man I found fascinating. I enjoyed watching him—the way he dressed, his actions, his wonderful golf. Everything he did was so dramatic. Tell me about him."

Fred thought quickly, wondering which of his hundred Hagen stories would amuse the priest. Instinctively, he turned to one that he thought the priest might relate to. "You know," he said, "Walter is not a religious man. I know he believes in God, but if I ever wanted to go looking for him I wouldn't start in a church." He thought a little and added, "I have an idea he's broken eleven of the Ten Commandments, but I'll tell you something else, Father, I think I'd like to be with Hagen wherever he goes when he dies."

Monsignor Barry's eyes followed him closely, nodding silently.

Fred went on. "Now, here's another thing. He's done more for people than anyone I know. For instance, he always takes good care of his caddie. If the boy needs a lift into town, Walter will get him a ride. He always remembers to give the boy a little gift. And he's like that with the other players. Always giving, not only his money, but himself. Now, I'd like to ask you this: How are we going to be judged?"

The monsignor didn't hesitate a moment. "I'll answer you, Fred, by saying the Walter Hagen you have just described has the quality we all must have to earn Heaven. That's charity." Faith, hope and charity, he pointed out, abideth. "And the greatest of these, as the Gospels tell us, is charity."

Well, Fred found this conversation very interesting, and the next time he saw Walter, he reported it. Hagen sat quietly for a moment, looking down at his feet, and then said softly, "I'm not a very saintly person, I know, but I've tried my best to go through life without deliberately hurting anyone."

Chapter 12

Everywhere Fred went, he met more memorable people. In 1940, he started a lasting friendship with the Duke of Windsor, after meeting him during the 1940 Miami Open. The Duke, who was then Governor-General of the Bahamas after abdicating his throne, was visiting Miami and called him to ask if he could arrange a game with Sam Snead.

"Who do you want me to play with?" Sam asked.

"Edward, the former King of England," Fred said. Sam was not particularly impressed, as if the word "former" took all the shine away from the penny. He was more concerned with the fact that he had no car and was worried about getting back to the hotel from the club. He had some mysterious appointment.

"Don't worry," Fred told him. "I'll see that you get back all right. I'll have a car there to pick you up. It will be waiting for you, I promise."

Sam agreed and on that day shot a brilliant 65 with the Duke exclaiming in admiration on every hole. On one tee, Snead rifled out a 300-yard drive and the Duke was ecstatic. "I've seen all the great ones since Harry Vardon," he said, "but I've never seen anyone strike a golf ball like that!"

Fred was waiting with a car and rode back to the Biltmore with Sam and the Duke after their round. When they got to the hotel, Sam excused himself and darted off to keep his appointment. The Duke and Fred chatted for a while in the lobby.

"How old is Sam?" the Duke asked.

"Oh, 26 or 27," Fred said.

The Duke looked somber for a moment. "Then he'll be shouldering a gun soon," he remarked quietly.

"We're all living on borrowed time," Fred answered.

The Duke broke off with a shrug and changed the subject. "What should I do for Sam?" he asked. "Should I offer him something? Say, fifty dollars?"

"No, no, that's not necessary," Fred protested. "I'm sure Sam would much rather have some kind of souvenir of the day. Perhaps an autographed picture of you."

The Duke's face lit up. "Oh, I say, of course. I'll just be a minute." He went upstairs to his apartment and returned in a few minutes with a photograph which he had inscribed to Sam. Fred thanked him and they parted.

Later, Fred gave the picture to Snead who stared at it glumly while Fred told him of the conversation in the lobby.

"Look," Sam said, "next time, get a check. If I want to start a picture collection of former kings, I can buy a deck of cards at the cigar counter and get four more."

During another conversation with the Duke, Fred proposed the idea of bringing the four men the Duke had seen win the British Open—Hagen, Armour, Sarazen and Jones—to Nassau for a Red Cross benefit exhibition match. The Duke was delighted with the prospect.

Fred flew to Nassau in advance of the match to complete the arrangements. At the end of the day, the Duke and he sat on the lawn of the Government House, chatting about golf and golfers. The Duke asked especially about Walter Hagen and Fred told him one story after another. Then he mentioned Hagen's philosophy of life. "He always says, 'Never hurry and don't worry. You're here for just a short visit. So don't forget to stop and smell the flowers along the way.'"

The Duke's eyes widened and he snatched a pencil from his pocket. "Oh, I say," he exclaimed, "this is just priceless! Priceless! Let me write that down." And he scribbled it on the back of an envelope. Then he jumped up. "I've simply got to read this to the Duchess," he said, excusing himself. "I'll be right back."

With that he sprinted for the house and went bounding up the stairs, waving the envelope and shouting for the Duchess. For the rest of his life, Fred recalled that moment every time the name of Walter Hagen came up in a conversation. Here was the King who had given up his throne, racing off to recite Hagen's philosophy to his bride.

Soon after, at the Masters in 1940, Fred had another idea. He was sitting around with a few of the writers, arguing playfully about who were the greatest players of the past and which of the current players would become legends when he proclaimed, "We need a golf Hall of Fame! Baseball has just started one. We need one, too."

Fred turned to Grantland "Granny" Rice. "Would you serve as chairman of a committee to make the first selections?"

Granny thought it over for a moment, and then said, "All right, I will if I can name my own committee. We have to have writers who have seen all the great ones, going right back to Vardon and Ray. It won't do to have these younger fellows on the committee because their range of choice is too limited." So Rice designated Linde Fowler of the old *Boston Transcript*, O. B. Keeler of the *Atlanta Journal* and Kerr Petrie of the *New York Herald Tribune* as the original selection committee.

Late that afternoon, the four of them held a lengthy meeting, and when it was over Rice handed Fred a folded slip of paper with the names of the players, in alphabetical order.

Fred opened the paper and read aloud, "Walter Hagen, Robert T. Jones, Jr., Francis Ouimet and Gene Sarazen."

That night, Fred announced the establishment of the Hall of Fame and the names of its first members. The story was carried on all the wires and, almost immediately, drew fire from the Chicago writers who protested that the selections were made by a packed jury of Eastern Seaboard writers. They argued that Chick Evans, two-time amateur winner of the Open and a Chicago District veteran, belonged in there and they accused Fowler, as a Bostonian, of pushing Ouimet at the expense of Evans. Fred thought this was an injustice to Fowler who was only one of four selectors and unfair to the committee itself, which was entirely justified in naming the one man who touched off the great American golf boom. However, the Chicago writers had a point in protesting the oversight of Evans. This was corrected in the fall of that year when the Chicagoan's name was added to the original four.

Any selection of this kind was an expression of personal preference at best and Fred, looking back on it, should have anticipated some outcry. But it just goes to show how the noblest of schemes can ricochet at wildly unexpected angles and you wind up, wide-eyed and puzzled, ducking hastily thrown rotten eggs.

Just as Walter Hagen had been applauded for opening the front door for the golf professional, and Ouimet and Sarazen had upped the respect of the caddie, the role of the early sportswriter was starting to receive its due, thanks to Granny Rice. While many writers persisted in looking the other way, Granny's syndicated "Sportlight" column helped lift golf to a status above that of filler material for a hole that needed plugging in the Sunday sports section.

Granny started writing sports in 1901 and playing golf in 1909. Gene Sarazen recalled Rice from his own caddie days at Apawamis, when he was assigned to carry a shabby old bag with the initials G.R. on it—and received his first $5 tip. "I learned right then," said Sarazen, "never to judge a person by his golf bag."

Granny often enjoyed a night of conviviality. He was especially devoted to a cocktail which may have been his own invention—straight gin chased with Coca-Cola, the native Georgia juice. Granny liked his formula best when taken from separate paper cups, but he wasn't a stickler for details. Bourbon or Scotch or gin, mixed or neat, would do nicely in an emergency.

As a sportswriter, he was equally as flexible, having been a football, baseball and track athlete at Vanderbilt. But he enjoyed playing golf and playing the races, especially the daily double which he won quite frequently. It was often debated whether the game of golf or the working press owed Rice the most. Fred always thought that Granny should have been named to the golf Hall of Fame, too.

That same year, a future Hall of Famer burst on the scene at the 1940 North and South Open—Ben Hogan. Here he revealed one of the greatest exhibitions of scoring, which most people, including Fred, had ever seen. Although this was not his first PGA Tour victory, it was his first solo win with an amazing score of 271, an incredible 17-under par, over the No. 2 course at Pinehurst. And while the numbers themselves were not impressive when engraved in the record books alongside much lower 72-hole scores, and even though Hogan's effort attracted very little attention at the time, Fred saw that 271 as the start of a new era in golf and an event that put another star on an even bigger stage.

Chapter 13

By the start of 1941, runaway horses were dragging America down the road to war, but many in golf didn't see it coming. The Royal & Ancient Society in Britain, which had cancelled its Open and Amateur championships in 1940, plowed under its courses, turning them into vegetable gardens, and filled the seaside courses with barricades to foil the expected German invasion. Henry Cotton, the British star, wrote to Fred saying that he had joined the Royal Air Force and was participating only in exhibitions on behalf of the Red Cross when he had time. Unbeknownst to the USGA, the R&A was about to play its last championships for the duration.

But the American band played on and one of the first stops in 1941 was the Hershey Open, which seemed typical of the period. Fred, as the Tournament Manager, was responsible for interpreting and enforcing the rules. Many a time, a pro insisted that Fred and only Fred make the call, and halted play until Corcoran was found and dispatched to the offending circumstance.

This time, Fred was summoned to the 16th hole because Byron Nelson had lost a ball under mysterious circumstances. The fairway followed a dogleg around a stand of trees and when he reached the scene, Byron explained the dilemma.

"I put my tee shot directly over that tree," he said pointing to the tall tree that marked the corner of the dogleg, "and it landed right on the fairway. But when I got down here, it had disappeared."

Fred walked the fairway from tee to the dogleg and back again, scouting the scene. Finally, he spread his hands in a gesture of helplessness. "Byron," he said, "if you can't find your ball, it's lost, and you have to go back to the tee and hit another."

Nelson knew this, of course. But he had called Fred over because he wanted an official ruling. Now he returned to the tee and hit an identical shot which cleared the same tree and rolled to the same spot on the fairway.

"I just don't understand it," Byron muttered as he walked to the new ball and finished out his round. The two-stroke penalty for the lost ball cost him $300 in prize money, which was dutifully reported as a footnote in the newspaper the next day.

A week passed, and then Nelson received a letter which read:

Dear Mr. Nelson:

I meant to write to you before this. I had a young lady with me at the tournament Sunday who had never been on a golf course in her life. Later, as we were driving home, she said, "Remember that lost ball they were all looking for?" And she opened her purse and proudly announced, "Here it is. I picked it up when nobody was watching."

I don't know how to apologize for her action, but I read where the penalty cost you $300 in prize money. At least, let me reimburse you for your loss.

The envelope contained three one-hundred dollar bills and the letter was unsigned.

Curious things were happening on the course this year. Fred was asked by the Ripley's Believe It or Not organization to referee a match at night in Cleveland during the Cleveland Open. This was a two-hole match between a pair of blind golfers, playing by flashlight, which of course, the gallery, caddies and assistants needed. The caddies and assistants told the golfers how far away the hole was and how the putt would break. Fred was amazed by the accuracy of blind men's putting.

The next day he found Ky Laffoon, a ten-time PGA Tour winner, on the practice green and he told him about his experience the night before. He demonstrated how one of the blind men putted beautifully, noticing that he never moved his head. Laffoon was interested enough to try it and found that it worked for him. He adopted the style and then went out and won the tournament. Fred, of course, had a field day with press, feeding them the headline, "Blind Man Teaches Laffoon How to Putt!"

Later, Fred told Ben Hogan the story. "Fred," Hogan said, "every mail brings me instructions on putting from all over the United States.

Every time I miss a putt I can depend on more mail, loaded with advice. Do this or do that. Stand on one leg. Cock your head, lock your knees, close one eye, or close the other." He waved him off. "But if I start taking putting lessons from a blind man, it's time to put the clubs away!"

Fred had another crazy idea that year that he knew was good for publicity. He suggested to Gene Sarazen, then U.S. and British Open champion, that he challenge Bill Cunningham, the sportswriter, to a match and offer to play him left-handed. Bill was a southpaw. Gene, one of the ablest space-stealers in sports, was always agreeable to a good publicity stunt. So Fred called Cunningham and proposed the match. Bill smelled column material, of course, and struck like a hungry tiger.

Fred set up the match in Florida and strolled along as a referee and one-man gallery as they played nine holes. Later, when he read the column Bill wrote, he began to have serious doubts that he was even there. Cunningham had an imagination with a four-way stretch, and he gave it quite a workout on this occasion.

Sarazen went on to have a terrible year, and later told Cunningham, "Bill, that left-handed round of golf threw me off my game for six months and cost me about $50,000!" This was worth two columns to Cunningham.

Product endorsements were becoming more common and every day a promising pro signed up with one company or another for a retainer to promote some sort of golf product. This, of course, limited the pros on what they could and couldn't do—a point many of them missed. And all hell broke loose when Johnny Bulla signed with a drug chain, which advertised that he played with a 29-cent ball sold by the chain. This wasn't important until Bulla won the 1941 Los Angeles Open and newspapers across the country broke out with drugstore ads picturing Bulla winning with the cigar-counter golf ball.

A howl of outrage from the PGA and the club pros from coast to coast broke out. They claimed this was ruining their golf-ball business. Fred received an urgent phone call from the PGA head office asking him to stop Bulla from further tournament play until it could be determined whether he actually was using the controversial 29-cent ball in tournaments.

Fred reminded the PGA officials that Bulla was not a PGA member and that the PGA could not decide who could and who could not play in an Open tournament. This had already been determined in a Massachusetts test case.

"And if you want to take this any further," Fred reminded them, "the additional publicity will only increase the sale of the drugstore ball. Maybe you should talk with a lawyer before you do anything foolish." On advice of counsel, the PGA decided to let the whole matter drop. Through it all, Bulla was cool and undisturbed. He said he was being well paid by the drug chain and the publicity was wonderful.

With a well-run tour, Fred was taking the game of golf from a minor curiosity to a major business, helped tremendously by a few well-placed stories and some big publicity events, like the match between Babe Ruth and Ty Cobb in the summer of 1941.

Over the years, Fred had been suggesting to Cobb that he play a match against Ruth for charity. Over both their careers, much had been made of their rivalry, and whenever Corcoran and Cobb were together, the subject would come up, with Fred goading Cobb endlessly.

"Why don't you face him on the golf course," Fred said. "Forget baseball. The history books will tell the story and the statistics will stand to time. What you need to do is take him out right now, beat him fair and square on the golf course. Just say the word and I'll set it up for you. Do you think you could beat him?" Ruth also played a respectable game.

"At anything," the tiger in Cobb snarled. "You name it," he snapped. He then signaled the bartender for another round of drinks.

A few months later, Cobb found Fred in a crowd at a bar. "Why did you ask me that?" he demanded to know, without even saying hello. "Why do you want me to play Ruth so badly?"

"No special reason," Fred said, playing Cobb like a fiddle, "except that I know Ruth likes the game and played fairly well at the charity match last year in Connecticut." He also knew that Cobb and Ruth's relationship was strained, at best, and the two rarely spoke. "Playing him would settle the score between you two. You know, I've been after you for the last four years to play him. Remember that night in Cooperstown when you wrote that note to Ruth?"

Cobb nodded, acknowledging him.

"I talked to him right after that. And I remember exactly what the note said." Fred was convincing. "It read, 'I can beat you any day in the week and twice on Sunday at the Scottish game.' Do you remember?"

"Of course I remember. And I *can* beat him any time."

"So let's get a golf match together," Fred said, hiding his excitement at the idea. "Will you do it?"

"Sure," Ty replied, "I'll play him anytime, anywhere, and for any amount. But he won't play me."

"You leave all that to me," Fred said, jingling his pocket to see how many nickels he had on him.

While the idea intrigued Ruth as well, the challenge lingered in barspeak for years. But when Fred arrived in Augusta for the 1941 Masters championship, Ty was on hand, and a plan was in the making.

Cobb was paired in the Pro Am with Sam Snead, the odds-on favorite, Sam Byrd, best known as a late-inning replacement for Ruth, and Charlie Yates, the British Amateur champ. Fred was with Henry McLemore, a great Irish sportswriter, and Henry was scratching around for column material, so they went over to watch the foursome warm up. Fred reminded Cobb of their conversation about the match with Ruth.

"You know, you two Hall of Famers really should meet together on the golf course. You can do it as a charity endeavor for the war effort," Fred said. Then McLemore started in on Cobb and, in a few minutes, he had Cobb repeating his challenge to Ruth—with fresh adjectives. Fred took this as the official word and the game was on—if he could get Ruth to agree.

Fred started pulling out all the stops as he wired Ruth the invitation. Everywhere he went, he talked about the match, harping on the tense nature and bitter rivalry between the two. He told a reporter, "I don't believe there are two other men who would draw as much attention as Cobb and Ruth. There have been 10,000 arguments as to which of the two was the better baseball player and that question never will be definitely settled. And in recent years, since they quit baseball, there have been arguments concerning their golfing skills. Now, we have a chance to settle that one."

Ten days later, Ruth responded to Cobb via telegram. "If you want to come here and get your brains knocked out, come ahead." And the match was on—as a 54-hole match in Boston, New York and Detroit, played for a war-relief charity.

Fred went back and forth for weeks, setting up the match. Ruth promised that he wouldn't give him any trouble on any points, but warned him about Cobb. "It's that Cobb who'll give you headaches about the arrangements. I see he's already saying he hopes he gets me on a golf course with narrow fairways and tight greens, so that I'll be in the rough all day." Head to head, Ruth had a five handicap and Cobb, a nine. Even Cobb conceded that Ruth might be the better golfer.

"Well, let him talk," Ruth continued. "I'll do my talking after the match is over."

And on it went, back and forth. The writers had a field day, bandying words like fireworks, showdown, historic matchup, fierce competitors. And beyond the hype, the truth was that both wanted to win—badly.

Cobb arrived in New York on Monday, June 23, for the Wednesday match in Boston. Fred tried to get Ruth on the phone for a few public taunts but Ruth had already left for Boston. Still, Cobb openly pledged, "I'll show that Ruth how to play left-handed golf," while privately admitting he was worried about the match.

Fred took Cobb to Toots Shor's restaurant that night. Shor, a giant of a man with a tremendous capacity for boisterous affection and equally boisterous animosity, was an unashamed worshipper of sports heroes. He also held the North American indoor brandy drinking championship title and was, without question, the greatest saloonkeeper on earth. Fred knew the place would be buzzing with reporters, mainly because he had called everyone he knew and told them they would be there at eight.

Toots put them at a remote table to keep the tourists from bothering Cobb, and then kept pouring tankards of beer into him, who was a pretty good suds man for his age. The more they drank, the more Cobb worried about his game. "Once you start to play poorly, you get in a rut and stay there for some time," Cobb said. "I haven't been hitting the ball that well."

Cobb continued his show of bravado but privately confessed to Fred, "I never worried before a ball game. I would just get up there and swing. But golf is different. I think it is a tougher game, especially on the nerves. And I'm beginning to take golf more seriously than those twelve batting titles I won."

"You'll do fine. And remember, this is for charity." Fred tried to calm him by reminding him of this, a point the fiercely competitive star was forgetting.

Cobb sobbed on, focusing on his problems—his swing, his putting, his sand play, his hands, his hips, his head. They drank and drank and barely managed to jump aboard the sleeper train to Boston as it began to pull out of Penn Station at one a.m.

The train arrived in Boston at dawn, but it was customary to let the patrons of the sleeping cars snooze until seven a.m. when the porter made the rounds, routing people out.

Cobb and Fred had opposite lower berths, and Fred was awakened by the most awful commotion in the aisle. He poked his head through the curtains to see Ty in his BVDs, his spike-scarred legs scrambling, as he chased the poor porter out of the car. He turned back, his face flushed and angry, and saw Fred. "Nobody puts his hands on me," he snorted.

Fred hurried and dressed and the two of them fled from the train to the Ritz Carlton to change before going out to the Commonwealth Country Club for a practice round. At the hotel, Ty remarked that he didn't feel too well and complained that he had drunk too much beer the night before.

"Say," he said thoughtfully, "you don't suppose that guy Shor has a bet on Ruth, do you?"

Ruth had arrived at the Ritz Carlton the day before, and after his practice round, he returned to the hotel where friends and reporters showed up in force. Ruth took a table on the rooftop bar, where he fended off taunts intended to add fuel to any fires. Fred and his brother John joined the party and kept the conversation going from baseball to golf and back again and kept the waiters on a short path between their table and the bar. John told Ruth how well Cobb had played in practice, but Ruth saw through it and tossed it back, recalling how he had thrilled a crowd in front of the clubhouse, pitching to the cup from 100 yards out.

"I put everything I had into the shot," Ruth said, "but the damned ball stopped on the lip of the cup. It looked like it was going to roll in, but that Cobb or somebody must have stuck some glue there and stopped it." The banter and the booze flowed for hours, and a few reporters, as they had been known to do, failed to meet their deadlines.

Cobb arrived later, as Ruth's party was well underway, and sat at a different table, seeming more interested in the young Cuban dancers and a hearty meal than he was in Ruth. As loud remarks were hurled across the way, it became an evening that sportswriters only dream of. Bill Cunningham wrote in the *Boston Herald*, "This is no autograph carnival. It's a golf match for blood." John Kieran of *The New York Times* wrote, "Don't stand too close!" Stanley Frank of the *New York Post*, gave it his perspective when he wrote, "Compared to Ruth and Cobb, Churchill and Hitler are old chums temporarily estranged by a slight misunderstanding."

"I've got a chunk of dough that says my game is better than yours," Ruth shouted across the room. Cobb heard him but headed back to his room to study his meticulous course notes and review his strategy for the match. This, after all, was a competition above all others.

Luckily, Fred had the foresight to schedule the match for the afternoon, giving them all a few hours to recover before heading to the course.

By tee time, a thousand spectators, who had paid their one-dollar admission fee, were milling around the first tee. Among them were Joseph P. Kennedy, a Ruth fan, and Jesse Guilford, the Massachusetts Amateur Champ, as a referee. Fred had also brought in Arthur Donovan, the noted boxing referee who had officiated at many Joe Louis fights, and prepped the press, pointing to his professional expertise should tempers flare.

The game, which went back and forth, moved slowly but Cobb took the match, three and two. Upon sinking the winning put, Ruth turned to the crowd and said, "He's a putting fool," and then offered his hand. Cobb shot an 81 and Ruth scored an 83.

"Well, now I've got something to show my grandchildren," Cobb beamed, after accepting the silver trophy donated by actress Bette Davis in support of the Golden Rule Farm, an orphanage in New Hampshire. Clutching it, he went on. "I finally have beaten the Babe at something."

Cobb later told reporters, "This exhibition golf is more punishing than baseball. During my twenty-four years on the diamond, I was never under such terrific pressure as I was while coming from behind to beat the Babe. Maybe it was because both of us were so gentlemanly. He was awfully nice to me, and I tried to be equally so. Neither of us acted that way in a ball game." He ended the interview saying, "It was a great pleasure to play with him and a much greater pleasure to beat him."

Ruth turned to the group and responded, "Don't get too excited about it, Ty. We play again at Fresh Meadow in two days." Ruth took off shortly after the match and headed to New York. Cobb and Fred stayed in Boston, celebrating, before boarding the overnight train.

Two days later, the second 18-hole match was set to go on Long Island. It had been years since Cobb and Ruth had dominated the sports pages as they did prior to the match, and this match, being in New York, meant more press and more fans. Ruth, fearing the large number of fans, had Fred issue a notice that he wouldn't be giving autographs. He claimed the last match left him with a kink in his arm. "They had me signing 'Babe Ruth' on everything from match covers to handkerchiefs," he barked.

The match went to the 19th hole with Ruth taking this prize. They were now tied and headed for the rubber match in Detroit, with a few weeks to prepare.

Fred needed to do some work because the crowd at Fresh Meadow wasn't exactly the crowd they had expected. For whatever reason, the crowd was more like a few people in the gallery. He, along with everyone else, didn't want a repeat of this. So in an effort to bolster attendance, he put in a call to trick-shot artist John Montague and Walter Hagen to play alongside Cobb and Ruth. Hagen and Ruth were old buddies, and together "helped make the 1920s roar," as Tom Stanton wrote years later in *Ty And The Babe,* his book about their rivalry and this match.

With everything in place, Fred arrived in Detroit and met up with Cobb early in the evening on the night before the final match. After dinner, Cobb wanted to visit Hagen so they went over to the Detroit Athletic Club to find him.

"I'm very sorry," said the clerk, "but Mr. Hagen is sleeping."

"Nonsense!" bellowed Cobb. "Give me his room number because we need to talk to him right away."

Fred, sensing a problem, called the clerk over to the other end of the desk. "Do you know who this is?" he asked politely.

"Why of course," the clerk nodded, "but I also know who Mr. Hagen is and I'm not letting you two up there."

"I understand," Fred said, "but this really is an unusual situation and Mr. Cobb does want to talk to Mr. Hagen, and I know them both very well so I can take care of any problem that might arise." Fred dangled his arm across the desk and gently placed a neatly folded twenty dollar bill in the clerk's hand. "Do you think you could just look the other way while I look at your guest book right there on the desk? I won't touch a thing."

The clerk pocketed the cash and walked off in the other direction without saying a word and a few minutes later, Fred and Ty found Walter's room. Cobb turned the door knob and it was open, so they walked in. And there was Hagen in bed.

"Walter! Walter! Wake up!" Cobb shouted, but Hagen didn't move a muscle. He just went on snoring peacefully. Cobb studied the sleeper and shook his head in admiration. "There's the most relaxed man I ever saw," he commented. "See how he sleeps all rolled up in a ball? Any time you have trouble sleeping, just try it. It's complete relaxation."

Hagen finally woke up and without getting out of bed, said hello to Cobb and Fred. "And lock the door on your way out," Hagen said. "I don't want you two coming back here in the middle of the night. I don't care what you want."

On Monday, July 29, at the Grosse Ile Golf and Country Club, 2,500 fans arrived and witnessed the final match, which got underway around four p.m. in front of a sizable gallery. Cobb and Ruth did not play great golf, but Cobb came out on top, with a score of four and three, despite the fact they clipped innocent spectators with their drives six times between them.

Later, Ruth called it the "Left-Handed Has-Been Golf Championship of Nowhere in Particular," much to the crowd's pleasure. Cobb may have won the match, but Ruth won over the crowd with his light-hearted antics.

Later on, Cobb said the series was one of the highlights of his life. "You know," he said with that competitive glint in his eyes, "I got a special kick out of beating Ruth because I outfoxed him. I started using an iron off the tee and that bothered him. I kept saying, 'I don't want to hit this shot too far.'"

"Competitive? Cobb had the killer instinct, in spades," Fred said of the match. "I often found myself comparing him to Hagen. They both made a million dollars in sports, but unlike Hagen, Cobb invested his at six percent or better and left $10 million. And where Walter was meticulous in his dress, Ty Cobb is the only millionaire I ever met who wore a rusty paper clip for a tie clasp until I replaced it."

Cobb obviously treasured some things above others. It was reported that wherever he lived after 1941, he kept two things on his mantle—his Baseball Hall of Fame plaque and the Betty Davis trophy from the first leg of the "Left-handed Has-been Golf Championship of Nowhere in Particular."

The three matches were played in front of a total crowd of just over 4,600, with the proceeds going to Bundles for Britain and other charities.

CHAPTER 14

CRAIG WOOD WON THE 1941 U.S. OPEN AT THE COLONIAL CLUB IN Fort Worth even though he had a bad back and his threesome never knew that play had been halted for an hour due to a Texas thunderstorm. Way out on the course and not hearing the siren, they just played on.

Bill Cunningham was covering the event for the *Boston Post*, and he accepted Fred's invitation to drive downtown with Craig after the win. Fred figured it would provide Bill with a chance to work up a column on Wood.

"Craig," Fred said as they rode along, "there's a driving range up ahead. Don't you want to hit a few balls?"

Wood fell right in step with Fred. "By all means," he said. "Pull in." They turned into the parking area and Craig drew a bucket of balls from the astonished range operator who never dreamed he'd have as his customer the United States Open champion.

After Craig banged out the balls, they climbed back into the car and resumed their trip to town. Cunningham, of course, found this performance a little hard to take. "Why did you do that?" he asked.

Wood turned a poker face to the sportswriter. "I didn't want to lose my touch, Bill," he said gravely.

Wood was that kind of a guy. And Cunningham was the kind of a writer who could build a whole column, or even a six-part serial, out of just such an incident. Bill always argued that the facts alone weren't enough. If you expected to hold the reader's interest, he maintained, you had to embroider the facts a little. You had to stretch the truth as far as it would go without snapping.

With the help of publicity stunts and an eager press, money was coming to golf through tournament sponsorship. But there was also a lot of money around golf through betting.

Since the prize money could only support about ten players, it was a common practice for two or three players to form a syndicate and split the money, regardless of who won the tournament. Bets were also placed on practice rounds, and frankly, side shows were stealing the game's thunder. Fred took the unpopular stance when he and the PGA finally banned bets and winner-take-all contests during the first days December of 1941.

"The gambling angle has no place in the game," he remarked after stepping in to call off a $1,000 side wager in an exhibition, matching Sam Snead and Clayton Heafner against Ben Hogan and Byron Nelson in Miami Springs. In his official capacity, he vowed to use his powers not only to stop heavy gambling, but to keep out all the promoters who wanted to get into the game now that the purses for the year totaled $200,000. He then learned how to nurse a permanent crick in his neck from watching his own back.

"That's big money," he told a reporter from *The New York Times*, "and they have all kinds of schemes for cutting in. No matter what the promoters want, we're going to have no burlesque, no hoopla, no circus, no masked marvels, no headless wonders." The Snead-Heafner against Hogan-Nelson match had been billed as a "feud" and he wanted nothing to do with that. "Golf is a gentleman's game," he reiterated, and the grand gentlemen, Nelson and Hogan, won the highlighted match, three and two.

During that friendly but spirited four-ball exhibition match at the Miami Springs Golf Course, word came that the Japanese had bombed Pearl Harbor. Almost immediately, Fred announced that in lieu of playing the Miami Open for cash, they would play for war bonds. The Miami Open was the tournament scheduled to kickoff the PGA's winter tour, and 213 professionals and amateurs had entered, the largest field ever for a medal-play tournament. Hogan, Nelson, Snead, Wood, Sarazen, Runyan and Picard competed strongly as Nelson defended his title. And the PGA officially pledged to President Franklin D. Roosevelt that it would support the country's crisis with nationwide War Relief Days.

In the weeks after America's entry into World War II, the question arose whether it was appropriate to play golf during these times of sacrifice. John B. Kelly, a former Olympic gold medalist in rowing and current Philadelphia construction executive, was named Assistant U.S. Director of Civilian Defense in charge of physical fitness. In one of his first actions, he called Fred.

"I want to offer you the position of Golf Deputy," he said. "I've been in close touch with President Roosevelt, and we want to suggest that the USGA encourage its member clubs to conduct patriotic tournaments as fund-raisers for war relief."

"Well, I'm pleased to hear this, but many of the better players will be going off to enlist."

"I know that," Kelly replied, "eight million people will be going into the armed forces and my job is to look after the 124 million that won't or can't go. They can keep fit by playing golf." He went on to explain why he thought it was important to keep the game going in the foreseeable future and he proposed a set of tournaments called the Hale America tournaments.

"Okay, but I suggest we get some others on the committee," Fred said. "I'd like to see Bobby Jones, Craig Wood and Ed Dudley, the current PGA President, brought on as advisors for the event."

"Why, sure, we'll take all the help we can get," Kelly agreed. And he even went a step further, urging golf associations and golf writers to expand and enlarge their programs. Golf contributed to the nation's physical fitness and this was of the utmost importance to the nation, he said. "No work can operate efficiently without regular periods of recreation. And America, now more than ever, cannot risk inefficiency when wartime production requires peak performance," he wrote on Office of Civilian Defense letterhead to golf associations and writers.

At the start of 1942, Fred was nearly 40, and he knew his patriotic duty would not be fulfilled in the trenches. So he headed to Hollywood to talk to Bing Crosby about an exhibition war bond tour with Ed Dudley, Bob Hope and Lawson Little. Bing was making a picture called *Here Come the Waves*, with Sonny Tufts. Fred had known Sonny's father, Bowen Tufts, as the president of Belmont Country Club when he was a caddie.

After finishing the day's shooting, Bing changed into his loafing clothes and he and Fred walked down the street to a big sound studio where he had to cut a record. The place was empty except for the band, the Andrews Sisters, and a man who sat at the far end of the studio. It was Jerome Kern, the songwriter. Bing and the girls hummed the song over a couple of times, and then cut the record with the band. Then they hummed it over again and made another cut. That was it. The whole business took no more than ten minutes and the record sold in the millions. It was a song called, "Don't Fence Me In."

Both Bing Crosby and Bob Hope wanted to enlist but like Fred, they were all a little too old for active duty. So they put together their

Victory Caravan and planned to travel to military bases and perform a show before or after playing a golf exhibition.

By February, when the PGA Tour stopped at Crosby's Pro-Am at Rancho Santa Fe Country Club, Fred had an idea. With Ed Dudley's blessing, he invited the famed duo to play some matches under the wing of the PGA during their Texas swing.

"We'll pair each of you with a tour star and increase the gate beyond fans of golf." Fred explained. They quickly agreed and signed on for the stop at the Brook Hollow Golf Club in Dallas, Texas, where they joined with Hogan, Nelson, Lawson Little and Jimmy Demaret. Actor and former Olympic swimmer Johnny "Tarzan" Weissmuller also agreed to play.

Instead of the anticipated 4,000, a crowd of 7,000 showed up. The next day, they moved to Brae Burn Country Club in Houston and 10,000 showed up, which became the largest gallery in Texas golf history. Between the gate and an auction the next day, where buyers bid for sets of Crosby albums they could buy in a store for a lot less money, the three days of exhibition golf collected $50,000 for the war effort.

Some say it was here that golf and Hollywood found each other. Playing golf for charity, and in this case, for the Red Cross, USO, Bundles for Britain or war bonds, became an event for publicity. Win or lose, the stars looked good swinging a golf club, striding down a fairway, and holing a putt, and with their appearances, the game spread to a larger and wider audience.

The success of the Victory Caravan brought other Hollywood stars to help the war effort through golf. Fred Astaire, Mickey Rooney, Gene Autry, Jack Benny, Ronald Reagan, Humphrey Bogart and the Marx Brothers got involved, along with Katherine Hepburn, Jane Wyman and Ruby Keeler. It also brought out celebrities from other sports like boxer Joe Louis and Gene Tunney, and of course Babe Ruth and Ty Cobb. Golf became the new arena for celebrities and competition, something the country was craving.

But with the war on, the sponsors were out of business, and sports were taking a back seat. Aside from the perception that golf was an elitist sport, there were some logistical problems to keeping golf and the tour going. Many of the golf pros enlisted, and caddies, who also enlisted, became scarce. Transportation to golf courses became difficult as gas was rationed. Some clubs bought horse-drawn carriages and picked up members at the railroad stations. Once at a club, however, the waiters and course workers were gone and so was most of the Scotch. Golf balls, because they had a rubber core, became precious. Some stores like Modell's and Macy's began buying balls back to repaint or refurbish them.

In January of 1942, the USGA decided to cancel its tournaments until further notice. Even though this didn't affect some PGA events, like the PGA Championship and several other Open events, the game had reached the end of an era.

CHAPTER 15

IN APRIL OF 1942, FRED AND WHAT WAS LEFT OF THE CIRCUIT HEADED to Augusta for the Masters, which had decided to stage their event this year, making it even more important. During this time, practice rounds were a big deal as newspapers covered them, hoping to get a lead on who might take the championship.

Two days before the Masters was to begin, Fred was on the practice tee with Sam Snead and as any good agent would, he was goading a few sportswriters.

"Sam is playing exceptionally well," Fred told the press. "Why, I'm betting, if I were a betting man, and if betting were still allowed, that he could win the Masters...," he hesitated a moment, sorting out the blarney in his head, "...barefooted."

"You mean without spikes?" one reporter asked.

"No, I mean without shoes."

"No way," they hollered back. "He'll break his toes."

"Sam, I know you can play without shoes," Fred said, hoping Sam would follow his lead. "Why, didn't you tell me you played five holes in practice in your socks before the Canadian Open last year? And you won it!"

Ignoring Fred, Sam continued to hit practice shots, with his shoes on.

"Yeah, Sam, kick off those shoes," one of the writers teased.

Fred called to Sam. "You've told me a hundred times that you used to play barefooted. So take off your shoes and socks and put your toes in the grass. Let's show 'em what you're made of."

"Fred, we know he's you boy and all," another one of the reporters said, "but this is a lot of bull."

Fred finally pulled Sam aside. "Sam, can you do this for me please?"

"But Fred, this is Augusta." Sam worried that playing barefoot might be frowned upon at such an austere club as Augusta. "I might get kicked out."

"Yeah," came the voice of Gene Sarazen, who had picked up on the commotion and joined the group. "Who do we have here, Huckleberry Finn?"

But Fred egged Sam on. "I'll take care of it. Don't worry. Have I ever let you down? Just play a few holes and you can put your shoes back on."

Sam finally agreed and walked off the practice tee toward his golf bag. There, he sat on it and carefully unlaced his shoes, giving the reporters a full show as he stripped off his socks and wiggled his toes.

"You know," Sam said, standing on the grass, "it sure feels good to get your feet on the ground. I used to play barefoot all the time back home in Hot Springs, Virginia." He then stepped up to the tee and hit a perfect drive and followed it with another.

Barefooted with a gallery of sportswriters on hand, Sam teed off on the first hole with a strong drive down the center of the fairway and followed that with a beautiful second shot that left the ball about 20 feet from the hole and putted for a birdie. He went on to the second hole and scored another birdie!

Snead went around that course in 68 that day and hinted at the idea of playing the tournament barefoot. But when word of this got back to the clubhouse, it didn't sit well with Gene Sarazen who accused Sam of acting like a barefoot hillbilly. "Can you imagine Walter Hagen or Henry Cotton playing barefoot on this course?" he asked anyone who would listen.

Of course, Fred sided with Snead which drove Sarazen crazy. "You know, Gene, I'd bet on Snead barefoot over you." He cited both their records and compared them, even though Snead hadn't won that much. But Fred was in his element, enjoying the digs his impish humor hurled at Sarazen.

And the press had a field day. Bill Corum in the *New York Journal* wrote, "Hagen would play in a bathing suit if the mood struck him. Sarazen would, too, if he thought it would help him win." The California Golf Writers also sided with Snead, thanking him "for putting the game back on its feet."

Neither Snead nor Sarazen won that year at Augusta. Hogan went on to beat Nelson in an 18-hole playoff, after five days of superior golf that helped elevate the Masters to one of the premier tournaments in the world and the most important of its time.

Golf balls, in short supply because of the war, also made the headlines at Augusta that year. Snead and Sarazen were recruited to test a batch of Wilson balls that had been refurbished. Balls with slight cuts or dings were placed in a machine that peeled away the cover so they could be recovered with balata, a hard rubber. "They rolled out of the box lopsided," Snead teased.

But when the duo hit these balls, they found to everyone's surprise that they performed just as well as new balls, even proving to be more stable in the wind. Sarazen was so encouraged with these balls that he played the second round of with one, shooting a 74. He urged everyone to save their old balls.

Snead once claimed to use the same ball for 54 straight holes, saying it was so soft by the end that he could pinch it between his fingers. The balata-covered ball really couldn't withstand the pressure from a professional golfer but Sam continued to use it nonetheless.

On the road with exhibition golf that raised money for war bonds, Fred moved on to Ohio that next month. The year before, he had met a woman, Jean, who worked at the Youngstown radio station. He had kept her number and when he found himself alone one evening, he gave her a call at her home. Fred wasn't a big womanizer, and living the life of a golf gypsy didn't help his social life, but he did occasionally get lonely on the road.

Jean's mother, Wanda Allison, answered the phone when he called. "Oh, Fred, I'm sorry but Jean got married and joined the Marines."

"Oh, I was hoping to take her to dinner," he said, using his most charming voice. With a little more chit chat, he found out that Jean had a younger sister, Nancy. "Why don't you and Nancy meet me for dinner?" he suggested.

Nancy was a beautiful young girl who had just turned 18. Fred was 36 and Wanda was just over 40. They all had a very nice evening together and when it was over, Nancy told Fred her news.

"I'm moving to New York in September and going to Katie Gibbs to become a secretary. I'll be living at the Barbizon Hotel for Women at 63rd St. and Lexington Avenue."

Fred told her he would call her when he got to New York and left town the next morning for the next stop on the tour—the 1942 PGA Championship.

Right before this tournament was to start, Sam received a draft notice. He planned to answer it, but using the excuse of his travels, he figured he could delay his answer until after the tournament. And as much as Fred told stories about Sam's hillbilly naivety, the truth was, Sam was as sharp as a pitchfork. He had a keen eye and could spot a stacked deck from a mile away, and he could also negotiate his way out of most circumstances. So when a Navy recruiter tried to sign him up a few days before the PGA, saying he could play and then ship out, Sam had the sense to walk away.

And it was a good thing he did. Fred had just agreed with Wilson Sporting Goods to give Sam a $2,000 bonus if he won the tournament. That, along with the $3,000 first-place prize money, gave Snead 5,000 reasons to delay his enlistment. Snead hadn't won a major at this point but he was ready and he made it to the final round of match play.

His competition was a local Army corporal, Jimmy Turnesa, the younger brother of Joe and five other golfing Turnesa brothers. The family brought along a gallery of some 7,000 soldiers who traveled from Fort Dix to the Seaview Country Club to watch the match. Each time the hillbilly civilian teed off, the Fort Dix boys would start jabbering, booing and caterwauling.

"The crowd isn't exactly pulling for you," Fred heard Ed Dudley say to Sam.

"Pulling for me? I'd settle for less pushing!" Sam said. "They almost knocked me down twice. I've never seen a gallery so ornery. You'd think I was a German or a Jap."

Snead went on to beat Turnesa when he holed a 50-foot chip shot on the 35th hole, winning him his first major championship. "In a way, I felt like I'd done my part for the war effort," Snead said. "I knew that once those Army boys got themselves some guns, God help any enemy that got in his way."

The next day, Snead joined the Navy where he would spend most of the war playing golf with Navy brass. Turnesa shipped out, Hogan went to flight school, hoping to apply his teaching skills to pilots, and Nelson stayed home, being classified as 4-F. And Fred felt a patriotic pull as well, so he made his way to New York.

CHAPTER 16

NANCY ALLISON ARRIVED IN NEW YORK IN SEPTEMBER OF 1942, AND Fred called her a few weeks later. She met him at the Savoy Plaza hotel, his New York address, for a drink, which of course, turned into two. They then walked over to Toots Shor's for dinner. Shor's had become a regular stop for Fred. It was a place where sports celebrities gathered, the press loitered, and deals were done. Nancy was impressed with the way people came to greet Fred as they arrived, and how Toots himself took them to a booth near the front so they could see and be seen.

After dinner, they hurried over to the RCA Building to sit in on a radio broadcast. Fred Waring had left tickets for them so they went right up to the second-floor broadcast studio. Nancy was in heaven. Coming from Youngstown, Ohio, she had only dreamed of an evening like this, with all the laughter and celebrities. Fred seemed to know everyone everywhere he went, and he told story after story so she didn't have to worry about what to say. The last time she had been out with a man, they had to struggle to find things to talk about, but this wasn't the case with Fred. He was charming and entertaining and fun.

They caught a cab after the show and Fred instructed the driver to head to the Barbizon Hotel for Women. Fred, too, had enjoyed Nancy's company but worried that she was so young. At 18, she was half his age and she had mentioned that she had never been with an older man. Fred wasn't sure how to interpret this. Did it mean that she had never been with a man or just one his age? Regardless, as the cab paused at a red light, he leaned over and kissed her and was a bit surprised when she kissed back.

He saw her to her door and thanked her with another kiss, but didn't call her for a few weeks. What with the war and his schedule, the last thing he wanted was a young girl on his hands, even though she was delightful.

Fred went back on the road with exhibitions for the benefit of various war funds. He tried to establish himself with the War Department, but nothing happened. "We'll call you when needed," they'd say.

"You know what the problem is," Bing Crosby teased Fred on one of their many phone calls. "The generals are scared to death you'll wind up in some critical theater of operations and tie up all the telephone lines."

Fred laughed at his own image. He was one of the first to admit that telephones did cast a strange spell over him.

"Why, someday," Bing continued in jest, "I hope the American Telephone & Telegraph Company will have the common decency to erect a memorial to you. Why, I bet you've trained more telephone operators than Ma Bell."

"I confess," Fred said, admitting he never looked up phone numbers. "Remember the time when I was at Augusta and I told the operator that I wanted to talk to Mr. Bing Crosby right away, and she came back and said, sorry, there was no 'Mista' Ri-da-way' staying at the hotel."

"Well, you know I told Bob Hope about you, about that time we were walking through the lobby of the hotel and you went over and picked up the phone and told the operator, 'Get me anyone.'"

"I was calling the press room!" Fred protested in his own defense, between gasps of laughter.

Still looking to get involved in the war effort, Fred next called his friend, Joe Cronin, manager of the Boston Red Sox. Cronin had an assignment from the Red Cross to set up a military sports center in London. Fred offered to ship out, and Cronin said he'd see what he could do. Meanwhile, sportswriters John Kieran and Grantland Rice had been named to head up a sports section for the American Red Cross and had issued a call for volunteers. Fred offered his help there.

Finally, a summons came and Fred joined the Red Cross as a volunteer without pay and took a six-month leave of absence from the PGA, boarding a lice-infested ship for an 18-day trip to London. If they had passed an island halfway, he would have jumped off, he said, comparing this trip to his one in 1937 with Snead going to the Ryder Cup.

When Walter Hagen found out Fred was going to England as a Red Cross volunteer, he called to say goodbye. "Promise me, Freddie, that you won't get yourself in trouble," he said with a chuckle. "And be sure to stop at the Savoy, my favorite place in London, and look up Karl Hefflin, the manager."

Fred arrived at the Savoy in due time and asked for Mr. Hefflin, who met him in the lobby with a puzzled frown. "Walter Hagen sends his best," Fred said, extending his hand.

Hefflin's puzzled look vanished. "Oh," he said, "the boy must have misunderstood. He thought you were Walter Hagen. And you know, we've had three bombing raids today, and as I was coming to meet you, I was asking myself, How can I take these air raids and Walter Hagen, too?"

Fred set up a command post at the Cumberland Hotel, and armed with some letters of introduction, presented himself to Harvey Gibson, head of the Manufacturer's Trust Company, which handled the Red Cross funds. Gibson's office was like a par-five hole with a dogleg leading to his desk. The distance gave him plenty of time to look Fred over before motioning for him to sit.

Fred handed him his letters and began to introduce himself but Gibson motioned to him to stop while he opened the letters, one by one, and scanned them swiftly. Then he looked up at Fred and said, "So you're in golf, are you?"

"Why, yes, I am, but I'm interested in all sports."

The banker just sat there for a moment, staring coldly at him. "Well, I think I have just the spot for you." He fanned the letters and settled back in his chair. "We have a lot of pinball machines over at Rainbow Corner, and they're not getting the play they should. Maybe if you went over there, you could take charge of the pinball-machine program and stimulate some GI interest."

Fred couldn't believe his ears. "You mean," he faltered, "you want me to run a pinball room?"

Gibson nodded. "Did you have something else in mind?" he asked dryly.

"Well," Fred said, "I sort of hoped I might be able to set up some kind of a sports program that would reach more men…men who were fans of golf, baseball, boxing and so on."

Gibson stood, thus signaling an end to the meeting and said, "Perhaps we'll find something else—later on."

Fred walked out of there feeling pretty low and headed over to the bar at the Savoy. After a drink or two, he struck up a conversation with a British man named Romney, who apparently had a lot of contacts among the military camps around London.

"What is it exactly that you have in mind?" he asked Fred.

"I was thinking about a live show, sort of in the style of a radio show, where I could talk about sports in the form of a story-telling session. I could take some questions from the audience, or even better, do a stump-the-expert type thing."

"And you're the expert," Romney said with an inflection that didn't deserve a question mark.

"Well," Fred hesitated, a bit embarrassed. "I've been called a lot of things in my life," he laughed, "but I guess I can call myself an expert."

Romney started asking him some questions about the 1937 Ryder Cup and Walter Hagen, which led to another round of drinks. As Fred satisfactorily passed his test, Romney proclaimed, "We'll call it the Fred Corcoran Sports Show."

Within a few days, Fred picked up Tommy Farr, the British Empire heavyweight champion, and later on, Jimmy Wilde, another fine British boxing champion. His friend and sportswriter Henry McLemore, who was in London as a war correspondent, joined up as a voluntary Masters of Ceremonies.

One of the first shows was scheduled for an air base south of London. The Yanks used to bomb by day and the British would take over at night with their speedy Mosquito bombers. Fred arrived at this base and was heading for the office to report when a crippled B-29, stumbling home, suddenly wheeled over and dove into the ground with a blinding flash, killing the entire crew. Fred sought out the Commanding Officer.

"Maybe this isn't a good night to put on a show," he suggested.

The C.O.'s face lifted. "Tonight," he said, "of all nights, we need a show. What's more, I'll throw in a keg of beer."

McLemore was a little undependable and tended to go missing around the time of his deadlines. He missed the show that evening, which turned out to be a good one. He also missed meeting one of the biggest fans of his column—Clark Gable, who had just arrived at the base as an assigned Air Force officer. While he and Fred were having a sandwich together at the officers' mess, the public address system played a recorded announcement for the show that evening, mentioning that Henry McLemore would be the evening's host.

"Is that McLemore, the writer?" Gable asked and Fred said it was. Gable laughed. "He's a great writer and a great humorist; I'll be looking forward to meeting him."

As soon as they finished eating, Fred called McLemore in London. To bypass the long ears of the censor without mentioning Gable by name, he told McLemore to be sure and come out for the show that night. "*Gone with the Wind* is here," he said.

McLemore failed to make it for a number of reasons, not the least of which was that he had been less discreet about revealing the arrival of Gable and someone in Intelligence took official notice of his story, hauling him in for questioning—and a lesson—which lasted way past midnight. But the show went on and was a good tonic for the bomber crews and support personnel. Many of the crews were going out again in the morning, and everyone knew that not all of them would be coming back.

By the spring of 1943, Fred got a notice from a Chicago attorney, hired by the PGA as its Executive Secretary. As soon as he got his business cards, he called Fred and asked him to sign a release from his PGA contract, which had three years to run.

"Why should I?" Fred asked, not unreasonably. His salary in 1943 was still $5,000 a year, the same as it had been when he started with the PGA some six years before.

"Since the start of the war," the lawyer said, "the PGA has held few, if any, tournaments and your contract calls for you to serve as tournament manager."

Fred told him he would call him back, and he had barely hung up the telephone when he had another call from Chicago. This time it was from one of his favorite secretaries in the PGA office.

"Fred," she said hurriedly, "don't you dare sign your release. They're trying to force you out."

So now it was his move. He called Francis Juggins, an attorney friend in Boston, who in turn, called the Chicago lawyer.

"I understand you're calling Corcoran's contract invalid because there won't be any tournaments during the coming year," said Juggins.

"That's right," said the new executive secretary.

"Just one question," said Juggins. "Is the PGA still collecting dues from its members?"

He said it was.

"Then, the contract is still good for three years. I've just finished reading your bylaws and there's nothing in there that says there shall be tournaments—nothing that says Corcoran has to arrange any," Juggins asserted. So that squeeze play failed.

The weeks dragged on and the only one Fred heard from with any regularity and thoughtfulness was Nancy. Fred would write back via "Victory Mail," a process the War Department used to save money. With V-mail, they photographed a typed or hand-written letter on microfilm and shipped to film to the U.S. where it was developed, printed to the size of a postcard and delivered to the recipient. Fred's read:

Dear Nancy:

Your nice letters have been forwarded promptly to me here. Believe it or not, your letters have been the only ones I have received with the exception of one from my brother John. I understand all my friends are out of the Savoy which is too bad. It looks like I'll have to get in the Barbizon. If you invite me. Or I might even go back to the Ritz.

I have been very busy with the sports programs which are going well. I'd only bore you with the details. The boys seem to like it. I meet a lot from Youngstown. The Crosby-Hope pictures are the most popular here. I saw the "Road to Zanzibar" the other night.

Please write me and give me all the latest news from school. Be sure to study hard. When the war is over, business will start again and many men will need secretaries.

I'm feeling fine and enjoying myself but naturally, I miss my Youngstown beauty queen. (I don't mean maybe.) I hope you don't forget me.

Oceans of love,
Fred

P.S. Give my best to your mother.

In the coming weeks, Henry McLemore and Fred became constant companions. With a lull in their schedule, they crossed over to Ireland to take a look around. In contrast to London, everything in Dublin was lighted up. The war was not evident there. But it almost broke out when Fred and Henry hailed a cab at the railroad station. As the cabbie, who was built like an NFL linebacker, flung their suitcases in the boot and they started off, McLemore leaned forward and remarked to the driver, "Why aren't you Irish bastards in the war?"

The cab spun to the curb and the Irish giant was out like a panther, hurling their luggage onto the sidewalk. Fred watched McLemore, who showed surprising early foot as they say around Aqueduct, flee down the street with his suitcase sailing after him. Over his shoulder he shouted, "Box him, Fred, box him! Don't fight him!"

McLemore could run, and he also had what Dubliners would describe as a powerful thirst on him. He couldn't buy enough of that Irish whiskey to haul back to London. Trouble was, he forgot that the customs guards would come through the train at the Ulster border, slapping duties on every quart. This left him without a farthing, and a strong need to finish off a few bottles before they hit the border.

Once in Greenock, which was a naval base, they saw a battleship berthed with a submarine alongside. Talking their way aboard, something that Fred was very adept at, they went down into the sub and stumbled onto a fast crap game which proved to be another temptation for McLemore.

"I gotta get into that game, Fred," he said, rubbing his hands together as if to warm them up and bring on luck. "But I don't have any money. I gave it all to the bastard border guards. Give me your money. I swear, I'll double it!"

Well, he lost it. All of it. So into Glasgow they went, penniless, with only their military passes. They holed up at a hotel which didn't have a single pane of glass left, only sugar sacks fluttering in the window casements. But they slept well and had a complimentary breakfast in the military mess.

Before catching a train back to London, they found their way to the telegram office and proceeded to write to everyone they knew to send them money.

Fred thought a minute and then had an idea. "Let's write to Crosby. I think one of his horses just won the Kentucky Derby."

"Then he must be rolling in dough right now. Great idea, Fred," Henry urged, slapping Fred on the back and knowing this would be good for some sort of story.

Fred waived the pen above the paper twice before he collected his thoughts and dashed off a telegram to Bing, asking that he send a hundred pounds to help old Corcoran and McLemore get out of a sticky situation.

By the time they got back to London, there was a message waiting from Bing. "You didn't say a hundred pounds of what so here is a hundred pounds of cheese." Stacked behind the desk at the hotel were four boxes, each with twenty-five pounds of cheese inside. After a good laugh, they bought some wine and some more whiskey and had a party in Bing's honor with everyone they knew.

Fred's leave of absence was about up when he received a telegram in June, which read, "Come home at once—urgent." It was signed, Ed Dudley. So he made his second pilgrimage to Harvey Gibson's office and showed him the cable and inquired about transportation. Mr. Gibson wasn't too concerned. Fred didn't blame him, but there he was, a volunteer, traveling on his own bank account. He expected some consideration.

"You'll just have to wait and take your chances," Gibson said. "We have a lot of ranking military officers with higher priorities."

Fred left his office and wandered down the street to the Officers' Club where most of the important Anglo-American drinking was done during the war. It was a Friday afternoon and clerks and undersecretaries of one kind or another were spilling out of the War Ministry offices and sprinting for the railroad station. Officially, the war stopped about four-thirty p.m. on Friday and didn't resume until nine a.m. on Monday. On weekends everyone went to the country.

At the Officers' Club Fred found Col. Earl E.T. Smith, who later became the U.S. Ambassador to Cuba. "How soon can you be ready to leave?" Smith asked after Fred described his problem.

"I'm ready right now," Fred said. And within an hour, he was aboard a C-54 flying out of London. Twenty hours later, he was back in New York, jingling nickels in his pocket. His first call was to Dudley who was quite surprised to hear from him.

"What about the cable?" Fred asked.

"I don't know anything about any cable," he said. "But welcome home anyway."

The puzzle cleared up when Fred caught up with Walter Ring, a dear and close friend. Walter admitted sending it. He said he was getting lonesome.

The six-month tour in England had taught Fred one thing. The American kids were starved for the sights and sounds of home. The USO shows, with the singers and the dancing girls and the comedians, were a wonderful tonic. The boys loved them. But they were hungry for sports and loved the bull sessions on all kinds of sports. And Fred also witnessed the positive effect that golf had on wounded soldiers. Golf would get them out of bed and putting into a tin cup across a hospital floor. This convinced Fred that he should get back to work and rev up the tour and promote golf. It was a patriotic thing to do. Plus, golf was how he made a living.

Chapter 17

AFTER PUTTING A FEW PIECES OF GOLF BUSINESS TOGETHER, FRED HAD an idea. He went to Chicago and called on Judge Kenesaw Mountain Landis, the Commissioner of Baseball. "I want to bring some players overseas and tour the bases," Fred proposed, expanding on his idea of sports as therapy for the soldiers.

Landis made notes while Fred talked. "It would mean so much to the men overseas to have real live baseball stars walk in and visit them. It doesn't matter whether they're in uniform or not. There are plenty of major leaguers in the service and the troops understand the conditions."

Fred was floored by Landis' response. "Corcoran," he said, "I certainly want to cooperate a hundred percent. But right now, we have an All-Star Game coming up next week. Let me get in touch with you when I get back from Pittsburgh. In the meantime, I'll ask just one thing of you. Please don't talk about this, will you? Don't even tell anyone you were here today."

Fred agreed and returned to New York to keep his vow of silence.

About two weeks later, he opened the newspaper to see a wire story out of Pittsburgh under a headline that read, "Landis to Send Baseball Players on War Tour." Somewhere between Chicago and Pittsburgh Corcoran got written out of the script.

So Fred went another route. The USO was shuttling off packaged shows to overseas bases and four New York sportswriters—Granny Rice, Joe Williams, Dan Parker and Bob Considine—were serving as a sports advisory board for that organization. With their assistance, Fred was able to recast a second edition of the Fred Corcoran Sports Show under USO auspices. He then went looking for volunteers.

Jimmy Walker, the dapper little ex-mayor of New York, wanted desperately to go along. They sat together in Toots Shor's one evening and he pleaded to make the tour. He'd have been a great addition to the troupe, but he couldn't get an okay from the Pentagon and had to stay behind.

Next, Fred went to Boston and called on Jack Sharkey, the old sailor and former heavyweight boxing champion, at his bar. Jack was enthusiastic. "But let me talk to my wife," he said.

He went off and made a phone call and returned about twenty minutes later. "Okay, I'm in."

"What did your wife say?" Fred asked.

He hemmed and hawed for a moment and then ordered a drink. "Well, she asked me why I want to go and I told her that I feel it's the right thing to do. Once I said that, she said if I felt that way, I should go. So when do we ship out?"

Lefty Gomez, the former Yankee pitcher, was working in a defense plant when Fred found him. "What'll we do?" he asked.

"Oh, tell a few stories and answer some questions," Fred told him. "We will get transportation and room and board."

"How long will we be gone?" Fred guessed, offering four to six months as the answer.

"Alright," Gomez said. "I'll start packing."

Fred picked up some prints of sports films—the heavyweight title fights including the Sharkey-Dempsey and Tunney bouts, the Byron Nelson golf film made at Pinehurst by Joe Walsh, some World Series baseball films—and they shipped out to Casablanca in North Africa in December of 1943. They traveled under a USO unit number, without names, and when the Special Services officer, Colonel Sid Piermont, met them at the gangplank, he looked quite bewildered when they called to him.

"What's the matter," Fred asked, sensing something was wrong.

"Oh, nothing," Piermont said, as Sharkey, Gomez and Corcoran reported for duty. "It's just that I was expecting dancing girls," he said with a touch of disappointment.

The men worked up a routine that included showing films and telling stories. Then they'd challenge the boys to stump the experts with questions. It was a simple format, but the boys enjoyed it. Lefty Gomez, Jack Sharkey and Fred used to throw occasional curves at each other on stage.

One night, before thousands of troops, Lefty selected his all-time baseball team and came up with an outfield of Babe Ruth, Joe DiMaggio and Hank Greenberg. Fred protested, "What about Ted Williams?"

"Look," said Gomez, "I'll pick my team and, when I'm through, you can pick yours." While that doesn't sound particularly humorous, coming from a former New York Yankee great—who was a contagiously funny man—it brought howls of delight from keyed-up, homesick GIs, so they kept it in the act. Fred didn't actually know Ted Williams at that time. He was just a name on the sports page. But as a Bostonian and a lifelong Red Sox fan, he felt a certain possessive pride in Williams.

At the end of the show, Fred would take the stage. "I'd like to thank everyone for coming tonight," he'd say, "and let's have a hand for Jack Sharkey, the former Heavyweight Champion of the World, and Lefty Gomez, one of baseball's greatest players." After a round of applause, Fred would continue. "Are there any questions before we go?"

On one particular night, a boy in the audience stood up, cupped his hands to his mouth, and yelled, "Yeah, who's you?" Forever the man behind the scenes with the ideas that deserved the spotlight, Fred carried on with a smile, a good laugh and a story he'd tell for years.

On Christmas Day, they caught up and shared a drink with Bob Hope who, like Fred, had put together a show and had just performed it for the troops. Then the sports trio followed the Fifth Army to Italy.

It was in Naples that Fred caught up with Humphrey Bogart and his third wife, actress Mayo Methot. They wound up together at a big theater for an evening of entertainment for the paratroopers who were scheduled to make a combat jump the next day. Bogart spoke briefly and after the show, they all headed out to the local watering hole. The specialty of the house that night was some kind of Italian explosive that was smuggled down out of the mountains and passed around in a bowl. The idea was to polish off the bowl while the others tolled a count on you. It was some sort of elimination round, where amid much counting, some were counted out.

The evening wore along and they finally returned to their hotel where they sat around until three a.m., when the party began to break up. Fred got up to go to his room and as he passed Methot, she side-slipped on the takeoff and he caught her. She was headed for the powder room, and since she was wobbling in the same direction and already in his arms, he gallantly offered his services as a navigator. He left her at the door to the ladies' room and went on to bed.

He dropped off to sleep instantly but bolted upright when he heard the pounding on his door, like the whole Fifth Army wanted in immediately. Amid muffled shouts of "Let me in!" and "sonofabitch," the door shook under the buffeting.

Fred was still debating whether to open the door or ignore the intruder, hoping he'd go away, when the door flew open and in staggered Bogart, with a pistol in his hand and a wild look in his eye.

"Where is she?" he howled, looking around without focusing. Then he lunged into the closet where he fought it out briefly with a pair of slacks. He came back to the bedside and waved the gun at Fred's chest. "Where's my wife?" he shouted.

"I don't know where the hell she is!" Fred told him, holding up his hands without being asked. "I left her at the girls' room."

Bogart lurched back and there was an explosion. A deafening roar and a blinding flash filled the room as Fred saw a large chunk of wall fly away. Apparently the shot startled Bogart, too. Or else, satisfied that his wife wasn't in the room, he decided it was best to just leave.

Fred didn't see him the next day but he learned that his wife had simply reached the sanctuary of the little girls' room where she quietly folded up and went to sleep.

Fred wrote in *Unplayable Lies* that he bumped into Bogart in an elevator at the Shamrock Hotel in Houston many year later. Fred greeted him cordially and Bogart flung an arm around him.

"You mean you're not sore after what happened in that hotel in Naples?" he asked. Fred answered that it could happen to anyone and that he had no hard feelings.

"My God!" Bogart exclaimed. "And to think I might have killed you!" He turned to his friend and told him the story. Then he turned back to Fred. "Didn't you ever tell anyone this story?"

"Upon my soul," Fred assured him solemnly, guessing that he had told a thousand people. But Fred never gave Bogart's name in print, calling him a "prominent actor" in *Unplayable Lies,* even though Bogart had passed away five years before the book's publication. This leads to a slightly different story, one that left Bogart terribly embarrassed and begging Fred not to reveal his identity. And keeping his word Fred never did, but he did call in a favor when Bing Crosby wanted some extra publicity for his Pro-Am tournament when it started again after the war.

"I can get you Bogart to hand out the trophy," Fred told Bing.

"No one can get Bogart," Bing said, dismissing the idea. Bogart was then the hottest star in Hollywood, just coming off *To Have and Have Not* and *The Big Sleep*.

"I can get Bogart. He owes me a favor." Fred repeated and a day later, news came that Bogart was on board, with his Naples secret safe with Fred.

But back at the front, the Corcoran team went on to spend a few days in Naples, which at this time was the nerve center of the American push up the Italian boot. Naturally, it was the target of a lot of German bombing runs, and at night, the blackout was total. This always struck Fred as odd: You had to hide in a closet to light a cigarette, but Mt. Vesuvius stuck up there like a giant beacon, smoking and belching. But he supposed the brass figured there was no point in making things any easier for the enemy.

Fred fell ill with a fever and had taken to bed when they had a raid. They had called a doctor when the sirens began screaming and the lights blinked out automatically. Finally the medical captain arrived with a flashlight, took Fred's pulse, and said he belonged in the hospital up the hill. Sharkey and Gomez were standing beside the bed when two showgirls from a USO unit came in to ask if there was anything they could do.

"Yes," said the doctor, "get him some fruit juice."

The girls said they'd be back and when they returned a little while later, there was a resounding crash just as they reached the door. With that, they turned and scampered back downstairs to the protection of the hotel cellar, leaving a big enameled basin behind at the door. The medic flashed his beam on it and remarked, "Ah, there's the fruit juice." He carried it into the room, sniffed it approvingly, and remarked, "Smells like lemon juice. Here, drink this." And he scooped up a glassful.

Fred tasted it and his stomach sent up flares of distress. "I can't drink this, Doc," he said, "it's awful." The doctor explained that he had given him some pills which spoiled the taste.

"You try it," Fred moaned.

"No, you drink it; you need it. It's lemonade and it's good for you," the doctor said before ending the conversation.

Well, Fred forced down three or four glasses of the stuff. He would drop his arm over the side of the bed, bale up a glassful, drink it and choke. Meanwhile, the bombs were bouncing around Naples like hail stones. But at last, the all-clear sounded and the lights came back on.

About ten minutes later, the two pretty blonds came back to his room, looked at the basin, and let out a howl.

"What happened to our lemon hair rinse?" one of them screamed.

Hair rinse! An hour later, Fred was rushed off to the Fifth Army hospital suffering from an acute case of hair-rinse poisoning. The wounded were stacked in the lobby of the hotel in five-tier bunks and the doctors never did get around to Fred. And after being violently ill all night, he began a slow recovery in the morning. The doctors thought the whole incident was hilariously funny, confirming his worst suspicions of their sadistic tendencies.

On another night the bombs were banging around the Parco Hotel worse than usual and they were all down in the catacombs, riding out the storm. It was pretty bad and they were all worried. Sharkey, who was a very devout man, dropped to his knees and prayed.

Fred seized the moment, figuring it was a good time to ask a question that had been nagging him for a long time.

"Jack," he said, "give it to me straight. Did you take a dive for Camera in that second fight?" It was a reasonable question since he had handled the Italian circus giant so easily in their first meeting.

Very solemnly, Sharkey said, "I swear I didn't, Fred." A really close miss shook the whole building. He decided Sharkey had to be telling the truth.

Lefty Gomez left the troupe after six weeks and returned home. Sharkey and Fred stayed on for awhile in Italy. Finally, however, by February of '44, they decided to pack it in and headed back by way of North Africa where they picked up a ride in a Sikorsky amphibian plane flying over via Bermuda.

As they winged along across the Atlantic through a heavy overcast, Jack coiled up and fell asleep. Fred was bored, so he stepped up the stairs to the flight deck for a chat with the pilot and the navigators who were as bored as he was. They had the plane locked on automatic control, and when Fred discovered this, he had an idea.

"Look," he said, "how about letting me sit there in the seat with the helmet and headset, goggles, and all the rest of it. Then you go back and wake up Sharkey. Ask him how long his friend has been a pilot. Tell him I offered to relieve you and now you're worried because you think I've gotten you lost"

The boys fell in with the plot right away and positioned Fred in the seat with the controls. Then the pilot went down the aisle and shook Jack awake, feeding him the story. They must have sounded convincing because Sharkey let out an ear-splitting screech. "Has he lost his mind?" he screamed. "He can't even fly a kite!" With that, he came storming up to the flight deck, his eyes bugging. "Get out of there, you damn fool!" he shouted. "What're you trying to do, get us all killed?"

Fred, looking a lot like Charles Lindbergh, took his hands off the controls and held them up. "Look, Jack," he said, "No hands!"

Sharkey turned to the two officers. "Get him out of there before I drag him out and dump him overboard," he said hoarsely.

Fred went quietly. In fact, that would be a fitting epitaph to his contribution to the war effort. He went quietly, and he came home the same way.

Chapter 18

Back in the States in the spring of '44, Fred caught up with the tour at a tournament the following week, one that guaranteed to pay the top twenty finishers. With most of the pros still away, the field was light and only eighteen players showed up. But Lefty Stackhouse was there. Lefty had quite a temper that was often fueled with alcohol. He had a party the night before the final round that ended only when he showed up at the first tee the next morning. At the end of nine holes, Fred ran into him.

"Lefty, you look terrible. Are you okay?" Fred said, genuinely concerned.

"I'm okay," Lefty grumbled. "Just didn't get enough sleep."

"Well," Fred offered, "you know you're guaranteed a check just for finishing. Why don't you go into the locker room and take a little nap before going back out to play the back nine." This was actually allowed at the time.

Lefty nodded and changed directions, heading for the clubhouse. Alvin York, a true war hero, was standing with Fred, listening to this whole thing. It was the first time he had ever seen golf played. As Stackhouse slumped off, Alvin turned to Fred. "Oh my," he said, "I had no idea golf was such a strenuous game!"

Stackhouse, upon reaching the men's locker room, curled up in a couch, only to wake up at nightfall and miss out on the back nine and his check.

In between tournament stops, Fred was still arranging shows for the military. At one stop in Corpus Christie, Texas, he was thrilled to see their theater packed with 2,800 servicemen, Navy brass and Waves for an 8:00 p.m. show. He just couldn't believe the turnout of a crowd so thick that they even had to turn away 600 people. Later they learned that Bing Crosby's latest movie, *Here Come the Waves,* was scheduled to start in the same theater at 8:30 p.m. They all got a big kick out of that.

By now, the PGA had elected to resume tournament play and Fred went back to work, doing what he did so well—finding money and sponsors and staging tournaments. He told anyone who would put up $10,000 that the boys who were around would be there to play, even though the big guns—Ben Hogan, Jimmy Demaret, Sam Snead, Jimmy Thomson, Lawson Little, Paul Runyan and Horton Smith—were still in the service. Regardless, Fred was able to put together a schedule of twenty-three tournaments that year, twenty more than they played in 1943.

And Fred's persistence and persuasion paid off when he brought in a record purse of $20,000, double the amount of any previous tournament. He signed with the Spokane Athletic Round Table to host the 1944 PGA Championship, the first major to be played in two years. The Round Table was comprised of a group of influential business men from Spokane with a passion for golf and a bankroll from a legal slot machine operation. But Fred worried about the location, a remote spot some 275 miles from Seattle. He felt it was risky to take the tournament there, and he was right when the competition turned out light. Many pros had war-related commitments and others just couldn't get there. The anticipated field of 140 fell to 100, then 85, and finally to 66 players, with many slots filled by club pros.

From there, Fred went to Portland to met Bob Hudson, the fruit-packing tycoon, who had sent word that he was interested in sponsoring a tournament in 1945. Arriving in Portland to discuss contract terms with Hudson, Fred came away from that meeting dazzled by his generosity. What started as a pleasant surprise grew to an overwhelming delight as Fred went over each point in the tournament agreement, which started with a minimum purse of $7,500.

"We'll make it $10,000," said Bob, drawing a line through the original figure. Then he came to the clause specifying an entrance fee for the players of one dollar per one thousand dollars of prize money. Hudson drew a line through that. "No entrance fees," he said. "The boys just register and play for the prize money."

Next came the line that established caddie fees of three dollars per round. The Hudson pen made another stroke. "I'll pay the caddies," he said.

The agreement also carried a provision requiring the sponsor to set aside a suitable room where the players and their families could eat lunch with some privacy and be assured of prompt service. The new sponsor stroked his chin. "What does that mean?"

"Just that," Fred shrugged. "They want a place where they can eat with their families without being disturbed by a lot of well-meaning people."

Hudson waved an expansive hand. "Oh well," he said, "I'll set aside a private dining room for them and they'll all be my guests."

Now Fred had a $10,000 tournament with no entrance or caddie fees and free meals. It was like stumbling on Blackbeard's treasure chest. But people are funny, and it's the nature of man to be perpetually dissatisfied. Fred's next tournament stop was in Los Angeles and he arrived on the scene to find a rump session of the Locker Room Congress. Some of the players complained chronically that the purses should be higher, and all Fred could do was agree with them and point out they were increasing steadily.

But this time, he arrived just in time to walk in on the locker-room meeting and hear the remark, "If that blarney bag Corcoran was on the job, he'd find us a Hudson in every town."

So there you are. Instead of a jolly-good-fellow cheer for coming up with the unprecedented Portland contract, Fred was being roasted over a slow fire. Sometimes you wonder!

The fact that Sam Snead returned to the tour the next month, when he was discharged from the Navy due to a bad back, thrilled Fred to no end.

Chapter 19

Fred had just played a tournament in Philadelphia in 1944 when he was approached by Tom Yawkey and Joe Cronin, the owner and manager of the Boston Red Sox, to become their road secretary at considerably more than he was being paid by the PGA. Fred liked baseball and the prospect of working for the Red Sox had its attraction. But golf was his game and there was no sense in kidding himself.

"Thanks, but I don't think I'm ready to leave golf," Fred told Yawkey, who dispatched Cronin to work on Fred. Cronin, who was filling in as a wartime third baseman, had broken his leg at Yankee Stadium so he was left behind as the team moved on. He went down to Philadelphia on crutches to press the case. Sitting outside the PGA meeting room, his broken leg propped up on a chair, he waited to talk further with Fred, and perhaps his mere presence had a certain effect on the committee. The PGA raised Fred's pay to $7,500 dollars and kicked up the per diem allowance from a ridiculous ten dollars a day to a more realistic twenty-five dollars a day.

The end of the war in 1945 brought times of general unrest and turbulence on the tour. Men were pouring back into civilian life, hungry to make up for lost time. Scores of pros, including players like Ben Hogan, Porky Oliver, Jimmy Demaret, Sam Snead, Vic Ghezzi, and Lloyd Mangrum were among them. Many, like most returning servicemen, carried a smoldering resentment because fate had chosen them for military duty while others stayed home and advanced their careers. They were in a mood to listen to agitators and conversations were often heated.

The 1946 U.S. Open had its own controversy. Byron Nelson was leading when his caddie inadvertently stepped on Nelson's ball as he climbed under the marshals' rope fronting the green, making this another Open championship lost by the thin margin of a penalty stroke. The penalty threw Nelson into a three-way tie with Vic Ghezzi and Lloyd Mangrum, who won.

"I can still see Byron," Fred told the press, "with his arm over the youngster's shoulders, comforting the weeping caddie with the empathetic words, 'I was a caddie once myself.'"

With the war behind them, postwar tournament golf was beginning to come on strong. But the heat was beginning to scorch, and Fred had a few other fish he was interested in frying. He was tired of traveling, fed up with the politics, and he had a lovely woman in New York who he rarely saw. In June he went before the PGA Tournament Committee and proposed that he leave the tour, set up a central office in New York, and put Gerry Moore, a Boston sportswriter, on the road as tournament director.

"Who would pay this man's salary?" the committee asked.

"I would," Fred said. The committee then said they saw no reason why Moore couldn't handle the position of tournament director, and they agreed that Fred could function more effectively as a tournament promoter operating out of a fixed address. So Moore took over the balance of the 1946 tour.

It was then that Fred did get involved with baseball—and the Red Sox—in a big way. John, Fred's brother, ran the Ford dealership in Wellesley, Massachusetts, and had sold a car to Ted Williams. Ted and John developed a friendship and Ted would stop by the Corcoran Ford agency almost every morning until it was time to go to Fenway Park. He complained to John that hustlers were constantly punching his doorbell and camping on his lawn. Everyone was waving a contract at him and he wanted no part of this business.

"These goddam guys won't let me alone and I don't want them bothering me. I'd like to find somebody who could deal with these sons of bitches and get 'em off my back." Even at this time, Williams was famous for his short temper and foul mouth.

"You should talk with my brother Fred," John suggested.

"What's he do?" Williams looked blank. If Fred tied trout flies or stocked ammunition, Williams would have known him. John explained Fred's function with the PGA and Ted looked skeptical. "But that's golf," he said. "My game's baseball."

John shrugged. "You said you wanted a manager. That's Fred's business. And he's the best there is. He knows everyone."

Williams finally leaped to his feet. "Okay," he said, "I'll call him."

Fred was in Chicago for George May's tournament at Tam O'Shanter when he received a call in his room at the Blackstone Hotel. "This is Ted Williams," said the voice. "I want to meet you."

Fred told him to come right over, and in a matter of minutes, there was a knock at the door. When Fred opened it, Ted seemed to spring into the room like a panther. Fred immediately felt a high-voltage energy fill the room. Williams was tall and lean and had the keenest pair of eyes Fred had ever looked into.

Ted explained his problem, saying that he had a lot of people running at him with contracts, and he was not a guy who liked to be jostled by a lot of people.

"Have you signed anything yet?" Fred asked him.

"Nothing," he said, "except my baseball contract. I'll take care of that myself." They talked some more and, finally, Ted turned and asked, "Are you interested?"

"Of course, I am," Fred said.

"Now, what do you want from me?" Williams asked.

"I'll take fifteen percent," Fred told him.

"Fifty?" he replied. "Okay."

"Not fifty," Fred corrected him. "Fifteen."

Williams let out a loud laugh. "Whatever you say. If you want to make it fifty that's all right with me."

"I assure you, that fifteen percent is a generous working margin." Fred stuck out his hand and the two shook. "Shall we draw up a contract?"

"We don't need any contract," Williams said. "John says you're for me and that's all I have to know."

But Fred insisted on calling in a public stenographer and dictating a note authorizing him to act as his sole and exclusive agent. If he had known then what he'd know later about Ted Williams, he would have realized that this kind of legal gibberish was totally unnecessary. Williams was a big leaguer all the way.

Fred then turned and picked up the phone and called L.B. Icely at the Wilson Sporting Goods Company and told him he could add Williams to his sports advisory staff. He named a price.

"If I had it to do over again I might have done it a little differently," Fred confessed later on, "But L.B. was always a true friend and a reliable adviser through the years, and also one of the most acute promoters in the sports equipment field."

Icely called Fred back a few minutes later. "I'll give you a $30,000 guarantee with three percent on all sales," he said, "but I want a ten-year contract." They signed with the Wilson Company that evening.

Reaching for the door Williams had an afterthought. "Let's keep this arrangement between us, if you don't mind. I don't think we ought to have any publicity about your being my business manager."

Fred suddenly felt pale. "How can I act as his representative if nobody knows about it?" he protested. After a back-and-forth for a few minutes, Fred finally agreed to play the game Ted's way. He knew it wasn't a secret that would keep for long. And sure enough, a week later he was in Portland, Oregon, for the PGA Championship, and he had a call from a wire service for a comment on an Associated Press story out of Boston to the effect that Fred had signed as Ted Williams' business manager.

"What does Williams say about it?" Fred stalled.

"Williams says you've signed a five-year contract to handle his affairs," replied the reporter.

"If Williams says it's true, it's true," he told him.

There were some strong feelings about this arrangement in Boston. Tom Yawkey, the Red Sox owner, was quoted as saying that Joe Cronin was still Ted's manager. Of course, Yawkey had a fatherly concern about Ted and felt that he should have been consulted before Ted took a step like this. But the first rush of anger passed quickly. Later, both Cronin and Yawkey agreed that this arrangement was in Ted's best interest and in the best interest of the Red Sox, and their association worked out well.

But Williams could be the most exasperating person in the world, and much the same could be said for Fred. "I walked away from him more times than I can remember," Fred told others. "He walked away from me a few times, too."

Meanwhile, Fred was still dodging an occasional bullet from the Corcoran's-gotta-go faction of the PGA. Things had become so farfetched that Fred was summoned one day to defend himself against a paragraph written by Bill Cunningham in the *Boston Herald*.

Bill, an old friend and staunch champion of Fred's from the outset, had come up with one of those hometown stories in which he identified Corcoran as "the man who took the golf pros out of the caddie sheds and back seats of automobiles and put them in saddle shoes." Granted, the line was in bad taste, but Fred had no control over Cunningham's typewriter, a fact which should have been obvious to the players. But some of the status-hungry boys were infuriated.

"What's the idea of saying a thing like that?" they scolded. "Who do you know who ever slept in the back seat of an automobile?"

"I didn't say it," Fred protested, declining the open invitation to recite a pretty good list of seat-cushion sleepers. "That's Bill Cunningham saying it. It's not in quotes."

"The hell you didn't say it! There it is—in black and white."

"But it's not in quotes," he argued.

"The hell it isn't," came the reply. "It's in print!"

Amid all this silliness, Fred still held the writers in high esteem and often said that if he hadn't taken the roads he had, he would have liked to have been one. And after this particular incident, he realized he really wanted these writers on his side, so he proposed the idea of a Golf Writers Association and launched it during the 1946 PGA Championship at Portland, Oregon. With all due respect to their profession, sportswriters loved to pat themselves on the back.

The Association, at the time, was set up to honor great writers and provide a sense of membership to this loose band of solo players. They were often the underpaid secretaries who recorded history with verbal pictures and articulate yarns. And they were a loyal bunch who were known to help each other out on the rare occasion when one missed a deadline due to an overactive thirst. Often, one would awake with a big headache only to find his story had been submitted while he slept.

Fred loved the writers and they cared a great deal for Fred because he was the closest thing they had to a golf encyclopedia, and not only did he have the facts and figures, he could weave them into entertaining stories and anecdotes—like the time in 1945 when Bing Crosby won the Academy Award for his role in *Going My Way*. He told Sam Snead about it and urged him to wire his congratulations to Bing. Sam's reply was a laconic, "Okay...did he win at match or medal play?"

Stories like these, all authentic, were accepted as legal tender by the golf writers who, knowing Sam, believed most of them, and by their editors who probably didn't believe any of them. But they were true and they made good copy. The editors welcomed them as "brights"—little chuckles that could be boxed to dress up the sports page.

Paul Gardner in *Liberty*, a magazine of the day, wrote, "Fred is the answer to the rainy-day prayers of the nation's sportswriters. Any one of them, beset by a calm in the news, knows that if only he can get to Fred Corcoran, he's got a story. For Corcoran is an encyclopedia of all sports, has a gift for thinking up 'angles,' and has a memory as accurate as it is long."

So the Association was formalized in the locker room, where most of Fred's business was done. But the credit for force-feeding it in its infancy went to Charley Bartlett of the *Chicago Tribune* and Herb Graffis, another Chicagoan and the freestyle champion of golf journalism. Others who nursed the baby through a perilous infancy included Russ Newland of the San Francisco AP bureau, Hal Wood and Oscar Fraley, Charley Curtis of the *Los Angeles Times*, Lawton Carver of International News Service, Art Rosenbaum of the *San Francisco Chronicle*, Harry Grayson of Newspaper Editors Association, Holly Goodrich of the *Portland Oregonian,* San Francisco scribes Roger Williams, Nelson Cullenward and Harry Hayward, Prescott Sullivan of the *San Francisco Examiner*, Braven Dyer of the *Los Angeles Times* and Leo Peterson of the United Press.

Things rocked along into 1946 with Fred stationed in New York, away from the fray. Meanwhile, a power struggle was building up within the PGA, between the touring pros and the rank-and-file club pros, with control of the tour at stake. The touring pros were still making more money to come off the tour and play an exhibition somewhere rather than compete in the next town. A tournament without the big names, of course, would not draw as many spectators and the sponsors would not make as much money.

Everyone, too, knew that Fred was handling the business affairs of Ted Williams. Fred had gone to the PGA officials at the time of his contract discussions and asked if there were any objection to such an arrangement with Williams. They had none. But inevitably, the chronic agitators began screaming about his "divided interests" and implying that he was being paid by the PGA, but working for Williams. During the war, the same cry was raised by a club pro who objected to Fred's travels around the country with Bing Crosby, Bob Hope, Lawson Little and Ed Dudley on a bond-selling exhibition tour. He wanted to know whether Fred was working for Crosby or the PGA. It made no difference to him that Fred was paying his own expenses on that tour, a fact that was pointed out repeatedly. This was characteristic of some pros. At home they were full of humility and deference to the members. But turn them loose in an association meeting of their peers and they became tigers, growling for blood.

Even Sam was giving Fred some trouble. He had gotten over his fear of flying and almost ruined Fred when he flew off to South Africa with a tennis promoter named Jack Harris, who had guaranteed him $10,000 for a series of matches with Bobby Locke. Locke was the first international golf star who later followed Snead back to the U.S. and went on to win Opens all over the world.

Fred was furious when he found out and Sam tried to reason with him. "I'd have to win five tournaments on the PGA winter tour to make that kind of money and here it is being handed to me with no sweat and tears," he said.

Fred couldn't really blame Sam but his timing was bad, as this occurred during one of Fred's skirmishes with the "mashie Mafia" in the PGA. The defection of the Number One gate attraction put Fred in a bad spot, leaving him with a swarm of angry sponsors who blamed him personally for not being able to deliver the star. He was not only embarrassed by this maneuver, but he was raging at Harris. Here was a guy who never did a thing for the game of golf, but who stepped in and made a quick score by snatching the big attraction.

Sam had put Fred on the spot another time, on the day before his scheduled departure for the British Open. During the last round of the Inverness Four-Ball tournament, Sam came to Fred at the ninth hole and said, "Fred, I'm not going to St. Andrews. I'm just not putting well and there's no point in me going all the way over there if I can't get the damn ball in the hole."

Well, Fred was furious. Their plans were already made. He was supposed to fly that evening to New York and take off for England the next day. After an argument, Fred stormed off to the clubhouse and the first person he met was Walter Hagen and Fred unloaded his story.

"Oh, what a shame!" Hagen said, "With his touch he'd putt those greens at St. Andrews as if they belonged to him."

When Snead came off the course, Walter was waiting for him. He drew Sam off to the far end of the locker room and said, "Sam, let me see you putt." He watched Sam stroke a few balls, and then he stopped him.

"Raise your blade just a little, Sam," he told him. "Try to slap that ball just above the equator. All you want to do is get it rolling…rolling …rolling…." Over and over, he had Sam stroke balls on the carpet until Sam was snapping his putts with a new crispness. Then he stopped him and said, "All right, you've got it now. Go ahead over there to St. Andrews and win it."

Fred duly told the newspaper boys about the episode in the locker room and the next morning the local paper carried a sports page headline, "Snead to Play in British Open—Takes Putting Lesson From Walter Hagen." This was all right, but at the same time, Snead was syndicating a series of instruction pieces and the gospel for the day was set up in a two-column box next to the main golf story. The headline over there read,

"How to Putt, by Sam Snead"!

Any good story has to have a happy ending, and this one does. Snead went to St. Andrews and won the 1946 British Open. He never putted better.

Fred caught up with him afterwards, and said, "Sam, give me the ball you won with." Sam looked at me quizzically and then pulled it out of his pocket with a smile. "Let me have it," Fred said, reaching for it.

"That's my lucky ball," Sam said, tossing it in the air and catching it in one hand, before returning it to his pocket.

"Give it to me," Fred demanded. "You don't have a lucky ball. You have a lucky putter."

Sam thought for a moment, and suspecting Fred was up to something, handed over the ball. Fred added to the others in his pocket. "I can get you some great press by handing these balls out as 'your one-and-only lucky ball,'" he said, slapping him gently on the back.

"Just don't go signing my autograph to any dinner checks," Sam added.

That year, 1946, was busy, alright, but it wasn't all storm and stress. Fred was around for a 36-hole match between Dick Burton, the holdover wartime British Open Champion, and Byron Nelson. The group was sitting around Ed Wyner's Ritz Carlton Hotel in Boston on the eve of the match when Fred sensed that Byron was a little nervous about the coming match because he hadn't had a chance to see Burton play. Fred could almost hear his sigh of relief when Burton said he had come directly to Boston from New York when the Gripsholm docked, and he hadn't had a chance to warm up.

"Well, that's no problem," said Wyner. "Come on up on the roof and hit some."

With few nightclubs worth mentioning in Boston in those days, The Ritz Roof was Boston's swankest dining-and-dancing spot. What the guests didn't know was that Wyner had set up a complete private driving range on the Ritz Roof. It had everything, including a magnificent view of the Back Bay.

Burton was the first to hit a few balls off the roof with a swing so rusty from wartime disuse, you could hear it creak.

Nelson turned to Fred and said softly, "Now I can sleep tonight." The next day he went out and opened up a four-hole lead on Burton at Charles River and extended it at Winged Foot two days later.

It was a terrible thing for golf when, in 1946, Byron decided to retire at age 34. He always said his goal in golf was to make enough money to buy a farm, and by this time, he had and he did. But who knows what he could have gone on to win if he had stayed with it. Just the year before, he won eleven consecutive tournaments in almost as many weeks and eighteen for the year. And two weeks after Ben Hogan set a 72-hole scoring record of 261, Byron broke it with a 259.

Fred often posed the question, "Who's the better golfer, Bobby Jones or Byron Nelson?" His own opinion usually caused any nearby golf writers to sit up and sharpen their pens. "What a match that would be! Why it would be the Dempsey-Louis battle of golf. If they played a 72-hole match, honest, I wouldn't bet a nickel on the outcome. On his record, you would have to give Jones the edge. Bobby won thirteen major titles before his retirement and was runner-up in other main events. But Nelson's mission was an economic one, not an historic one. Each week he set out to win enough money to buy a ranch and retire from golf. In the process, he assembled the greatest year in the history of the game, both royal and ancient."

After the match at Winged Foot, Fred drove into New York City to celebrate the event. Bing Crosby was in town, having just returned from a trip to Europe where he had entertained the troops, and they arranged to meet at John Bruno's Pen & Pencil with a host of others. Fred called Nancy to join them, who by now was used to the late-night, last-minute dates. In fact, they added a bit of excitement to her life which was more-or-less built around Fred. By now, she had a job as a secretary at the International Chamber of Commerce but handled most of Fred's paperwork and correspondence as well. But he still lived at the Savoy Plaza, with no plans to settle down, and she was still at the Barbizon, with all the hopes in the world.

With everyone sending over drinks in celebration, they began an impromptu sports quiz, just like they had done for the troops. Bing surprised everybody by coming up with the answer to Ty Cobb's favorite baseball stumper: How can a club make six hits in an inning and still not score a run? Crosby had quite an inventory of sports trivia that impressed even Fred.

Bing told Fred that he had promised to send General Omar Bradley a golf club so he could practice his swing for exercise, and Fred jumped at the opportunity to have one of his equipment manufacturers send the club to the general. Then Crosby had a tougher request, this one from General Eisenhower, who asked him to send some whole hominy. Not hominy grits, mind you, but whole hominy. "I haven't been able to find any," Crosby confessed.

"I'll take care of that, too," Fred said, only to call Bing the next day at the Waldorf and say, "Bing, you'll never believe this, but you're going to have to sing for your whole hominy."

Fred had found the only wholesale grocery house in New York that handled whole hominy, and when he gave Crosby's name and address, the woman who ran the business thought it was a joke and refused to accept the order. In desperation, Fred asked the woman if she would recognize Bing's voice if she heard him sing over the phone. When she said, "yes," he told her he'd have Crosby call her and sing. When Bing heard the story he went along with the gag. He called the woman and sang a parody of an old favorite. "Hominy hearts have you broken," he crooned, "with those great big beautiful eyes."

CHAPTER 20

FRED SPENT A LOT OF HIS TIME IN 1946 WITH TED WILLIAMS—AND HE loved every minute of it. Ted had a widely publicized problem with the Boston press which Fred tried to ease. And Williams didn't like some of the fans any better than he did the reporters, something Fred could never understand about him—nor about a few other athletes for that matter. They never seemed to realize that without spectators you have nothing, whether you're on a golf course or in a ballpark. The spectators made it possible for Williams to become the first player to be paid a salary above $100,000 a year, followed by a long-term contract with Sears, Roebuck for money in six figures, starting in 1960 when he left the game.

Williams' attitude never changed and sometimes he went out of his way to show how he felt. He was reprimanded and fined for his behavior in response to heckling from Boston fans in the stands and for spitting at Kansas City fans. He had a favorite, unprintable term of endearment for some of the spectators.

In fact, Fred claimed, Ted never seemed to get any real pleasure out of baseball in general. When they were together, he rarely talked about it. The only aspect of the game that interested him was batting. Occasionally, he would discuss the mechanics of hitting, and he used to complain that he never got enough batting practice.

"Look at Snead and Hogan and those guys," he would say. "They get out there and practice hitting balls forever. I'm lucky if I can stand in there for fifteen practice swings a day. If I could get an hour's batting practice every day, I could hit .450."

He had some justification for this thinking. In 1941, when he broke his ankle just before the season opened, his spring training consisted of staying in Boston and spending hours in the batting cage at Fenway Park. A big strong-armed youngster named Joe Dobson was detached to serve them up to him, and Ted just stood there by the hour and took his cuts. That year he wound up with a .406 average to be the last man in the majors to hit above .400—a record that stands to this day. He went on to become one of the greatest hitters in the history of the game.

"Hitting was almost an obsession with Ted," Fred said. "He often spoke of his childhood, during which some bitterness was worked off by swinging a bat. As far back as he could remember, he would coax others to throw to him until he achieved the only real ambition he ever knew: to be a great ballplayer. As a fielder, he was much better than he looked. He had a good arm, good judgment on balls hit to him, and he was deceptively fast, being lanky and limber.

"He was born with talent, but he didn't rest on it," Fred said. "He honed it to a keen edge through those endless hours of hitting during his teens when his playmates were dissipating their time and energy on other things. In addition to other physical attributes, he had outstanding vision, vision found in only one in 100,000, according to Navy medical reports, and reflexes that made it possible for him to hit a ball after it passed him, according to catchers. Yogi Berra once said, 'He'll reach back with his bat and take the ball right out of your glove.'"

Fred introduced Williams to Sam Snead and they became good friends, spending many days together—fishing—and developing a lasting, friendly rivalry. In 1960, Fred got a call from *Golf Digest* to get the two of them together to analyze each other's swings. Sam wrote about it in his book, *The Game I Love*.

"Ted might have been the first southpaw golf champion. He had that delayed-hit action, holding his wrists back until the last second. But Ted was also a stubborn pull hitter in baseball (remember the famous "Williams Shift"?) and would have been a hooker in golf. He concentrated well, crowds didn't bother him, and he had a good touch. Ted would have been an aggressive player on the Tour."

He continued, "Ted said I would have made a king-sized Yogi Berra if I had played major league baseball—a strong arm behind the plate to gun down stealing base runners, and that I'd hit the ball a mile. We used to argue about which hand provided the power in the swing. I felt it was the left because you can pull more than you can push. We also argued about which sport was more difficult."

Fred took Sam to a Red Sox game around the time they first met, and they stopped by the dugout before the game. Ted and some of the

Red Sox players were jockeying Sam about the soft touch a professional tournament golfer has, compared with the life of the ball player.

"Aaah," Williams said, "you golfers are soft, tip-toeing around on the grass, all whispering to each other, being nice and saying 'after you.' We got guys throwing hard balls at our heads! And many of them don't like me."

"Yeah," Snead rebutted, "but you guys have eight other teammates to take up your slack and cover for ya. And you got that whole back fence as your target. I have to get a ball in a little 4-inch hole—eighteen times!"

Williams continued to needle, "You use a club with a flat hitting surface and belt a stationary object. What's tough about that? I gotta stand up there with a round bat and hit a ball that is traveling at me 110 miles an hour—and curving. And then we have about a tenth of a second to decide whether to swing or not."

Snead looked at Ted for a moment, then drawled, "Yeah, Ted, but you don't have to go up in the stands and play all your foul balls. I do!"

From their lips to the UPI and AP wires, via Fred Corcoran and his pocket full of nickels.

Williams was named the league's Most Valuable Player twice, and missed by only one point on another occasion. He led in Home Runs and in Runs Batted In five times and as Batting Champion seven times.

"But I prefer to remember 1941," Fred said, even though he didn't know Ted then. "That was the day he became the first .400 hitter in a decade and the last one since then. On the final day of the season, going into a double-header, he was hitting .39955, which would be .400 in the records. The Red Sox weren't fighting for anything, and Manager Joe Cronin advised Williams to watch the game from the bench and protect his place among the .400-batting elite. Williams elected to play, and went six for eight to haul his final average up to .406."

"But he wouldn't tip his hat when the fans cheered him," Fred said with a shake of his head.

Ted's performance in the 1946 World Series that first year with Fred was miserable: five singles in twenty-five times at bat for a .200 average. But the fans never knew that Ted played through that series in excruciating pain from a badly bruised elbow. Because the Dodgers and Cards wound up deadlocked, calling for a playoff, the Red Sox set up a game in Boston with an all-star American League team to fill the time. While he was at bat in this meaningless exhibition, Williams was hit on the elbow by a pitched ball. For several weeks after that he could barely pick up a bat, let alone swing one.

Every night during the World Series, he sat with his elbow packed in ice to relieve the pain and reduce the swelling, but it didn't help much. He failed to hit in the series and then, not only the Boston writers but sportswriters all over America, gave him a pretty good raking over. "I never saw Ted so depressed," Fred said. "He said he didn't care if he never played baseball again. And he meant it."

Ted needed someone to talk to so he and Fred talked and talked and talked. Fred told him about Ben Hogan missing an 18-inch putt to lose the Masters tournament that year, and what it cost him. He told him story after story of golfers who had dragged through some pretty low points in their lives. Williams seemed to perk up a little, but when he left Boston for a trip to California via Minneapolis, there was still some doubt that he would ever return to baseball. He was hurting, both physically and spiritually. All that really mattered to Ted was fishing, and occasionally hunting. He could fish for ten hours a day, seven days a week, and he thought there was something wrong with anyone who didn't like fishing.

Fred often visited Ted in the Florida Everglades and always came back with a story about it. "Ted was living in this swamp cabin near Everglades City," he began, pretending to swat mosquitoes as he told it, "and was awakened by the sound of somebody—or something—prowling across the metal roof. Ted slipped out of bed and took a shotgun from the wall rack. Then he returned it and grabbed a revolver. Then he had second thoughts about that and put it aside for a lead-weighted baseball bat he used to swing every day to strengthen his wrists. With the bat and a flashlight, he stepped outside just as the creature leaped from the roof.

"In the beam of the flashlight, Williams found himself eye to eye with a snarling Florida bobcat that made a fatal mistake—it came in fast, high and on the inside—right down Home Run Alley and got clobbered. With a bat in his hand, Ted Williams was one of the most dangerous men in the world. Ask a generation of American League pitchers...and that bobcat."

Fred could tell stories about Ted for hours. And what did this say about the man who befriended on the left, Ted Williams, and on the right, Ty Cobb—two of the orneriest men to ever run around third base. "I'm attracted to people with a temperament," he said often, admitting he was attracted to their energy, their passion and their brilliance.

The greatest admirer of Ted Williams as a hitter was Ty Cobb, who himself was among the .400 hitters, batting .420 and .409 in 1911 and 1912. "Cobb was an admirer who also was his most persistent critic," Fred said. "I remember their first meeting during the 1946 World Series. Ted and I were walking down the ramp after a game at Yankee Stadium and Granny Rice brought Cobb over to meet Ted. Williams grabbed a rolled-up newspaper I was carrying and drew Ty off to one side."

"Show me how you stand for a slider," he asked Cobb, who was happy to demonstrate.

"My boy," said Ty in a later session, "you're one of the greatest natural hitters I've ever seen. But why don't you ever hit to left? If you'd hit to left field, you'd break up that shift they pull on you and you'd break every record in the book. You could hit .500!"

Cobb embarked on an extensive correspondence with Williams, offering him batting tips and scolding him for looking at the first pitch. The pitchers, Cobb pointed out, knew he wouldn't swing on the first pitch and always slipped that first one in for a strike, making a two-strike batter out of him. Ted was grateful to Cobb for his interest and always listened patiently to him, but never accepted his advice.

"Fred," Williams said one day, "I'm not going to hit to left. If I do, these guys will start pitching to me differently. Right now I know where they'll pitch me—outside." Nor would he change his habit of taking the first pitch. "I know it's my home-run pitch," he said, "the best one I'll get. But I look it over because I know that if I just wait, it's going to come up again—and that's when I'll belt it."

Not until he reached the twilight of his life did Ty Cobb discover the real meaning of frustration. That was when he tried to remodel Ted Williams' batting style. Ty was determined to make Williams the first .450 hitter since they had stopped winding baseballs by hand. Like everything else he did, Cobb tackled this assignment with missionary zeal. He later branded Ted a wild stallion and tossed in the sponge.

In the spring, Fred received a long letter from Ty Cobb, in his usual green ink, suggesting that he was beginning to despair of ever changing Ted's batting habits. He went into a lengthy character analysis of Williams which could be summed up in these lines, extracted from the heart of the letter:

"Ted is like an outlaw horse that has certain fine ability but rears and pitches in the harness of society and gets many burns and wounds. But that means nothing to him. He retires quickly to those who fawn upon him. Neither you nor I nor anyone else with the interest or desire to help Ted can ever accomplish one thing for him…so it's better to endure him and save one's self."

"Williams, despite Cobb's biting analysis, had great personal charm. You couldn't remain angry with him," Fred said. "He had a boyishness that never left him, and a grin that lighted up the whole place when he turned it on. I would get telephone calls at all hours of the day or night and a voice would come on. 'This is Billy Graham,' or 'Mahatma Gandhi speaking,' and it would be Ted, being coltish."

"Much of how Ted viewed the world came from which way the wind blew on any particular morning," Fred wrote. "The wind was his first concern when he bounced out of bed. A 'coffee' wind, sweeping up from Boston Harbor, meant he'd be hitting into the teeth of it and might go zero for four, batting some long fungo shots. Curiously, an east wind meant you could expect a call from Ted that evening suggesting dinner.

"When Williams had a bad day at the plate, he wanted company around him that evening. On the other hand, if he clouted a couple of home runs, nobody could ever find him. He went into hiding. It was as if he felt that nobody would bother him when he went hitless and he could circulate freely in public without being crowded. But if he had a big day at bat, he knew he'd have people running at him all evening to shake hands with him and rub elbows. This he hated.

"Golfers, I find, are like that, too," Fred added. "You'll find all the 76-shooters around the club or the hotel lobby at night. But you'll never find the guy who came in with a 68. He's under the bed some place."

Chapter 21

Fred's replacement on the tour resigned for health reasons in December of 1946, so Fred hit the PGA Tour again in the spring of 1947. Nancy, of course, wasn't pleased to learn the news. She was in love with Fred and wanted to get married. Wanda, her mother, tried to counsel her in a letter she wrote, saying:

"He's a nice, quiet, well-mannered man and I could certainly fall for him myself if I was younger. He's so interesting, too, and if he does ask you to marry him, go ahead and say yes. I know you will be happy with him because you have always loved him, and I suppose always will—marriage or no marriage! I have secretly wished you would marry him but haven't told you. I can't see you with a boy from Youngstown after Fred. Fred is a celebrity and a 'catch.' If he does ask you to marry him, do it in a hurry and don't bother with a wedding or any fuss. I'm sorry I can't be of more help. Getting Fred to marry you is up to you!"

Fred certainly was a catch, leading a celebrity's lifestyle. In fact, he had recently been named that year as one of America's most eligible bachelors. But while he didn't date other women as seriously at Nancy, he just wasn't ready to settle down, especially now that he was going back on the road.

And on the road, he stepped right back into the thick of it. Ed Dudley, the President of the PGA, had disclosed after a big powwow in Chicago that the tournament players were seeking to control the tournaments. Ben Hogan took the lead for the players and called for the election of seven players to work with the PGA on all matters concerning tournaments.

"The player board," Hogan said, "would in no way be set aside from the parent body and will only be an added instrument of the PGA to improve the overall tournament picture." Hogan didn't name the other players who had signed the recommendations, but Dick Metz stepped forward to say that forty-five players had signed on.

The cabal within the PGA tried again to break Fred's contract. They said he broke faith by returning to the tour. Fred defended his action on grounds that it was an emergency measure, adopted when his replacement withdrew. He was caught in the middle again, with no special interest in the civil war. By this time, he was looking off in another direction, wondering if he could get any money from selling all those knives in his back.

"There's been talk that the PGA and USGA would split wide open," he told one reporter. "But I can't see it. We've had some differences but they've never been so serious as to go its separate ways as governing bodies. Our differences are mainly about rules. Right now, the code is being re-written."

"The PGA," Fred continued, "is pretty much in the same position as professional and collegiate football. The two groups do not play under the same rules. However, they're gradually getting together. It's the same with golf. The professionals believe certain practices should be permitted. The USGA disagrees, but when the new code is announced, I believe we will operate in an accord."

Tensions rose over the next few weeks and came to a head in Carmel, California, in January of 1947. Dick Metz was in town and had announced that he and at least four other players would not play the tournament circuit. Metz said that a full-scale player revolt was in the making and it was time the news spread.

Until that point, Fred ran the show, and even though he was tired of the travel and the lifestyle, he didn't want to go down without a fight. The problem arose with the pros who had been away in the war. Upon returning they wanted a players' committee to lay out the schedule and mediate disputes. That was what Fred had been doing for the past ten years.

"Look," he told Metz, "if you're going to play a game, you can't be the one to make the rules!"

Metz and Fred argued for days, and that Friday night, Dick invited Fred to ride with him and Horton Smith and another pro golfer to dinner. A heated discussion occurred in the car and when they reached the restaurant, Metz took Fred by the arm and said, "Let's take a walk."

After they walked a few steps, Metz wound up and without a word, punched Fred in the face, knocking him out cold, loosening his teeth, and nearly breaking his jaw. Fred went to the hospital where he was treated for this unprovoked, sneak attack. Metz was later suspended from tournament play for two events but allowed to play in the Pro-Am events, which appeased the sponsors somewhat.

Metz, of course, told a different story to the press. "An argument took place on Friday night. I understand Mr. Corcoran was slightly injured, which I deeply regret. In the midst of the argument, Mr. Corcoran turned around toward me in a manner judged to be a menacing one. I reacted spontaneously in self-defense. Following the altercation, we spoke briefly and went our ways."

Fred was capable of a menacing look, but he never once acted on it. When he was mad, he'd bite his lower lip and clench his fists, and he would pace, as his face would turn bright red. Obviously, his style angered some people, and he was known to have a drink or two, as most people did in those days, but he had more imagined enemies than real ones. Why, he had even reached a common ground of understanding with Bob Harlow. "I'd be out of bounds to say our relationship ever ripened into a profound friendship. But we came to know and respect each other, and even to enjoy each other's companionship," he wrote.

After this Metz incident, which did make the papers, George Schneiter, a pro from Utah who had begun to take a prominent part in running things, came to Fred with an offer to continue his salary for the duration of his contract if he would stay away from the tournaments. In the spring of 1947, the Tournament Committee formally changed Fred's title from Tournament Manager to Promotion Director, and he was exiled to New York to open a publicity office where he was simply cut adrift without the approval of the PGA directorate. His check came regularly every week, but he couldn't attend tournaments, and during this period, he missed the Masters tournament for the first and only time. Schneiter was one of the tournament players who later succeeded Fred and unsuccessfully tried to lead a players' revolt against the PGA, for which he was banished.

So now Fred was officially the PGA's publicity guy, and he went about doing what he did best, drumming up publicity. He was in the Pen & Pencil Restaurant in New York one evening when Bing Crosby tracked him down by telephone from California.

"Fred," he said, "is there any reason we can't move the tournament to Pebble Beach and play it over the three peninsula courses?"

"Not that I can think of," Fred replied.

"Joe Novak says he thinks all the players have to play the same course every round," Bing said. Novak was then president of the PGA and a California professional.

"Well, I agree with that, but, mind you, the British Open has been played over a couple of courses any number of times. If you structure your tournament so that all of the players are required to play an equal number of rounds on all the courses, I don't see why there needs to be a problem. Once at Pebble Beach, they could rotate around the three excellent courses with the survivors taking a second crack at the Pebble Beach layout on Sunday."

They shifted the tournament up to the Monterey Peninsula later that year where they renamed it the "Bing Crosby National Pro-Am." Bing's annual celebrity clambake was played this way for decades.

Later that same evening, Fred met up with Jack Sharkey after the Louis-Walcott fight. It was a great fight, with Walcott slipping Joe's best punches, then moving in with solid combinations. It went the full distance. And when Louis got the decision, Sharkey was furious. He was still raging when he met up with Fred and Lawton Carver, the former International News Service sports editor, who was in complete agreement with the decision.

"Why, Walcott counter-punched him silly," growled Sharkey. Then, in a typical Sharkey burst of anger, he snapped, "You're like all the rest of those boxing writers—you probably don't even know what a counterpunch is."

"The hell I don't!" Lawton shouted back at Sharkey. "Stand out here and I'll show you!"

He and Sharkey lurched from the table and squared off in the center of the floor while the patrons stared at the ceiling with that inevitable New Yorker indifference. The best part, however, was the expression on the face of Lawton Carver's wife. To her, this was not an overweight sports editor and an overage former world heavyweight champion arguing and shadowboxing ten feet apart. It was her husband against the champ.

"Nobody got hit, but I had to give the decision to Sharkey on vocabulary," Fred joked.

Without an office or a home for that matter, Fred would work from his hotel room, making and taking calls and being where ever the action was. In the spring of 1947, he got a call from Tom Shehan, a writer who was traveling with the PGA Tour, doing a daily newspaper column for Ben Hogan. When Fred invited him to ride to the Red Sox training camp in Sarasota on opening day, Shehan jumped at the opportunity. But when they arrived at the Sarasota ballpark, Joe Cronin, the Red Sox manager, let out a bellow from behind first base.

"Sure, Corcoran," he yelled. "You're here, but where's Williams?" Cronin, it turned out, had granted Ted permission to duck the opening day of practice for another day's fishing in the Everglades, but he made a commotion as a cover-up. Ted objected to the first-day foolishness which was devoted to uniform-fitting, wind sprints, and fielding a lot of questions from reporters and photographers.

"The writers will see me talking to you, and with no Williams," Cronin groaned, "they'll start adding two and two, and come up with five or six. God only knows what they'll write."

Feeling unappreciated, Fred and Shehan turned around and drove back over the Tamiami Trail and turned off toward Everglades City where Ted was living in a typical swamp cabin with a corrugated tin roof. When they learned he was fishing in one of the drainage canals, they plunged off through the sawgrass to find him.

Arriving at the canal, they saw Williams in the distance and shouted to him, but got no reply. Together they pushed on through the thick growth and finally came up to him. He was wearing high boots and toting a revolver. A snake-bite kit hung from his belt.

Ted shook his head as they approached. "I don't know how you did it," he said, "but you just came through the most heavily infested snake pit in South Florida."

Fred looked at Shehan and they both shuddered, thinking how the hell were they going to get out of there? Then Williams grinned. "When I saw you coming," he said, "I thought you were a couple of newspapermen and I was trying to make up my mind what I'd do if a rattlesnake bit you—whether to help you or just let you die, slowly."

CHAPTER 22

IN JUNE OF 1947, TEN YEARS AFTER GETTING NOSED OUT IN HIS FIRST Open by Ralph Guldahl at Oakland Hills, Sam Snead almost won the U.S. Open in St. Louis. The optimum word here is "almost" because it's a title that eluded him all his life. Fred said many times, "Snead was the best player to never win the U.S. Open."

This year, Snead came right down to the 18th green of the play-off round needing only a half to throw the match into a second 18-hole play-off round. And he almost won this time, except for a bit of gamesmanship from his opponent, Lew Worsham. Tied and even on the last hole, Worsham chipped to within three feet of the hole. Sam's putt missed and ended up about the same distance away. Disgusted with himself, Sam went to hole out.

Suddenly, Worsham stepped in front of him. "What are you doing?" asked Lew.

"I'm puttin' out," Sam shot back as he started to address his ball.

"Wait up," said Lew. "Are you sure you're away? We better have the distance measured." He called for a referee who brought out a tape measure while Sam stood off to the side, fuming. And sure enough, Lew's ball was one inch closer to the pin than Sam's. Sam putted first and missed. Lew putted after that and won the Open.

"I, along with many others," Fred said, defending Sam, "always believed that the interruption for the measurement shattered Sam's concentration at a critical moment."

The summer of 1947 opened another door for Fred. Babe Didrikson Zaharias won the British Women's Amateur Open. She was aware that the men golfers—Hagen, Snead, Bobby Jones, Gene Sarazen, and Ben

Hogan—had all added to their celebrity by taking home trophies on both sides of the "pond." And with this victory, she was treated like a star.

When she arrived in New York in November, her phone rang off the hook with all sorts of offers. After a few days of these interruptions, she and her wrestler husband, George, called Fred.

"Why, Fred," she said on the phone, "George and I are wondering if you'd be interested in handling me. I need someone to book my matches and take care of all this other business stuff. I swear, these people are pests!"

It took Fred about ten minutes to get over to her hotel to shake on the deal.

"It nearly kills me to give up the amateur standing that I struggled so hard to get," she said, "but I don't see any other choice. Sometimes the offers get so big you just have to take them!"

Fred promptly arranged a press party at Toots Shor's to make an appropriate announcement and had a great turnout of New York sportswriters and golf figures. Standing together, Fred told the press that Babe was turning pro for the second time. But just before Babe got up to speak, Fred had an idea. He quickly leaned over to her and said, "Babe, wouldn't you like to play in the U.S. Open?"

Babe was never one to fumble a hand-off. She stood up, tall and strong, straightening her skirt around her waist and announced, "Not only am I now a professional golfer, but I intend to enter the USGA Open Championship."

This caused a 24-hour sensation. No woman had ever played in the tournament, and there was nothing in the eligibility rules that said the competition was restricted to men. And even though this was just a publicity move, Fred was satisfied that if Babe could play, she would have wound up a long, long way from the bottom of the scoring list.

"If I continue to play the game as I am now, I think I could qualify," said Babe. "I don't expect to win, but I'll do my best and see if I can finish in the money. After all," she added," I have had rounds of 67 and 68." She had also won seventeen tournaments in a row.

The USGA, after a hurried consultation, came out with an announcement that the United States Open Golf Championship was closed to all but male golfers. Within 24 hours, the Royal & Ancient in Scotland issued an edict of its own, closing the British Open to women. Nevertheless, Babe's ringing declaration of independence at Shor's that day was a battle cry of sorts. Women and golf were together to stay. Within a couple of years, Joe Dey, the USGA Executive Secretary, had complete matched set of Open championships—for men and women.

By then, Fred had had it with the PGA, so he submitted his resignation effective June 1, 1948. This ended his eleven years as PGA Tournament Manager and gave him the time he needed to devote to his other work and to his love, Nancy, who was still patiently waiting for him in New York. His job now, in addition to managing the business affair of Sam Snead and Ted Williams, was to line up and publicize Babe's shows and exhibitions, along with whatever appearances George set up for her. Fred would tell the press where they'd be and they would all show up to talk to her and go home with a story.

While Babe was the greatest women golfer who ever stepped on a tee, she wasn't invincible. It was golf that reduced her to human dimensions. She could be beaten, and often was. That first year, there were few tournaments open to the woman professional. They made an exception in the Texas Women's Match-Play Championship that year, declaring it an open tournament, and invited Babe to play. George and Fred were in New York at the time, having dinner together at Al Schacht's Fiftieth Street restaurant, awaiting word on Babe's progress.

George had telephoned one of the newspapers earlier, hoping for a report on Babe's 36-hole match, but there had been nothing on the wire as yet. Now they were finished with dinner, and George turned to Schacht and asked him if he would call one of the newspaper sports departments again and see if the result was in.

"Did you get it?" asked big George, when Al came back upstairs after making the call.

Schacht nodded. "Yeah," he said, "and Babe lost. But it was a close game—ten to nine!"

Zaharias leaped to his feet with a strangled cry and lurched off into the night, his napkin still tucked under his chin, heading back to his hotel with tears in his eyes. Al looked at Fred, puzzled. "Did I say the wrong thing?" he asked.

"No," Fred said, "except that the score was ten and nine, not ten to nine—and it wasn't close."

Schacht groaned. "Maybe I shouldn't have told him, huh?"

Fred shook his head. "You just shouldn't have come back so soon. I think George was going to pick up the check!"

Babe was a grand "showman." She had a flair for the dramatic and a raw, earthy sense of humor. She loved life and loved people. She loved the color and glory of the passing parade and wore her role of champion as naturally as Walter Hagen did. When Fred signed her there was no women's tour, of course. That lay ahead. The only money for a woman professional was in exhibitions.

Fred was able to line up some fun exhibitions that promoted both her and golf, like the one at Yankee Stadium before a game, where she stood out on the diamond and hit golf balls out of sight. Then, when the Yankees took the field for infield drill, she called for a glove and stepped in at third base where she handled herself like a big leaguer. Again hobbled somewhat by her skirt, she ripped it up the front and went back to scooping up ground balls and firing them across the diamond to the first base. The crowd went wild.

Then she called Joe DiMaggio out of the dugout. "Joe, darlin', come on out here and hit some of my pitches, will ya?"

DiMaggio didn't move off the dugout bench.

She called to him again and when he waved her off, she walked over and gently took him by the arm and led him over to the stand of bats, much to the crowd's approval. Selecting a bat and handing it to him, she then steered him over to home plate and walked back to the mound to a huge round of applause. Then she turned and bowed to him, getting down real low. "Are you ready?" she called.

He didn't answer but he nodded, and she could tell by his stance that he was.

Babe let loose with a few pitches. The first one caught DiMaggio looking. He fouled away the next two and on the last, he missed. When she witnessed her strike out, she smacked her fist in her glove, giving herself a big tap of congratulations. Fred headed to the pay phone to call in the story.

That night, Fred and Babe went to dinner where she ordered a steak and when it arrived, even she was taken aback by the size of it. Eating half of it, she pushed the other have to the side of her plate. "Can you wrap this up for me, sonny," she said to the waiter as he lifted to plate off the table.

The waiter smiled knowingly. "You got a dog," he announced.

"Dog, hell!" Babe exploded. "I'm gonna have me a midnight snack at the hotel, that's what."

This was Babe—honest, direct and tough-minded. On the surface, there was no sign of feminine softness. But under the hard bitten outer shell you got an occasional glimpse of a gal from Texas named Mildred who married Big George and settled down in a bungalow in Tampa, Florida, where she made frilly window curtains, played the harmonica, and baked up quite a storm in the kitchen when the mood struck her.

"Babe was a promoter's dream," Fred said often. He signed her to a lifetime contract with the advisory staff of Wilson Sporting Goods Company, marketing Babe Zaharias golf equipment, and he got her a deal to write a golf-instruction book. They were on a roll.

By the end of 1949, things were looking good for Fred. Sam had won both the Masters and the PGA Championship. Babe was as hot as they came, and Fred had the pleasure of calling Ted Williams to deliver some good news.

"Ted, sorry to wake you up but I couldn't wait to tell you. You've won the Most Valuable Player award."

"It's not possible," he growled through a bad connection on the phone. "You better have a good reason for waking me up. I'm in no mood for one of your jokes."

"I'm not kidding!" Fred shouted in the phone. "You're it! You're the MVP!" It took Fred about two minutes to convince him he wasn't pulling his leg, something he admittedly did often.

CHAPTER 23

OFFICIALLY, THE LPGA STARTED IN 1950, BUT IT ACTUALLY CAME together about two years before that. A women's pro tour had been in existence since 1944 through the support of three women—Hope Seignious, Betty Hicks and Ellen Griffin. They held four major tournaments and a few smaller ones. Hope Seignious was a pioneer professional, and with her father, they used their own money to fund the tour. But by January 1948, she was nearly broke and the Women's PGA was only a name.

Patty Berg and Babe Zaharias joined forces at that point and called Fred to a meeting at Miami's Venetian Hotel, along with Babe's husband, George. Berg was the WPGA president and Babe was its biggest star, so this meeting was a mutiny of sorts. They decided then and there that they wanted to revive the association and they needed Fred's help. But they had no money to pay him.

"You've gotta get all the ladies on board, first," Fred said. "I've had enough knives in my back. I don't want to find any with lipstick on them."

"Oh, we will," Babe assured him. "That will be our first priority. You find the money and we'll get the girls, right Patty?" Berg was in total agreement, pledging to spend the next year talking to the other women about joining the new tour.

About a year after this meeting, in April of 1949, Fred's phone rang. It was L.B. Icely, president of the Wilson Sporting Goods Company. "Fred," he said, "how about coming back into golf?"

"My horoscope this morning said I was going to hear some good news," Fred replied. "I'm listening."

"Do you think you could do anything with women's professional golf?" Icely asked.

"Well, I have Babe under contract, and after running back and forth between amateur and professional golf, she's decided to play for pay. With the '47 British Women's Amateur Championship and the Olympics under her belt, there aren't really any more worlds for her to conquer."

"I know," said L.B. "That's what gave me the idea. If I can get the other manufacturers to come in, will you set up a women's tour?"

"I'll give it a try," he said, more or less knowing that the girls were on board.

Fred called Hope Seignious and her dad in Greensboro, North Carolina, and when he asked them if they would surrender the charter, they said, "No!' They had sunk a lot of money into a Women's PGA magazine. So Fred called his attorney in New York and told him his problem.

"Where's the problem?" he said. "Start a new organization and call it the Ladies' PGA."

A few weeks later, in the winter of 1949, Fred found himself in Florida for an organization meeting with the seven charter members of the new women's golf association, the LPGA. They included Babe, Patty Berg, Louise Suggs, Betty Jameson, Helen Dettweiler, Betty Hicks and Betty Mims Danoff.

The new LPGA's first tournament at Essex Fells, New Jersey, was memorable if for no other reason than the fact that it produced the first tournament money winner in history who never teed off. And it was the only tournament in the annals of golf in which a player was scratched because of illness—to her dog.

Helen Dettweiler, one of the pioneers, called just before the starting gun and said she wouldn't be able to play because her dog was sick. But the group had $3,500 in prize money to split up six ways and, because a prize was allocated for every entry, Helen got a check for $350 without swinging a club.

The actual announcement that they had formed the Ladies' PGA touched off a national storm of indifference. Potential sponsors were polite when Fred called them, but he could hear them stifling a yawn at the other end of the line. Wilson walked alone this first year, while the other equipment firms dragged their feet, coming in a year later through the Athletic Institute, a cooperative promotion

Fred, however, pressed on, making contacts and doing business wherever he was, and continually marveling at what he called, "Corcoran's

Law of Improbability."

"What is it," he posed, "that makes a man walk down 51st Street, where he meets someone who changes the course of his life, instead of walking down 52nd Street, where he gets hit by a bus?"

"I remember flying back to New York from the 1950 USGA Women's Open Championship in Wichita," he continued, "which Babe had won by nine strokes. I got back into town about 10 p.m. and I couldn't get a room at my hotel. But I was assured they'd have one for me in about an hour, so I went down to Toots Shor's to kill time over a drink and see who was there."

The Sportsmen's Show was running at the Grand Central Palace and Shor's was crowded with sports people. Fred found a seat at the bar and was ordering a drink when Al McCann of the Bristol Company pushed through the crowd and came up to him.

"Fred," he said, "come over to the table. I want you to meet Graham Treadway, president of our company." So Fred joined McCann at his table and met Treadway. As they talked, Fred learned that Bristol not only manufactured golf club shafts, but also fishing rods.

"You ought to have Ted Williams on your team," Fred told the Bristol president. "Think what he could do for you at that show…and in here tonight, talking Bristol rods." He waved to the crowded room.

The next day, Fred got a call from Treadway. He'd been thinking over what he said and he wanted to meet with him. The upshot of it all was he signed Williams to a ten-year contract for $100,000.

"I never cease to wonder about this Law of Improbability," Fred said. "If I had decided to stay overnight in Wichita, or if the hotel room had been available when I got back to New York, I wouldn't have been at Shor's that night. For that matter, what if I had decided that evening to go down to John Bruno's Pen & Pencil or over to Al Schacht's?"

The next month brought Alvin Handmacher, the Angel from Seventh Avenue, to center stage. Fred had a phone call one day from Herman Barron, the Fenway Club pro who had been a member of the 1947 Ryder Cup team. He had just won the Palm Beach Round Robin, and one day, he would become Teacher's PGA World Senior Champion.

"Give this guy Handmacher a call," said Barron. "He wants to do something in golf and he has the money to do it right."

So Fred called Handmacher who, he learned, manufactured women's Weathervane sports clothes. "I guess you might say that Weathervane suits belonged in a mixed foursome with men's Palm Beach suits, and I think it was this distant relationship that fired Handmacher's imagination. He wanted to use the round robin-tournament format and dress it up in women's clothing," Fred recalled.

Well, Handmacher was a very busy man, but he and Fred finally managed to make a date to meet for lunch at the Pierre, and while Fred arrived in ample time, Alvin was late. This got them off on the wrong foot because Fred didn't like to hang on the hook for anybody.

While waiting at the bar, Fred started a conversation with Joe Creavy, who was also standing around. Fred knew Joe's brother, Tom, as the youngest winner of the PGA Championship in 1931. What he didn't know, until he pulled him into the lounge, was that he was Handmacher's personal pro and aide-de-camp. He, too, was standing by and waiting for Alvin.

In the rich fullness of time, Handmacher swept in, made a commotion, and ordered champagne.

"Now, I'm a plain man," Fred wrote. "I rarely, if ever, make a lunch out of champagne. But Alvin always liked to give it that Metro-Goldwyn-Mayer treatment and it was amid the bubbles that he announced he would like to stage a women's round robin tournament."

"Not so fast," Fred said. "You can't move in like that. To begin with, there aren't enough women professionals to fill out a field for a round robin format. For another thing, the round robin format was something special that I dreamed up for Elmer Ward of the Palm Beach Company." Elmer and Fred had now been friends over a long period of time and Fred wasn't in any mood to let someone walk in and steal Ward's show.

That first meeting with Alvin didn't improve with the champagne either. Handmacher drummed thoughtfully with his fingers and kept glancing at his watch as they talked. Suddenly he lurched to his feet. "I've got to get upstairs," he said abruptly. "I have a showing. Give me a call when you work something out." And he was gone.

Fred went back to the Savoy, angry with Handmacher and angry with himself for being snookered into such a waste of time.

A couple of weeks passed before Barron called Fred again and asked him why he didn't get in touch with Alvin.

"I did," Fred snarled, "and we went to a fashion show together." Fred recalled the champagne. "We played to a tie in the Lawrence Welk Open," he added.

"He's very much interested in moving into golf," said Herman, "and in a big way. I thought the two of you would get along together."

Nothing like two characters getting along together for fun and profit! Well, time passed and then, one day, the phone rang, and it was

Handmacher.

"I thought you were going to call me," he scolded. "What's the matter?"

Fred told him he didn't think they would be able to get together. "You didn't have much time for me that day," he reminded him, "and I went to a lot of inconvenience to keep that appointment."

"I'm sorry I had to run off on you," he apologized. "Let's make it for another day and we can sit down and have a long talk."

Fred told him he was sorry, too, but he was headed for the Havana Open. That left the whole business hanging as Fred went on his way.

While in Havana, Fred received a cable, forwarded from the Kenilworth Hotel, his winter headquarters in Miami Beach. It was from Alvin, asking to meet him at the Boca Raton Club, about thirty miles up the coast from Miami Beach, upon his return.

Back in Miami, Fred hired a car and drove up to Boca where he found Handmacher coming in off the course with Tommy Armour, now the Boca Raton pro. Fred walked with them into the clubhouse where Alvin and Tommy sat down at a table and began shuffling a deck of cards.

"Order a drink, Fred," said Handmacher with a wave, "while I get some of my money back from Armour."

"I don't want a drink," Fred said, beginning to simmer. "I thought you wanted to talk to me."

Alvin raised a hand. "Just a couple of games," he said. So Fred sat there with smoke coming out of his ears while they played gin. Finally, the card game ended and Alvin stood up. "Let's go out to my yacht where we can talk," he said.

Once aboard a yacht that was rocking at its mooring in the lagoon, they settled themselves in a couple of lounge chairs on the fantail. Alvin broke open a bottle of Scotch and studied Fred narrowly. "Why didn't you ever call me?" he asked.

Fred shrugged. "I didn't see any point. We seem to have a lot of trouble getting together and I'm not sure I know what you have in mind."

He poured a couple of drinks and tipped his glass in salute. "What I want," he said, "is to get into golf some way that's never been done before. I don't want just another tournament. I want something big…and national in scope. I've got the money, but I've got to get value for my money."

Fred hadn't really pushed Handmacher out of his mind, and he did have an idea. All these weeks he had been gnawing at the Weathervane bone between meals, so to speak. He had the vague shape of an idea and now it flashed into focus.

"How about a transcontinental tournament?" he said, improvising as he went along. "Tee off in California and hole out in New York. Have the girls play four 36-hole tournaments in four different cities with a windup on the East Coast and first prize to the low aggregate score."

The idea of a progressive golf tournament, like a progressive dinner, was a novel one and appealed to Alvin. His round face broke up in a broad smile. "Great!" he enthused. "We can open in San Francisco, then play Chicago and Cleveland, and on into New York. And we'll have a Weathervane suit promotion tie-in at each stop."

And so the first Weathervane Transcontinental Tournament was born. It became the skeleton of the women's professional tour, to be fleshed out with intermediate stops for other events. Fred wouldn't go so far as to say that without Alvin Handmacher and his Weathervane Championships, there wouldn't be a women's pro tour today. But make no mistake about it—Alvin put the Ladies' PGA in business. He set up $15,000 in prize money and a $5,000 bonus for the winner, and he spent three times as much just promoting the tournaments. In the history of tournament prize money for the ladies, it was Handmacher who cracked open the safe.

In addition, Handmacher paid Babe Didrikson Zaharias $10,000 a year to wear his clothes and when Jackie Pung, the jovial Hawaiian wahine, won the USGA Women's Amateur Championship in 1952, he signed her for $7,500 and put her on the tour.

Another who gave the girls a big lift along the road to self-sufficiency was Helen Lengfeld, the energetic California matron who published *National Golfer* magazine. Helen threw her boundless energy and enthusiasm into women's golf when the Weathervane tournament was announced and built a Pacific Coast spring tour around it with some $15,000 in prize money for the girls to compete for.

Now some of the fence-straddlers took the leap. There were a lot of women golfers who couldn't afford to go on playing amateur golf forever, but couldn't risk the uncertainty of a professional career without any prospect or hope of making it pay out. Handmacher's prize money and the additional tournaments along the way gave them the courage to take the step. Betty MacKinnon, a rangy and pert Texan, turned pro. So did Betsy Rawls, the Phi Beta Kappa from Spartanburg, South Carolina, by way of Texas University. Peggy Kirk, a Titleholders' winner, and Shirley Spork, a California physical-education teacher also joined the tour.

Meanwhile, the big attractions in amateur golf were the Bauer sisters, Alice and Marlene, daughters of a German-born golf pro who steered them into golf with the dedication of a Hollywood momma with a couple of latter-day Shirley Temples. The Bauer kids were attractive little teenagers who came out of the Dakotas to become giant-killers on the amateur circuit. Marlene, at age 15, won the first U.S. Girls' Junior Championship and had become the youngest player to ever move to the semi-finals of the U.S. Women's Open Championship, and Alice, at 22, was low amateur in the All-American Open.

Papa Dave led the girls out on the barnstorming trail as soon as they became hot gate attractions and this, naturally, brought them to the attention of the USGA policemen. When Dave received an invitation in 1950 to bring the girls in for a little talk about amateurism, he decided he had reached the point of no return. He called Fred and said the girls were turning pro and asked if he would act as their manager.

"I will," said Fred, "but because of their age, I don't want to take any money for it."

Fred held a press party in New York and took a lashing from one of the Manhattan sports columnists for aiding and abetting the professionalism of two little girls who, he said, ought to be in school. "He had a point," Fred admitted over a Scotch, "but then again, I wasn't a truant officer."

So now Fred had a pretty good group of women professionals and it looked as if the women's tour was on steady turf. Other equipment manufacturers wrote themselves into the act, but Fred still had a familiar old tournament problem: guaranteeing the appearance of the stars. The manufacturers were signing the ladies to their staffs and clinging to old thinking. From time to time, the leading gate attractions would be whisked off the tour to play exhibitions for a dozen people at the behest of their manufacturer. This, naturally, brought howls of anguish from the tournament sponsors which had sold tickets in anticipation of a field full of stars.

Right off the bat, the tour lost a solid sponsor this way. The Bobby Jones Golf Club of Sarasota raised $4,000 for a women's tournament. This was important money when you considered that the going price for a tournament stop then was $3,500. But when the tournament chairman called Fred to guarantee the appearance of the ladies under contract to the golf club manufacturers, Fred couldn't, and the Sarasota group canceled out. What's more, they fired a broadside in the press aimed not at the girls or their employers, but at Corcoran!

But Fred had a whole world to conquer. In 1950, Fred proposed to Handmacher that they take a team of women to England. This was a great idea, even though it turned out to be a goodwill expedition that threatened to set back Anglo-American relations a hundred years.

It all began innocently enough when they gathered the six low scorers in the 1950 Weathervane Championship—Babe, Betty Jameson, Peggy Kirk, Betty Bush, Patty Berg and Betsy Rawls— and headed for Blighty. Fred had traveled to England a few weeks earlier to line up a match with England's best amateur women. In the course of that visit, he fell in with Leonard Crawley, an able British golf writer and himself a former British Walker Cup player.

"Just how good are these girl professionals of yours, Fred?" asked Leonard.

"Good enough to beat any team of British male amateurs," Fred said without hesitation.

Leonard cocked an eye. "Oh, come on," he exploded.

Fred shrugged. "We'll challenge any team you can put together."

Crawley's mouth tightened. "You have a match," he said coldly.

Suddenly, Fred wanted to renege. Not that he had any doubts about his girls. He knew the caliber of British amateurs who are strictly weekend golfers, and he now feared the worst. Win, lose or draw, no good could come of the match. And, if his worst fears were realized and his girls thumped the men, every men's grill and lounge in the British Isles would be barred to Alvin and him. In Britain, women were tolerated, not worshipped. Fred told a tale of seeing one sign at a British golf course which read: "Dogs and women not allowed."

When Babe Zaharias learned of Crawley's attitude, her eyes glittered and her mouth thinned to a slit. "Save him for me, son," she said. In Babe's book, every male, regardless of his age, was "son." "I'll play in this h'yah match, but only if I can have Crawley."

Fred's fears were realized.

Leonard didn't pull any punches. He lined up a team of six former Walker Cup players, and away they went to Wentworth.

"I'll never forget the scene at the first tee as Leonard and Babe prepared to play away," Fred said. "Crawley gallantly pointed down the fairway and observed, 'There's the ladies' tee down there.'"

Babe smiled a cold, mirthless smile. "Ah'm playin' with you, son," she drawled. And it went downhill for Britain from there. Not only did Babe beat Crawley, outgunning him from every tee, but she fired a 74 over a real championship course. And all the American women, playing from the men's tournament tees, won their matches, running up a ruinous score of 6-0. That evening, Fred was probably the most unpopular man in England.

If Alvin Handmacher made the women's tour possible, it was Babe Zaharias who made it go. She was the color, the gate attraction. She was, without doubt, the greatest woman athlete the world had ever seen—and probably the greatest woman golfer of them all, although Fred ranked Glenna Collett Vare right up there with her. Joyce Wethered of England, Louise Suggs and Patty Berg were a half-step behind them. Others, like Mickey Wright, Nancy Lopez and Annika Sorenstam, were decades and generations away.

"But I can't shake the suspicion that Babe, on any given day, could beat any of them by sheer force of will. She had that special quality of champions. She could be as good as she had to be. It was no surprise to Babe that she could pick up a golf club and hit the ball with a ton of power. To the natural athlete, there is nothing difficult or complicated about a golf swing. For a person with good coordination, it's the most natural thing in the world," Fred said.

"It was Hagen who observed that if a ball rolls into the cup, it's a lucky shot. If it stops near the hole, it's a great shot. I believe it was this fine distinction that drew Babe Didrikson Zaharias into golf to the exclusion of everything else. For her, hitting a golf ball was as simple as hurdling, swimming, running or throwing a baseball. All it required was muscular coordination and a sense of timing. But she discovered that playing golf and playing championship golf were two different things. Here was a game she couldn't bully into submission. She found par a tireless and unyielding opponent. Golf offered a fresh challenge every time she picked up a club, and her fierce competitive drive relished the challenge."

Chapter 24

One of Fred's biggest problems throughout his career in golf was the weather. From his crayons that melted in the heat and the deluge at his second official PGA event to every thunderstorm that delayed play and caused havoc with tee times, Fred usually took refuge from the weather in the clubhouse and at the bar. In those days, there was nothing else to do but sit around and wait it out. And it was during many of these times that he had his best ideas and most productive days.

In 1950, during a rain-out of the Weathervane press party at the Scarsdale Golf Club, Fred proposed the idea of the New York Metropolitan Golf Writers Association. He felt there were enough writers in the New York area to set this group in motion, with Lincoln Werden of *The New York Times* and Guido Cribari of the Westchester-Rockland newspaper chain taking the reins. Also involved were Dave Eisenberg of the *Journal-American,* Dez Sullivan of the *Newark Evening News,* Larry Robinson of the *World-Telegram and Sun,* John Brennan of the *Long Island Press,* and Tom Paprocki of the AP.

Fred would have made a great sports editor and often said that if he had to pick another job, it would be that. He had all the instincts and the personality for the job. And he had lots of fun with the writers, especially the golf writers, whether he was uncovering, creating or just telling the story. For a golf writer, covering a tournament often meant a roadtrip where the group was together for a week at a time, eating together, sitting around in the press tent together, and often rooming together. Many friendships developed.

For many writers, covering a golf tournament offered sustained pressure, having to meet deadlines with fast and accurate news and color. Others exerted a real physical effort in scurrying all over the course because in those days, there was no on-course communication. There was also no training for these duties, except work. And like drama critics who can't write plays, the vast majority of golf writers might have trouble breaking 100 on a carpeted golf course. But that didn't stop them from enjoying the game—and there was a rivalry there to be counted on for some fun at times.

"Jimmy Burns, the *Miami Herald* columnist, was instrumental in setting up a farewell testimonial dinner for Clure Mosher, the popular and outspoken sports commentator. I was one of the group of about eighty sports fans and sports-page figures who turned out for the event," Fred said. "'Scrooge' Mosher was given a wild assortment of going away gifts—none very practical—and including a tired old plow horse. It was all very touching."

"Finally, the time came for the guest of honor to acknowledge the tribute and deliver his farewell address. Mosher arose, made his way to the microphone, and took a deep breath. By prearrangement, everyone at all the tables in that big hall stood up at once and left the room and went home," he chuckled.

Mosher's undelivered address has been ranked among the finest banquet speeches ever unheard. The fact that such a mad climax could be contrived for a solemn farewell party was what made the sports-writing gang Fred's favorite people.

One of the first things the Metropolitan Golf Association did was establish the Ben Hogan Award for the golfer of the year who overcame a great physical handicap to achieve golf distinction. Miraculously, Ben was back on the tour now, after suffering his near-fatal car crash the year before. He was now making his famous comeback, having won the 1950 U.S. Open at Marion in an 18-hole playoff. Bob Hudson, the open-handed packing-house tycoon from Portland, came to Linc Werden and offered to underwrite the cost of the award which was to take the form of a statuette of Hogan swinging at a ball.

Minute modifications of the statue were endless, with Ben himself carefully supervising the changes until he was satisfied with the grip, the stance, and the swing. Finally the casting was made. But time was running out and, on the eve of the New York dinner, Werden frantically called Chicago, asking for the statue.

"Don't worry," they assured him. "It's all finished."

"Yes," said Linc, "but it's all finished in Chicago! We're making the presentation tomorrow night here in New York. How are we going to get it here on time? And don't tell me about Railway Express."

"Don't worry," said the designer. "I'll deliver it personally."

And he did. Carefully stashing the beautiful trophy in the trunk of his car, he hit the turnpike and drove night and day to deliver the finished masterpiece to Werden at the dinner.

Fred believed that a good sportswriter was much more interested in a good story than a fancy meal or big party. "Many people make the mistake of trying to buy a friendly press with lavish luncheons and oceans of drinks—and neglect to offer a decent story to go with it. I'm proud to say that I've always been able to come up with a fresh morsel for a hungry writer," Fred said. But Fred did know how to pick up a check and throw a party, many of which were impromptu and some...changed his life.

A few weeks before the Masters in 1951, Nancy called Fred. They had been seeing each other regularly for ten years. She was now 28, still living at the Barbizon Hotel for Women in New York, and still working for the International Chamber of Commerce. She had become invaluable to him, as both a secretary and a sounding board, typing his letters, clipping his clippings, and forwarding his mail. She listened to his stories endlessly, without judgment of him and always in support of him. In short, she was madly in love with him.

But on this call, Nancy gave him a marital ultimatum he couldn't ignore. He flew to New York a few days later and they met for dinner. She wanted to get married and start a family. She told him that she had wanted to marry him since the day they met. But Fred thought he wasn't the marrying type. He was almost 47 and he still lived in a hotel. He was often on the road. He hadn't had a happy childhood. He didn't understand women. He was a bachelor!

The next day, Fred called his brother John in Boston, who was married with four children. "I just don't think this marriage is a good idea for me," Fred told him. "I travel too much to settle down."

"Marriage is a wonderful thing," John said in a reassuring voice. "You come home from work, the wife greets you, the kids all give you big hugs and kisses. What's not to like about that? And Nancy is such a wonderful, sweet girl."

"I know that," Fred conceded. "It's just that I don't see myself living in one place."

Finally, John lit into him. "What the hell's the matter with you? You've got a beautiful young woman who is totally in love with you. You are a successful man who has never been married. You've made a lot of money in the past few years. What is your problem? Marry her and get a home in New York for the summer and one in Miami in the winter. What's so hard to figure out!"

His words hit Fred like a ton of bricks, and dangling the change in his pocket, he hung up and called Nancy. "Let's get married next weekend," he said. "Do you think your mother can get here that quickly? I'll make all the arrangements."

Fred didn't want to leave the tour for very long, so they were married in a small service at St. Patrick's Cathedral that next week. With only a few days notice, they put together a small wedding party, consisting of his brother and a few friends, one of whom was Moe Berg.

Moe was known as the "brainiest guy in baseball." He had degrees from both Princeton and Columbia Law School, claimed to be fluent in seven languages, and would read ten newspapers each day. He charmed people with his charisma and wowed them with his intelligence. Along with the New York sports reporter Jimmy Breslin, Fred was probably Moe's best friend. Both were charmed by Moe's personality and intrigued by his quirks. One of his teammates, however, once remarked, "He can speak in seven languages but he can't hit in any of,'em."

Berg had retired as a catcher for the Red Sox in 1939, and was now rumored to be a spy. When asked what he did for a living, he would put his finger to his lips and not say a word.

Fred never mentioned where and when he first met Moe, but he had been a good companion for many years. Moe was around in 1937 when Fred first proposed to Ty Cobb the golf match with Babe Ruth, and Moe was also assigned to mentor Ted Williams when Ted first joined the Red Sox, so they traveled in the same circles.

Prior to World War II, Moe traveled to Japan and snuck up on the roof of the tallest building in Tokyo, St. Francis Hospital, and filmed an aerial view of the city to see if the Japanese had weapons factories. On a separate war mission, he was outfitted with a gun, sent to a lecture, and given instructions to shoot a German atomic scientist if he ascertained that the scientist was working on an atomic bomb. Moe determined he wasn't.

But more than these government achievements, Moe was known as a first-class character. Without any permanent home and with a penchant for long baths, he would visit Fred for weeks at a time, talking about his friends Nelson Rockefeller and Albert Einstein, and rinsing out his only white nylon shirt and gray suit in the sink of a hotel room. In the morning, he'd walk miles to find a specific newspaper, which he would proceed to read in a highly ritualized way. At the time of Fred's wedding, Moe was traveling with him.

Fred threw a wedding reception at the Stork Club and their guests included Nancy's mother Wanda, Fred's brother John and his wife Dana, sportswriter Joe Walsh and his wife Peggy, and Paul Brophy, who handled some of Fred legal affairs in Boston, and Louise and Lee Eastman, who handled some of Fred's legal affairs in New York and whose daughter, Linda, grew up to marry Paul McCartney.

"It's interesting that I had so many lawyers on hand at the wedding," Fred recalled. "I've never understood how lawyers charge for what they don't do. When I ask a lawyer to look into something for me and they come up empty-handed, I don't understand how they can still bill me for their time. When I look into something for someone and come up empty, I come up empty, too!"

The party lasted well into the night, and the following day, Fred took Nancy on their honeymoon to the Montreal Open. Moe went along, too. When Nancy asked why he was traveling with them to Montreal, Fred told her that he had nowhere to go and he didn't want to turn him out.

Fred and Nancy later took a quick trip to Europe together, with their friends Peg and Charley McAdam, who started the McNaught Syndicate, which was best known for syndicating Will Rogers and Dear Abby. In Paris, they stopped at SHAEF headquarters to visit General Eisenhower, who was a friend of McAdam, Fred and golf.

When Eisenhower was introduced to Nancy, he asked with his famous twinkle, "So you're married to that fellow who has to interpret the rules for the golf pros, are you?" And he added, shaking his head, "I wouldn't want his job for all the money in the world."

"Of course, at the time, Ike had his eye on a job I wouldn't want either, which makes the match all even," Fred said with a laugh. "And the job of Tournament Manager for the PGA didn't pay all the money in the world. In fact, it didn't pay well at all. The best I ever got out of it was $7,500 a year and a modest per diem for expenses. And I earned every nickel of it!"

When Fred arrived back in New York, Jack Sharkey called and invited him to the fights at Madison Square Garden. Jack was very fond of Joe Louis and was delighted when the usher took them down the aisle and sat them next to Louis, who had retired as Heavyweight Champion and was out of circulation. In the course of the general conversation, Joe said he was taking up light training and was planning an exhibition tour. At that, Sharkey grabbed him. "You aren't thinking of trying a comeback, are you?" he glowered.

Louis said, "Oh, no. I just have a chance to make a piece of money."

Sharkey released his grip and sat back, waving a finger at Joe. "Let me give you a piece of advice, Joe," he said. "Don't ever try to come back. They talked me into coming back and meeting you in 1936. I'd been away from it for a couple of years and it was awful. It was drudgery and hard work and my timing was off. But they told me you were a sucker for a counterpunch.

"I got it all set up in the first round," Sharkey went on, "but I missed you by about that much," and he held up two fingers, measuring off an inch, "and you nailed me. It was the worst beating I ever took. I woke up the next morning trying to put my jaw back in place."

Louis looked at him with those dreamy eyes and kept nodding his head.

"The same thing will happen to you," Sharkey continued. "Some young guy will come along and you'll see the punch coming but you won't be able to get out of the way."

Joe squirmed in his chair and tried to change the subject to golf, but Sharkey was hard to stop when he began to roll. "Someday you'll tell me, 'Sharkey was right.' For the few bucks I got for fighting you, after taxes, it wasn't worth it. The only thing I got out of it, besides a beating, was a picture which shows me with my nose buried in the canvas and you standing in the far corner while they're counting me out. I've got that picture framed and hanging over my bar at home. It's labeled, 'The Kid's Last Fight,' and my wife thinks it's great. She didn't want me to fight, either!"

Well, about three months later, Louis announced his comeback and he was promptly matched with a young bull named Rocky Marciano. Sharkey called Fred with tickets and they went to the Garden to see the match. Louis was going along pretty well, doing a good job of staying away from Rocky's blockbusters, while Jack kept yelling, "Keep your hands up, Joe. This guy is going to nail you!"

Early in the eighth round, Marciano knocked Louis out. Sharkey turned to Fred and said, "See, people will only remember him lying on the floor." Louis wound up tax poor and Sharkey woke up every morning with an earache.

CHAPTER 25

SAM SNEAD, WHO WON ELEVEN TOURNAMENTS IN 1950, PLAYED THE 1951 Ryder Cup contest, which as usual, the tournament-toughened Americans won. Afterwards, Snead and Fred crossed over to France for a series of matches with an All-European team. On the bus from the hotel to the St. Cloud Club for a practice round, Fred decided to have some fun.

"I'll play you for five dollars if you'll give me five strokes," he said to Sam, who was known to make a lot of money on the side by betting on himself in matches.

"I'll give you four," said Sam, who has the instincts of a used-car dealer.

"Five," Fred insisted.

"Four," Sam shot back.

And so it went, all the way out to the course where they finally paired off in a foursome with Ted Kroll and Jim Turnesa, two other members of the Ryder Cup team. On the first hole, Fred put his second shot in the woods and couldn't find the ball. While looking for it, he noticed a man off in the distance, sitting on a shooting stick and watching the play. He called to him and asked if he had seen his ball and he answered back that he hadn't.

When Fred came up even with Snead, Sam nodded towards the seated figure. "That's the Duke," said Sam. "Remember, you got me his autograph."

Sure enough, it was the Duke of Windsor. They exchanged greetings and Fred invited him to follow the match. As he fell in step with them, trailing along one side of the fairway, two other figures appeared. At the seventh hole, Jacques Leglise, the president of the French Golf Association, was waiting on the green with another gentleman, a man who was well along in his middle years.

"Fred," said Jacques, "would it bother you chaps if this gentleman walks along with you? He'd like to get some pictures of Sam."

"Of course not," Fred assured him. "Tell him we appreciate his interest."

Leglise beckoned the man over and introduced them to Leopold, the former King of the Belgians. Leopold and Windsor nodded majestically to each other and walked along with the foursome—with each holding to his own side of the fairway.

Sterling Slappey, who had covered dozens of Masters championships while he was with the Atlanta bureau of the Associated Press before being transferred to London, was waiting for them on the ninth green.

"This has been quite a day, Slap," Fred said as he greeted the small blond newsman. He nodded to Leopold and Windsor flanking the green on their shooting sticks. "Two ex-kings following four ex-caddies."

Slappey whipped up a delightful journalistic soufflé out of that.

Fred's daughter Marguerite, called Peggy, was born during the Ryder Cup in the fall of 1951, and as they moved into 1952, things continued to go well for Fred. He was booking endorsements for his clients and even landed one for himself when he appeared in the "Man of Distinction" ad campaign for Lord Calvert Whiskey. Nancy was thrilled when it appeared on the inside cover of *Cosmopolitan* magazine.

But for Fred, there was always something dark brewing, which he started to refer to as the "Corcoran Curse," and while he was wintering at Miami Beach early in 1952, it first reared its ugly head. Fred's phones went off like alarms when the announcement of Ted Williams' call-up came from the Marines out of Washington. Immediately, the Boston and New York sportswriters called and the photographers started pounding on the door. They all wanted to know where they could find Ted, who was fishing down in the Keys.

Fred called Williams to tell him about one of those calls, which came from a young Congressman from Massachusetts, John Kennedy. He said Kennedy had tried to do something for Williams but there was nothing he could do.

Fred was devastated about the news and Williams was bitter, to say the least. Here he was 34 years-old, having served his country gallantly during World War II, and he was being called again for the "police action" in Korea.

A professional baseball career is a short one at best. Most major leaguers put in ten to fifteen years, twenty tops in those days. They have only those golden years to create an impressive scrapbook. And here was one of baseball's greatest hitters, whose career had been interrupted already for a period of three years, from 1942 till 1945, being called to a war for a second time on the theory that he was needed in Korea.

"Needed?" Fred shouted across the bar. "Why, if they recalled all the World War II Marine pilots in alphabetical order they wouldn't have had any planes left for Williams to fly by the time they got down to the Ws."

Not only was Ted robbed of a rich baseball salary for two more years and a fair shot at several records, he also had thousands of dollars worth of endorsement contracts cancel out. Remember the Bristol rods for $100,000? This contract, along with a lot of others, carried war clauses, and Ted received payment for only one year out of his ten-year contract.

By now the Miami and wire-service cameramen were old friends of Fred's. They had produced a lot of golf pictures for Fred over the years, and now he wanted to help them. So Fred invited them to pile into a couple of cars and drive off to Islamorada, where Williams was hiding out at a fishing camp. Although Ted refused to come out of hiding, he did allow some photographs to be taken in the last week or two, showing him in various fishing poses. Fred distributed these among the boys, who pledged they would never disclose their source, and he passed along Ted's statement, which was a simple: "If Uncle Sam wants me, I'm ready."

Ignoring the personal consequences, Ted accepted the new draft even though he was advised that he could sidestep the recall on the basis of a cranky elbow. He had been injured in the 1950 All-Star Game when he banged into the wall going after Ralph Kiner's drive. But Ted would have none of that.

Fred flew back from Miami to New York with Ted. He signed him on the passenger manifest under a fictitious name to escape any public clamor. But when they landed at New York, there were dozens of newspaper photographers waiting for the plane to taxi to the ramp. Ted turned on Fred angrily.

"You told me nobody would know we were coming," he snapped.

Fred protested. "Ted, I can't prevent some guy with the airline in Miami from recognizing you and wiring ahead."

Ted grunted something, then turned up his coat collar and sprinted from the plane to an automobile that was waiting for them where he burrowed down in the back seat. Meanwhile, out of curiosity, Fred hung around the terminal and learned the cameramen were waiting for another passenger on that flight, the Italian movie star, Gina Lollobrigida. He reported this to Ted.

"Lollo!" he said, brightening. "Where is she?"

Going back inside and hoping to have some fun, Fred figured he would add to the confusion by having Ted Williams paged on the public-address system. This caused a mild outbreak of hysteria among the photographers who now concentrated on a search for Williams, hoping to make camera history with a film duet of Gina and Ted. After watching the show and retrieving their luggage, Fred jumped into the car, quite pleased with himself as they drove off to the city.

If Ted hadn't been snatched by the Marines in 1952 and pressed back into service in Korea for the better part of two seasons, there's no telling how he might have rearranged the record book.

"If I had to pick one man with whom to walk down life's highway, my choice would be Ted Williams—for his honesty, sincerity and charity," Fred told others. "Williams and I had a lot in common that drew us together. We both had known some rough early years after the loss of a parent. We were both pretty thin-skinned. We knew where to pick at each other and strike a nerve. Somehow, we knew instinctively just how much the other could take—and what he couldn't take.

"Ted was most honest guy I ever knew. In a world filled with so many phonies, he stood out like the Empire State Building. His word was good and if you asked him a question, you could expect an honest answer, which was a welcome change from many people who make promises after three drinks, get cautious after five, begin to back away after that— and the next day, forget they ever saw you. Not that Williams ever was a drinker. A little dab would do him now and then. He could get pretty upset around heavy drinking, and an upset Williams was a tart-tongued Williams—and let the chips fall where they may.

"Ted was a genius of sorts and, like most geniuses, liked to keep the world at arm's length. The world was the enemy and it crowded him constantly. He treasured his privacy, which I suppose, is why he was so passionately addicted to fishing. Williams, standing in left field surrounded by thousands of raucous baseball fans, was never a happy man. But Williams, bone fishing alone on the flats of the Florida Keys, was a guy at peace with the world. Once you understand this much of the Williams enigma, you're well along the road to understanding the person. Ted's idea of a big evening was tying trout flies in the basement.

"Whenever I was in Boston during a Red Sox homestand, I'd often wind up sitting there, watching him, wishing all the time I was out with the sportswriters and other convivial souls, talking and listening to the happy clinking of ice cubes in a glass. None of this interested Williams—especially of all the sportswriters."

Between Ted and the Boston baseball writers there existed what was perhaps the most protracted and bitter athlete-writer feud of all time. While you could build a pretty good case for either side, Fred's sympathies were with Ted, but he could appreciate the position of the sportswriters. Boston was then a very competitive newspaper town, with about nine daily newspapers at the time. The sportswriters, always fishing for an exclusive or scrambling for a fresh angle, would seize on any scrap of gossip or conjecture and blow it up into a headline. They fanned the flames of controversy without malice, but without rest, and they had no qualms about investigating an athlete's private life if it sold newspapers. Turn this crew loose on a guy like Williams who stubbornly insisted on his right of privacy and you had all the elements of a political battle.

And some columnists were just plain mean to Williams, like Dave Egan of the *Boston Record*. On the day Williams played his last game at Fenway Park before heading to Korea for his second tour of combat as a marine, many fans showed up to pay tribute to him. Everyone was well aware that this might be the final game of a brilliant career. No one knew how long the war would last and in what shape Williams would return.

The next morning, Egan wrote a column, saying Ted was a poor example for America's youth because he would not wear a necktie. "It seems disgraceful to me," Egan wrote, "that a person such as Williams now is to be given the keys to the city. We talk about juvenile delinquency, and fight against it, and then officially honor a man who we should officially horsewhip for the vicious influence that he has had on the childhood of America. Williams has stubbornly and stupidly refused to recognize this responsibility to childhood. The kid has set a sorry example for a generation of kids. He has been a Pied Piper, leading them along a bitter, lonely road."

"I couldn't blame Williams for hating that guy," Fred stated.

CHAPTER 26

IN 1952, CHICK HARBERT, WHO WAS NOW CHAIRMAN OF THE PGA
Tournament Committee, offered Fred a new contract at $12,000 a year
as its Promotion Director. The offer was made on a vote of four to three.
Voting against Fred was—Horton Smith.

"Don't you think you ought to have the unanimous vote of the
committee before you accept this offer?" Horton questioned Fred on a
call he made.

Fred laughed. "Horton," he reminded him, "you've just been elected
President of the PGA, but there were nineteen votes cast against you. I
only have three votes against me. Let's both resign."

But by this time, Fred was coming to the end of a long and difficult
road and his own interests were beginning to range beyond the narrow
confines of the PGA Tour. Now, when he met with sportswriters, they
wanted to know about Ted Williams and Stan Musial. Fred had met
"Stan the Man" Musial at a sports show and Stan had asked Fred to
represent him. Musial was a former National League MVP and current
St. Louis Cardinal All-Star. And Fred was also handling Babe Zaharias,
and women's professional golf. The PGA affiliation had become more a
matter of personal pride and identification than anything else.

By this time, too, the LPGA had taken off. By 1952, the tour boasted
twenty-one events, nearly triple the number only two years before. Babe
Zaharias had finished on top or near the top of every tournament in
1952 and by the end of April, she was the women's leading money
winner. But it was then that her troubles began. She entered a hospital
for hernia surgery and was diagnosed as anemic from overexertion and
fatigue. Sidelined for a few months, she returned for the tournament at

Tam O'Shanter in Chicago, and while she came on strong for the first two days, she faded over the next two and wound up third behind Betty Jameson and Patty Berg.

The ink was barely dry on the new PGA three-year contract when Fred had an idea. He went back to them and offered to tear up the contract in exchange for an agreement that was the most valuable document he ever held in his hands—at the wrong time. As he watched the phenomenal postwar growth of television, Fred thought, "What a great showcase for golf!"

Fred went to the PGA and swapped his new contract for an agreement that gave him the exclusive rights to PGA-sponsored golf tournaments on television and radio. Since this didn't add up to five cents at the time, he had no trouble getting unanimous approval for the agreement.

That agreement was worth millions. Under the terms of the agreement, Fred would receive fifty percent of the first $25,000 accruing to the PGA Tournament Bureau, one-third of the next $25,000, twenty-five percent of everything above $50,000 up to $125,000, and ten percent on everything thereafter.

Fred wore a path to the office of Tom Gallery, then the sports director of the National Broadcasting Company, and offered him professional golf on a platter. All he had to do was sign up and NBC would have owned television golf. But Gallery would have no part of it.

"Look," Gallery finally said, "don't bother me anymore. Golf is not a television spectator sport!" Others that Fred talked to followed suit, and the agreement that the PGA signed so eagerly turned out to be just an interesting document for the scrapbook. At that time, nobody knew whether people would sit and watch a golf match on a 24-inch black-and-white screen. Certainly, Gallery didn't think so.

"All he had to do was scratch his name and pick up an option. With that in my pocket, I think I could have sold the package to the Miller Brewing Company which was interested but shared the same doubts about the viewing habits of American golf fans. With Gallery's token of faith in hand, I believe the Miller people would have gone in and blazed the golf trail on TV," Fred wailed.

Fred was a little ahead of his time with this idea. He still held the TV rights in 1953 when he came back from the Ryder Cup matches, and Cary Middlecoff and Sam Snead went out to Chicago to make a pilot film for the *All-Star Golf Show*. But that was a wildcat deal that wasn't made through the PGA. The first U.S. Open was broadcast a year later, in 1954. The big boom in TV golf was several years down the road, awaiting improved camera techniques, equipment and, of course, color. But Fred couldn't and didn't know this then.

"Today, of course, golf has become one of the biggest sports spectacles on television," Fred said in the mid-1960s. "The pro golfers are about as well-known in American living rooms as most baseball and football stars. Jimmy Demaret, a three-time winner of the Masters, tells me he drives into a filling station now and the attendant greets him as a favorite TV personality."

That same year, Fred hit his best shot—literally. He was at Pebble Beach to kick off the 1953 Weathervane Transcontinental Championship when Alvin Handmacher and he went out to play a round the day before the tournament began. They found themselves playing behind Babe Zaharias, Patty Berg and a couple of other women.

Fred had just taken a 5 on the short 7th hole when they came up to the 8th tee. Fred hit his tee shot, which almost drifted into the ocean, but held steady. He took out a spoon and tried for the short cut over the cove. The wind lifted the ball and sailed it along, all the way to the green where it bounded once and rolled straight into the hole for a deuce—the first and only one ever scored on that hole.

Alvin and Fred finished out their round and came in, changed, and returned to the Lodge. By then, the word had spread to the wire services and Fred was receiving congratulatory phone calls from all over. Fred played golf for nearly a half century without scoring a hole-in-one, but he scored a deuce and wound up with national publicity! And, by the strangest of coincidences, it had to happen on one of the holes Craig Wood and he had picked for *Esquire* magazine's story about the best composite 18-hole golf course, which had appeared the year before.

With the TV rights-contract swap, Fred drifted out of the mainstream of PGA tournament golf in 1953. He retained the title of Promotion Director, but he had waived his salary in exchange for a due bill on the future that expired before he could ever cash it. Thus he ended twenty years of gypsy life that were filled with laughter and tears, turmoil and strife, triumph and disaster, war and peace. "And I had met everybody," Fred added in jest.

With Babe not feeling well, Williams in Korea, the lingering animosity between Fred and the PGA tour, and his idea that came too soon, Fred found himself in the dumps more often than not. The real light in his life was that Nancy was pregnant with their second child. During this period, Fred settled down, buying some land in Florida, a Ford dealership in Wellesley, and a house bordering the 15th hole at Winged Foot in a suburb of New York City. Fred was surprised at how comforting it was to come home to a wife, baby and house on a golf course.

"I wouldn't want to live my life over again, but I wouldn't have missed it for the world," Fred said. "I'll carry the emotional scars through life, but even the wounds become curiously precious with the passing years— like the loss of my first set of golf clubs, which also was devastating, and sad in a way. I loaned them to a kid and asked him to treat them as if they were his own. He did—he sold them."

CHAPTER 27

"THE CORCORAN CURSE" WAS IN FULL SWING AS FRED HEADED TO TEXAS in March of 1953 for the first "Babe Zaharias Open Championship" in Babe's hometown of Beaumont.

The first sign of trouble came when Marlene Bauer, one of Fred's other clients, discovered an extra putter in her bag at the 14th hole. Marlene recognized the club as belonging to the son of the club president who had been putting with her on the practice green before she was called to the tee. While she promptly reported it to the tournament director, the penalty at that time for carrying too many clubs was automatic disqualification from the tournament. The younger Bauer girl was leading the tournament and disqualification, under the circumstances, would have been brutally unfair.

The tournament director put in a long-distance telephone call to Richard Tufts at Pinehurst and described the situation. To his great credit, Tufts, who was then chairman of the USGA Rules Committee, proposed a special ruling. He cited the fact that the extra putter clearly was placed in the player's bag by an outside agency, and reduced the penalty to a total of two strokes.

Babe came through at that tournament, but the star who performed legendary athletic feats with special dash and bravado that the sports world came to know was fading inside. She was tired, achy, and "out of gas." But in typical Babe style, she put on a show at the final green.

After trailing through the early rounds, Babe staged a closing rally that carried her to the 54th and final green needing a birdie to win. Her second shot rolled to the distant corner of the green, leaving her an impossible 30-foot putt for the bird. Babe's was the last twosome on the course and now the entire gallery was wedged around the green, a dozen deep. A great hush settled on the crowd as Babe surveyed the putt and then took her stance. In a breathless instant, Babe stepped back from the ball and swept the gallery of home folks with a grin of pure delight.

"You don't think for one minute I'm gonna miss this, do you?" she called. With that, she stepped back up to the ball, sighted swiftly, and stroked it across the green and into the cup to win the tournament.

The drama of the moment acquired a secondary impact two days later when from the Beaumont hospital where she had gone directly from the golf course came the announcement that she had cancer. While they took some time to build up her strength, they performed a colostomy ten days later. The press reported that a "great athletic career was over," but with the prognosis hidden from Babe, she took the setback in stride, sending everyone a cheery "hello" from her bedside.

"I also got the call from Alvin Handmacher at that time," Fred said. After four transcontinental junkets, the honeymoon between Handmacher and the girls was over. The novelty of the Weathervane Tournament was wearing off for him, and I think he felt he had gotten about all the promotional mileage out of women's golf he was going to get. Moreover, the tour's biggest star, Babe, was now convalescing after cancer surgery and was out of golf, apparently for all time.

"In the final analysis, I think Alvin just got fed up with the locker-room meetings and the girls' rising demands. He announced that he was getting off, that it was his stop, after the final Weathervane Tournament of 1953 at Philadelphia's Whitemarsh Club where the girls staged a locker-room sit-down and refused to play until their demands were met.

"Golf pros are golf pros, it seems, whether they're dressed in Weathervane skirts or Palm Beach slacks," Fred said. "They're all addicted to locker-room meetings. The locker room is the Town Hall of American professional golf. It was bad enough dealing with the men, but the situation became insane when I had to deal with the women—because their meetings were closed to Alvin Handmacher and me. Of course, there's another way to look at it. The men's locker room often served as a convenient sanctuary for me when they came running at me, bristling with their sometimes incredible grievances."

Fred admitted that when it came to strikes, he had touched all bases. "I've been present at the first players' strikes in baseball, men's golf, and women's golf. The first took place at Fenway Park in the 1918 World Series between the Red Sox and the Cubs when the players refused to take the field unless their demands for a cut of the gate were met. The second was at Pomonoke in 1939 when two-time champion Denny Shute neglected to get his entry in before the deadline and Tom Walsh, the PGA secretary, refused to pair him. Walsh caved in, however, when the rest of the players struck and drew up a petition. The revolt of the ladies at Whitemarsh in 1953 also was short-lived. After a heated locker-room discussion, concessions were made and the show went on.

"But that was all for Alvin. I was sorry to see him back away, not just because he was a valuable client, but because, after a rocky start, we reached a reasonably happy working arrangement. He understood me and I understood him. Neither of us ever wholly understood the girls.

"And Babe was out and I knew I'd never see another one like her. Someday I suppose another woman super athlete will come along to send another generation of sportswriters digging back into the yellowing pages of the record books to make a comparison. But it will be long from now."

Fred went directly to the Masters after Beaumont and Nancy went to the hospital to deliver their second daughter, Judy, three days before Babe's operation. Fred then headed to Miami to meet up with Nancy and the baby, but his heart and thoughts were with Babe in Beaumont. He urged her to leave Beaumont and go to New York, but to Babe, Beaumont was home and where she belonged.

Nancy and the girls left Miami Beach a few weeks later and moved back to their house in Mamaroneck and Fred made his way to the Open that June. While Fred was no longer technically on the road with the tour, he still went to all the major tournaments, something he would do all his life, because that was where the action was.

As one star faded another appeared, and 1953 was Ben Hogan's brightest year yet. He won the Masters at 14-under-par, five strokes better than anyone else. And then he went on to win the U.S. Open and the British Open at Carnoustie. Hogan was unable to enter—and possibly win—the PGA Championship that year to complete golf's Grand Slam because its play overlapped with the British Open. But he went on to win five of the six tournaments he entered. It still stands among the greatest single seasons in the history of professional golf. It was the only time a golfer won three major championships in a year until Tiger Woods matched the feat in 2000.

"Hogan's success was not due to luck," Fred professed. "Hogan worked with a savage intensity and for countless hours to perfect his game. Nothing came easily for him. He even started out as a southpaw, and then had to learn to hit a ball right-handed. He never knew the meaning of an eight-hour day. For Ben, it was practice, practice, and then more practice—until the gathering dusk made further practice out of the question. When the time came, there wasn't shot on the course that Hogan hadn't played, in practice, a thousand times."

"Two figures in the record books, standing alone, would certify Ben Hogan as the greatest of them all. I'm referring to his record 276 in the U.S. Open at the Riviera Country Club in Los Angeles and his winning 274 in the Masters at the Augusta National Club," Fred said. Both scores would stand for more than a decade.

"I don't think either will ever be bettered, and I say this, fully aware that somewhere, an equipment designer right now is working on an improved ball or club and, somewhere, tomorrow's Open champion is batting a rubber ball across the back lawn with Grandpa's cane."

Usually, at this point, someone would interrupt Fred to say that Hogan lost to Sam Snead three times in head-to-head matches. "True, but Hogan won the USGA Open four times and the best Sam could do here was post four seconds," Fred would rebound. "Hogan won his share of the others, too—the Masters twice, in 1951 and 1953, the PGA in 1946 and 1948, and the British Open in 1953. He was the leading money winner on the tour five times.

"It's a strange thing, but Hogan never won an important tournament until he was 36 years old while Bob Jones at 28 had won everything in sight and then retired from competitive golf," Fred pointed out.

For Hogan, it was a long, tough climb from the caddie yards of Texas to the top of the heap. And it was an even tougher struggle to stay there. Fred said, "I have never considered golf a game that called for courage—not in the sense that raw courage is a necessity in the ring, hockey rink or on the football field. Golf is not a contact sport, and I can't recall a single instance where two players ever squared off and tried to settle the PGA Championship with brassies in the club parking lot.

"Golf is a game that requires nerve control which, I suppose, is a subtle form of courage. In the real champion, nerve control may very well be the outward manifestation of true courage. I am strongly persuaded to this belief because Ben Hogan was a little guy with tremendous physical courage and an ice-cold golfing temperament. So the two, apparently, go hand-in-hand.

"Hogan could win under any and all conditions. He had a fierce competitive drive that was almost frightening in its intensity. And he mastered the difficult art of concentration, blanking out everything but the immediate problem—the hole he was playing or the shot he was making. And nothing ever changed Hogan. He was the same in defeat as in victory. He filed them both away in some mental locker box after carefully analyzing them, and then went right along with the business of surviving. I had enormous respect for him and because of it, I could overlook the cold aloofness which at times exasperated me as a publicity-minded promoter."

When Hogan won the Masters one year, he was sitting for the customary locker room grilling after the final round. One writer, determined to capture every moment of Hogan's round, was digging at him with a series of questions that traced every shot, from tee to cup. Finally, running out of patience, Hogan stared coldly at his tormentor.

"Someday," he said, "a deaf mute is going to win this tournament and you won't be able to write the story."

"I never fully broke through that wall of reserve and never felt completely at ease with him," Fred said. "I was never sure, when he bared his white teeth in the suntanned face, whether he was smiling or unhappy. Mirth was a luxury he denied himself except on the rarest occasions, as though he were afraid it might corrode his zeal. Compete and work, compete and work...on the practice tee and on the practice green...then putt in the hotel room until bedtime while the others were relaxing. He even practiced in the rain so he could hold his game together under those conditions. Actually, Ben didn't leave himself much time for laughter, even though we did have a few laughs together."

By July of 1953, Fred got word that Ted Williams was coming home from Korea, and as soon as he landed in San Francisco, Fred got a call from Ford Frick, the Commissioner of Baseball. Frick was calling to see if Ted could fly to Cincinnati to throw out the first ball at the All-Star Game. Fred tracked Williams down.

"Everyone wants you at that game," Fred said, "and they want to see you play. You need to get back to Boston."

"Hell, no," Williams said. "I'm out of shape, tired and I'm not feeling well."

"But there's still two months left in the season. Everybody wants you back. I think you ought to try to play this year," Fred pleaded.

"It's the middle of July, already, Fred. The Red Sox aren't going anywhere. I'm not ready to play baseball and Mr. Yawkey says I can do what I feel like doing. I feel like fishing. I'm going fishing."

"But you're not a fisherman," Fred protested. "You're a ballplayer."

"You've never seen me handle a fly rod. I'm the best there is."

"I'm serious, Ted," Fred said. "You've got to get started. It'll be the best thing in the world for you. Work yourself in gradually, then be ready for a full season next year. Listen to me—baseball is your business."

Fred finally got through to him because Ted agreed to go to Cincinnati where the fans at the All-Star Game gave him one of the warmest receptions he ever got—not a boo in the crowd, and that perked him up some more. And during the second half of 1953, in this shortened season with only 37 games, Ted batted .407.

It was that summer, too, that Ted practiced batting so much to get back in shape that he often got blisters all over his hands. Fred happened to be with him on one of these days and gallantly pulled out a golf glove from his bag and suggested Williams wear it while in the batting cage. Williams did and as people around the league saw him wearing it during practice, they started wearing golf gloves. It's commonly acknowledged that this is how the batting glove was introduced to baseball.

During that same summer, Babe Zaharias staged an amazing comeback. She was back on the course, devoting her time to cancer activism and education, and raising money for the Damon Runyon Cancer Fund with the Babe Didrikson Zaharias Week Golf Tournament. She entered the Tam O'Shanter Tournament and finished third, enabling her to edge out Ted Williams, who made the appearance for charity, and she went on to win the Ben Hogan Comeback Player of the Year Award from the Metropolitan Golf Writers Association.

Fred then flew off to the one of the Ladies' PGA tournaments in New Orleans where Patty Berg was going through a high scoring slump. She met a local physician friend and told him, "I don't know what's wrong, but I seem to be tired all the time and I'm not playing well."

"There is no formula for winning golf because there is one variable factor that is invisible, uncontrollable and physiological. This is what we'll call, for lack of a better term, the Choke Syndrome," Fred told a crowded press room. "We've heard it said a million times, he 'choked' on his second shot. I'm sure there is an actual physical experience that takes place and it's actually and literally choking. Doctors, I think, will bear me out in this. They'll tell you that a person's breathing is affected by excitement. In some people the effect is more acute than in others. This is called choking.

"Well, the doctor followed Berg around the course. At one point, he stopped her and said, 'Walk along at your regular pace until you're about

20 yards from the ball. Then slow down or stop, and do some deep-breathing exercises.'"

Patty won the tournament and the newspapers reported, "Patty Wins by Proper Breathing."

Fred was often asked to pick the winner of an upcoming tournament, but he had learned his lesson early on. "Picking winning golfers and picking winning horses amounts to the same thing. You can make an educated guess, but you can't cut one horse out of the herd and hang the Derby roses around his neck before he goes to the post. Neither can you point a finger at any one young golfer and say, 'There goes tomorrow's Open champion.'"

The only thing Fred could ever bet on was bad weather. He saw more washed-out rounds and was blamed for more rainstorms that the Morton Salt girl. During one terrible storm, he flew with Ben Hogan and Jimmy Demaret from Houston to Dallas. The plane was tossed around like a basketball. Ben never changed expression and stepped off the plane as if he'd just come down in the elevator from the fifth floor at Macy's.

Demaret, however, staggered off the plane and croaked, "Lindbergh got a ticker-tape parade for less than this." This brought a bleak smile from Hogan.

"Excuse me a minute," Fred said. "I'm going inside to dig my rosary beads out from under my fingernails."

Hogan's wintry smile broke into a full-throated laugh, his usually icy shell shattered. Later he told Fred that the mental image of him actually digging rosary beads out from under his fingernails was too much for him.

Hogan held a pilot's license and served in the Air Force during World War II. Right after the war, Johnny Bulla bought a government surplus C-54 and one day flew a planeload of high-priced players from Miami to Fort Worth with Bulla and Hogan up front. They had forty of the leading tournament players aboard. Fred was the steward.

"The plane looked as if it had been rebuilt by the Crankshaft Pinball Machine Company," Fred joked. "I swear it flapped its wings to get off the ground. I remember the cabin door was fastened with a length of clothesline. Over Pensacola we ran into what the pilots simply call 'weather.' Well, I've seen all kinds of weather and if I had to stick a label on this mess, I'd have called it, without further ado, a hurricane. We were five hours overdue at Fort Worth and the plane was reported lost for a while, providing a macabre headline for a few of the bulldog editions that day."

When they finally landed, there was a wire from Ed Dudley waiting for Fred. The PGA president wanted him to call him immediately.

"Do you realize," Dudley shouted into the telephone, "that if anything happened to those golfers, it would set the PGA tour back ten years? I don't care if you fly, but keep those players out of that plane!"

"That struck Hogan as funny, too, but I can't recall him ever finding humor in anything that happened on the golf course. Golf was his business—a tough business, full of disappointments. And, as near to perfection as Hogan was, he had his bitter memories, like the two putts missed from 18 inches in the 1946 Masters and Open Championship. In each instance, he needed a par 4 on the last hole to tie, and took a 5. All of which seems to confirm that in the game of golf, even for the best of them, is only as good as his worst putt."

Women's professional golf reached maturity in 1953, too, when the United States Golf Association took over the four-year-old Women's Professional Golf Association Open Championship, and ran up the USGA flag.

"A USGA-sponsored Women's Open was bound to come, of course," Fred said. "And I believe it was due to my suggestion that Babe enter the Men's U.S. Open seven years earlier."

"I can't leave 1953 without the mention of George May and his Tarn O'Shanter Club," Fred added. "I still linger over the memory of that fantastic finish when Lew Worsham holed his wedge shot on the final hole to win the $50,000 first prize. He was the last player to finish. Earlier, Chandler Harper had almost holed a chip shot on the same green, and then dropped his putt for what appeared to be a certain victory.

"But when Worsham dramatically holed out to win, the crowd closed in and swept him up on their shoulders. I remember them surging across the bridge to the clubhouse with Worsham riding on their shoulders. They passed Cary Middlecoff who raised a drink to Lew as he passed. It was quite a parade. Meanwhile, what about Harper? In one fleeting second, he saw his prize money shrink from $50,000— and $50,000 in exhibition fees—to $10,000 as a runner-up. But there are no cheers for the runner-up. Fifteen minutes later I saw him walk slowly out of the club carrying a half-dozen pairs of shoes—alone. The winner gets to be toasted in champagne while the loser is off alone paying his caddie."

CHAPTER 28

HARDLY ANYTHING IN FICTION COULD BE MORE IMPROBABLE THAN Fred's encounter with John Jay Hopkins on the final day of the 1954 Open at Baltusrol. This meeting put him into international golf with both feet and changed the entire focus of his life. Ed Furgol had just won the Open and there was the usual milling around the new champion as he came off the 18th green. With a police line to cross, the direct route to the press tent was blocked, so Fred circled around the clubhouse.

As he passed the clubhouse door he encountered Hopkins, the financial genius who put together the industrial complex known as General Dynamics Corporation. They had met on a couple of occasions because Hopkins was a dedicated golf follower who had launched a tournament called the Canada Cup in Montreal the year before.

"Fred," he hailed. "Can you help me? I'm in real distress. I have a PGA badge and a ticket, but it won't get me in the clubhouse and I have to find a men's room."

The entrance was barred by a Pinkerton guard who took his job more seriously than his pay grade should have permitted. With a few stern words and an authoritative tone, Fred took Hopkins by the arm and escorted him inside, past the guard. They then walked over to the press headquarters where he introduced Hopkins to several of the golf writers and players as they came and went. For John Jay Hopkins, a starry-eyed golf enthusiast, this was Seventh Heaven.

"Fred," he said later, "what's the matter with my tournament? It just isn't going anywhere." The Canada Cup matched fourteen players from seven countries in team play to promote international goodwill through golf.

Fred, who seldom beat around the bush, knew what was wrong. "In the first place," he said, "it's played in Canada. Canada isn't a golf country. The winters are too long and the people spend too much time looking at skiers and hockey players. In the second place, it's being put on by a bunch of aircraft public relations people." This was all true. Among other toys in his corporate closet, Hopkins owned Canadair, the airline.

Hopkins looked thoughtful. "I'd like to talk with you at length about taking over my tournament," he said, "but I'm going to England next week."

"Oddly enough, so am I," Fred said, traveling for the Teacher Trophy special British-U.S. Senior match. "Let's meet there."

A few months earlier, Fred had received a call from an advertising agency that wanted an idea for a golf promotion. The agency wouldn't identify the client and Fred didn't have the faintest clue as to whether they made bread or hula skirts. But the PGA Seniors were playing an annual championship down in Florida each winter and nobody cared a hoot about it. Fred suggested that the agency's client put their name on it and take it over as a promotion.

"The reason nobody cared about the outcome of the PGA Seniors' Championship was that, with a few exceptions, the oldsters were a bunch of club pros with only local reputations. But I pointed out that the calendar leaves were falling steadily for the golden boys of golf—the Sarazens, the Runyans, the Demarets and Sneads and Hogans—and could bring a touch of headline magic to that obscure little mid-winter tournament at Dunedin, Florida," Fred told the agency.

The idea of a Senior Tour was greeted enthusiastically by the agency's client, Tex Bomba, of the Schieffelin Company, American distributor of Teacher's Scotch whisky. Ronald Teacher, the Scottish distiller, liked the idea as well. This became the Teacher Trophy and established the roots of the PGA Senior Tour.

To the Teacher Trophy and cash prize, Fred proposed they add a bonus—an expense-paid trip to England for the winner of the Dunedin tournament to play in the British Open and to meet the British senior champion in a special match. Since there wasn't an official British champion, Fred suggested the British golf writers make the pick, which then involved weeks of public dialogue. They finally chose Percy Alliss to meet the U.S. winner, who turned out to be Gene Sarazen. This set the stage for a dramatic reunion of these two 1937 Ryder Cup duelists over the same Southport course where Gene had defeated Percy two decades before, in Ryder Cup competition.

"I mentioned to Gene that I was meeting Hopkins and talking about the Canada Cup, and Gene came up with an observation that made the sports pages all over the world," Fred said. "Sometimes I think Gene and I are sprinting against each other to catch the next edition. But anyway, Gene predicted that the British teams would never again beat the Americans in the Ryder Cup, and that it was time to rewrite the rules. His point: The American supremacy is based on sheer weight of numbers."

"The Americans," Sarazen pointed out, "can draw from a much larger pool of polished pros." He recommended that the British teams expand to enlist players from Australia, South Africa and other far-flung outposts of the empire. And he was right. Twenty-five years later, the British team moved to add players from Ireland to become the European team.

Fred was in full agreement. "I think the great strength of the Canada Cup matches will lie in the fact that it limits one nation's quota of players to a team of two," Fred told Hopkins during a meeting at the Ritz. "This has the effect of strengthening the hand of the smaller nation. For instance, it would be impossible for Japan to field a team of ten top professional players. I doubt if there are that many pros in Japan who can play at par level with any degree of consistency. But Japan could turn out two pros good enough to win the cup. So could Spain. So could a number of countries."

Hopkins and Fred worked out an agreement, and Fred took over as Executive Tournament Director of the International Golf Association, the Hopkins vehicle for operating his tournament. And with that move, a whole new world of golf promotion opened up in very competent hands.

Hopkins was consumed with the idea that golf could play a role, however minor, in bringing nations closer together. He believed it was the only sport that really offered any hope of achieving this.

"I'd never seen a man so dedicated to this abstract idea," Fred said. "I'm sure he was conscious that the tournament also offered an excellent showcase for his aircraft and submarine factories because he was an intelligent man and a shrewd businessman, but that wasn't his mission."

Hopkins wrote, "I believe golf can be a powerful force for good in the field of international relations. When faced with the nerve-shaking dilemma of a ball buried in the confines of a sand trap and a seven-stroke score about to be recorded, all men are equal. Whether a person speaks Cherokee, Japanese, Saudi Arabian, flawless Persian or English, his problem with that ball is the same as the other players who find themselves in the same bunker. And he and his fellow sufferers will understand each other a lot more quickly after having faced the identical devilish quandaries that a golf course poses for all men."

The first thing Fred did as Tournament Director for the Canada Cup was move the matches out of Canada. He felt the tournament, if it ever was going to have any real meaning, would have to be played in the capitals of the world. So in 1955 they played at the Columbia Country Club in Washington, D.C. He also added the International Championship for individual medal play, upped the number of participating countries to twenty-five, and lengthened the tournament from 36 holes to 72. He had seen enough records broken in his time that he wanted to be in the same ballpark here as with any other tournament.

The 1955 Canada Cup wasn't the greatest. The field was not colorful, the publicity was only fair, and the gallery was slim. On the recommendation of the PGA, Hopkins had adopted a policy for that year of inviting the reigning PGA and USGA Open champions to represent the United States. It pained Fred to point out that the American team of Chick Harbert and Ed Furgol, the tournament winners, would not bring the crowds. Both were good men and personal friends, but to golf fans in the District of Columbia, they were just a couple of good professionals with no special glamour. Fred was a firm believer in the power of a well-known champion.

"Give me four big name players and let them play right here," he would say, "and you take all the others to the course across the street, and I guarantee you, I will out-draw you every day."

When Fred got back to New York, he got news that Babe was doing well, despite terrible back pain which she thought was due to overexertion while digging her car out of the sand with a shovel. She went on to win the Tampa Open and the Peach Blossom-Betsy Rawls Open, and she played well in some others. She was again elected president of the LPGA, but by June, her pain increased and she entered the hospital again. By August, they found a new cancerous lesion and started x-ray treatments. Fred didn't speak to Babe as much as he would have liked to during the next six months as she returned to her home to convalesce. Everyone had a hard time realizing that women's professional golf was losing its brightest star.

Fred went on to the 1955 USGA Open where the drama unfolded on the last day. Near the end of regulation play, Hogan was in the clubhouse and apparently had the winning score. Only a miracle could upset him at that point—or the obscure pro named Jack Fleck, who was enjoying a hot hand that week.

Hogan had felt secure coming down the stretch, and instead of gambling for birdies, he played it safe, figuring he'd win with par golf. And so did everyone else. But Fleck was still out on the course and he had a remote chance of catching Hogan—he'd have to finish the tough closing holes with a couple of birdies to tie. This was about as likely as having Monday follow Tuesday.

A television pick-up, one of the first of its kind, had been carefully scheduled for a time when they expected to announce the winner. Gene Sarazen was handling the commentary and he wrote off Fleck who was still on the course. As the show went live, Gene confidently announced Hogan as the winner. But Fleck soon pulled to one behind when he got his bird at the 17th hole. Then on the par four 18th, he put his second shot on the green, but left himself a long, difficult, downhill putt for his birdie. Against these staggering odds, the virtually unknown pro from Davenport, Iowa, canned the shot that sent the championship into an 18-hole play-off.

"I was with Hogan in the pressroom when a tremendous cheer went up from the 18th green," Fred reported. "Ben, gray with fatigue and suffering, blanched. Someone interrupted him in mid-sentence, shouting, 'Fleck has tied it up!' Hogan turned on his heel and strode out. He never completed the interrupted sentence. I think the prospect of another ordeal for his battered legs on the next day was a heavy blow."

During the evening, Fred found Sarazen in his room, ankle-deep in telegrams from angry residents of Davenport. They said they had turned off their TV sets, only to learn later, on radio, that Fleck was forcing a play-off. "Well," Gene said, "I just made a little mistake. I announced the winner 24 hours in advance."

That was the consensus of popular opinion. There was little doubt that Hogan, the shot-making machine, would grind the upstart Fleck into fine powder the next day. But Jack Fleck proceeded to astonish the golfing world by beating Ben Hogan in the 18-hole play-off, causing Hogan to miss winning a fifth Open Championship. Perhaps people failed to take into account the factor of Ben's physical condition.

"I must confess to a persistent private conviction," Fred offered. "I think it was Ben's brutally scarred and aching legs that beat him in the play-off round that year. Ben's great heart could carry him to the end of the world, but it couldn't do his walking for him. Those legs, mangled in a near-fatal highway collision a few years before, could barely carry him through the 72-hole tournament and to add an 18-hole play-off was a test of endurance. Nobody will ever know the cost in terms of agony and physical wear and tear.

"And I don't mean to downplay Jack Fleck's fine triumph here. Fleck had the misfortune to pop up from nowhere, topple a national sports idol, and drift back into obscurity. Poor Jack! He never really got the credit he deserved. Even the writers, who never quite warmed up to Hogan, treated Fleck as some kind of a villain who had cheated them out of a vicarious place in golf history as witnesses to Hogan's fifth Open championship."

In any event, Jack the Giant-Killer pulled the upset of the decade by knocking Hogan out of his big chance to become the only five-time Open champion. Fleck never won another important tournament and this, of course, made his upset victory in 1955 the more remarkable. This was too bad, too, because under different circumstances, Jack could have become something of a national image on his own merits—representing the triumph of the little guy who had just the one cartridge in his chamber and made good on it.

"I also had the feeling that Hogan would have won that Open in the regulation 72 holes if he had been playing behind Fleck," Fred said. "Hogan was a great come-on player. He had whatever shots were needed to win. He was one of the few golfers who always liked to play last. Snead, for instance, liked to get in early, post his score, then sit back and let the others gamble away their opportunities."

Sarazen's jump of the gun that reported Hogan the winner had another repercussion, this one on Bob Drum who was reporting on the tournament for the *Pittsburgh Press*. Bob, a former Alabama defensive tackle, was not above accepting a glass of schnapps on occasion, a failing that was known to his peppery spouse. Back in Pittsburgh, at this time, Mrs. Drum had been following the championship by television and had switched off the set after Sarazen's bland assurance that Hogan was the winner.

The next morning, after returning from Mass, she picked up the Sunday paper and opened it to the sports page and Bob's story. Drum, of course, had faithfully reported the tie and the forthcoming play-off. But his spouse, taking all the known factors into consideration, concluded that Robert must have plugged the gap again and stopped a bottle of bourbon in its tracks for no gain. This was the only way she could account for what she figured had to be some wildly inaccurate reporting. She rushed to the telephone, put in a long distance call to San Francisco, and delivered a Sunday sermon of her own. Poor Drum, dragged from the dark waters of sleep through a few time zones, had quite a job of convincing Mrs. Drum that he was a more reliable reporter than Gene had been.

The 1955 All-Star Game in Milwaukee put a spotlight on Fred's other baseball client, Stan Musial of the St. Louis Cardinals. Musial was one of only two players to ever hit five home runs in one day—in a double header against the New York Giants in 1954. Now, in this All-Star Game, Stan won the game with a 12th-inning home run.

Ty Cobb called Fred right after the game and said he'd like to see Musial, so Fred set up a breakfast at the Savoy for Stan, Ty and Red Schoendienst, the Cardinals' second baseman.

Seated at the breakfast, Cobb took over. "What kind of a ball did you hit yesterday?" he asked. Musial said it was a curve. "Hah!" Ty exclaimed with satisfaction. "I thought so." Then he turned to Fred and said, "This is the greatest player in the world, the greatest ballplayer I've ever seen. Ted is a great hitter, but this boy is the greatest all-round player."

Schoendienst was dozing and Fred reached over and tapped him. "Did you hear what Ty said?" Fred asked.

Red, who had quite a wit, opened one eye. "He said something about the greatest baseball player he ever saw and he wasn't talking about me."

Cobb sat back and speared Fred with a cold glare. "You manage both Williams and Musial," he remarked. "Why don't you do more for this boy?"

As Cobb pointed out, Stan Musial may very well have been the finest ballplayer who ever stepped out of a major league dugout. In addition, he was without doubt one of the finest men Fred had ever known. And, as a home-run hitter, he was a natural crowd pleaser. Yet he never moved people the way Williams did. Here again, he lacked that great intangible called "color."

"Williams had color even when striking out. You could walk down the street with Stan and few paid any attention or even noticed him. But Williams was a star, like Cobb or Snead or Jack Dempsey in this respect. Walk down the street with any of them and taxi drivers would blow their horns and wave. Traffic cops would shout greetings," Fred claimed.

Sheldon Fairbanks, promoter of the Boston and New York Sportsmen's Shows, gave Fred the answer to Cobb's question. Fred used to get $10,000 a week for Williams to appear in these two shows. One year Williams declined the offer, saying he wanted to stay in the Everglades and fish. So Fred called Fairbanks and told him Williams wasn't available. "But I can get you Stan Musial. What would he be worth to you?"

There was a pause at the other end of the line, and then Fairbanks cleared his throat. "Fred," he said, "without meaning to belittle Musial, great ball players I'm not looking for. Williams is different, especially in

Boston and New York."

When Fred told this to Cobb, as a sort of lesson in promotional values, he understood and conceded the point, remembering perhaps his own peculiar quality of color. In Cobb's case, the best definition probably was offered by Al Schacht, the New York restaurateur who was an American League pitcher and coach in Cobb's day. "When Cobb came to the plate," said Schacht, "it was like somebody turned on the electricity."

Fred signed a deal with a promotional baseball company that produced 10-inch-tall statuettes of both Williams and Musial in October that year. He had just received a shipment of them at his home in suburban Mamaroneck when his doorbell rang. Totally unprepared of Halloween and without candy, he and Nancy turned away the first group of trick-or-treaters with their apologies. When the doorbell rang again a few minutes later, he cracked open the boxes and handed out the statuettes, along with a few autographed baseballs he had in another closet. One little girl was unimpressed with the statuette, but the next set of boys offered to give Fred all their candy for a few extra baseballs. Fred fed that story to the press, too.

CHAPTER 29

INTERNATIONAL GOLF CAME INTO ITS OWN IN 1956. IN VIEW OF WHAT had happened in Washington, Fred told Hopkins it was wrong to take the PGA and Open champions automatically. "Let's go over to England and see what they say," he proposed. "Let's find out which American players they want to see over there, and then sign them up."

When they met with Brigadier General Critchley, the majordomo of British golf, he bellowed, "Get us Hogan and Snead and we'll stage a great tournament." This would be the first time that Snead and Hogan ever played together and it would also be the first time that Hogan ever played in England.

In those early years, the teams played 36 holes on the last day, which happened to be a Sunday. Until then England had not held golf tournaments on Sunday and there were doubts about the propriety, along with the legality, of selling tickets for that last double round. But Fred had an idea. He suggested they charge greens fees instead of admission prices and issue tickets entitling the purchasers to play a round after the tournament ended. On those terms, 20,000 joined the galleries, and five years later, Critchley reported golfers were still showing up to redeem those tickets.

Even with the objective of "international good will through golf," Hogan was the commensurate pro. He could tell you more about a golf course after one round than others could in ten. Fred saw him demonstrate this when on the plane together, Ben came down the aisle and slipped into a vacant seat next to Snead to have a little chat.

"Sam," he said, "you've played this Wentworth course. Tell me something about it."

Sam gestured vaguely. "Well, what can I tell you? It's tough, that's all.

It's a tough, tricky course."

Hogan was silent for a few moments. The he said, "Sam, I could make you the best player in the world."

Sam cocked his head alertly. "How's that?"

"Well," said Ben, "I'll give you one tip and you can win every tournament."

"Even the Open?" Sam grinned.

Hogan didn't crack a smile. "Even the Open."

Snead straightened up in his seat "What is it?" he asked.

But Ben waved him off. "Not now," he said. "I'll tell you some time during the tournament in England."

Arriving later that day, they went directly to Wentworth for a practice round, and on the way back to the hotel, Hogan got on Sam's case.

"Sam, you don't play this course right," he said, even though Snead had played the course many times and Hogan had just completed his first round over it. "To begin with," Ben went on, "you ought to leave your driver in the bag. It only gets you in trouble here. Now, take first hole—you've got to be down the right-hand side to come into the green. On the second hole, you've got to be short…all the way. Come into that green short of the flat. They're going to stick the pin up front and it's a whole lot easier putting uphill than to come in high and have to putt down to the hole." And Hogan went on, hole by hole, until he came to the 17th.

"Sam," he said, shaking his head, "you don't play that hole right at all." Snead had lost his singles match to Harry Weetman in the 1953 Ryder Cup matches at Wentworth, losing four of the last six holes. "Use your 4-wood from the tee, or an iron. Stay on top of that hill because you'll never get a good lie if you go over the brow to the far slope."

On the last evening, Fred saw Sam and asked, "Sam, did Ben ever tell you anything?"

"No," said Sam, "not that I can recall."

"Didn't he ever give you that tip during the tournament that he promised you on the plane?"

Sam brightened. "Yeah," he drawled. "Come to think of it, on the last round he told me to point my left toe down the fairway."

"Did it help?" I asked.

Naw," said Sam, "I don't think so." He had just shot a 68 on a tough course by pointing his toe down the fairway and unblocking his stance.

Twenty thousand golf fans descended on the fashionable Wentworth course in Surrey, causing chaotic conditions during the tournament. The majority of the crowd saw little of Hogan's and Snead's play, except the occasional flight of the ball in the air. With such a large and unruly crowd, a number of spectators were hit by stray shots. Some spectators climbed—and fell—from trees while others climbed—and fell—from ladders, with one on-looker breaking his leg. As enthusiasm for Snead and Hogan grew, a stampede from hole to hole occurred and continued for five hours.

Hogan set an all-time record for Wentworth, 31-36-67, on his second time around the course and he won the individual trophy. Both he and Snead shot final round 68s to win the team championships in a tournament that smashed all crowd records in the history of British golf.

And Hogan wowed the crowds. When Hogan holed a chip shot on the first green, an enormous cheer went up. Ben already had a record 282 in the 1953 British Open at Carnoustie, and now playing for the American side in the 1956 Canada Cup matches, he set a competitive record of 277, a number that may never be equaled over the tough course at Wentworth, England.

There were a few other "firsts" as well at this tournament. This was the first time a golf tournament was played in England on a Sunday. It was also the first Canada Cup event for a 19-year-old kid from South Africa who teamed with his internationally renowned partner, Bobby Locke. As the two finished play each day, the young man gobbled down a sandwich and bolted out to watch his idols, Snead and Hogan. The next year the young man, Gary Player, made his debut in the U.S.

Player later said that he waited for hours to get a photo with Ben Hogan because he was most interested in standing next to him to see who was taller!

And there was a last—the last tournament for John Jay Hopkins, who passed away in May. "When I drafted the plan for the Canada Cup," Hopkins had said, "it was my fond hope that the event would be played wherever the spirit of fair play and friendly competition made it a welcome addition to the sports calendar. More than that, it was my humble ambition that the tournament would contribute, in whatever small way, to a better understanding among peoples, regardless of race, language, creed or national aspirations."

"The success of the Canada Cup," he went on, "is not to be measured in terms of dollars, pounds, francs or marks, but only in terms of the mutual respect and admiration established between the players and among the spectators."

Frank Pace, a Princeton and Harvard graduate who had been Secretary of the Army under President Truman and the current CEO of General Dynamics, took over the Canada Cup. He and Fred got along, but Pace's personality was one that caused Fred to jump every time he called. Pace served as Chairman of the International Golf Association for the next ten years, before becoming the first chairman of the Corporation for Public Broadcasting. It was at this time, too, that Hopkin's secretary, Doris Sims, went to work for Fred at the IGA.

Late September of 1956 brought more sad news to the world of golf. Babe Didrikson Zaharias passed away at the age of 45. Fred was quoted as saying her funeral was surprisingly small. "Not many reporters showed up. Frankly, there were few people outside of her family," he said. "Others thought it drew a sizable crowd. Maybe I just didn't think any size crowd was large enough to pay tribute to the greatest woman golfer to ever walk this earth."

The Canada Cup crossed the Pacific in 1957 to a land that had never hosted a golf tournament and only a dozen years before, had surrendered to the American forces. And when Fred took the matches to Tokyo's Kasumigaseki Country Club, he staged a smashing success.

Sam Snead signed on early to represent the U.S. The Japanese golf committee also wanted Ben Hogan, who declined, so they settled happily for the colorful Jimmy Demaret. Both men proved to be wonderful goodwill ambassadors, endearing themselves to the Japanese people in many ways. While on the plane en route to Tokyo, the pretty Japanese stewardess asked them for their autographs. They wrote their names for her and then she showed them the corresponding Japanese symbols. Demaret and Snead painfully practiced their Japanese calligraphy for the rest of the trip, and when they stepped off the plane, they were able to dash off their autographs in Japanese. Sam was suddenly "Sa-mu Snead-o."

A reporter for the *Washington Post* wrote, "It's difficult to explain what a gracious little gesture this was and what giggles of surprise and pleasure it drew from an act of genuine and unstrained friendliness, a way of saying without words, 'Hey, Pal, let's see if we can't get together and talk the same language.'" By the end of the week, the Japanese idolized Snead and Demaret.

Even before the tournament began, interest in the game and its players grew. As word of Snead's practice round got out, Japanese golfers who were already on the course bagged their clubs and followed Snead. Other Canada Cup players joined the gallery as well, even though there was no advance notice of the round. By the last holes, a group of about 200 people let out 'ohs' and 'ahs' in several languages with every Snead shot.

Unlike other places, the Tokyo tournament used women caddies.

"They carry these big bags around as if they were purses," remarked Snead. "They never seem to get tired and they're always fresh and pleasant. Why back home I've got big husky guys who act like they're dying. They puff and pant and plop down on the ground every chance they get."

The young women made two hundred yen for an 18-hole round, which was about sixty cents. In America at the time, tournament caddies got a minimum of five dollars and the going rate was ten dollars. And the girls also gave their players gifts. One knit a set of club covers with the player's name on them.

Higa, the Japanese television network, claimed that an average of ten million fans per day watched the tournament on television. "We couldn't believe it," said Hal Wood of the *Honolulu Advertiser*. "We dropped in at an ice-cream parlor late one afternoon and couldn't get a seat because fans were watching delayed tapes of the action on a color set."

If Fred had any doubts or reservations about international goodwill through golf and John Jay Hopkins' sincerity or the soundness of his doctrine, the Tokyo tournament erased them. It was hard to believe, watching the teams chatting easily on the first tee, that many of these nations had been at war only a few years earlier. And the imprint the championship left on the Japanese sports scene made it all worthwhile.

"Watching the sudden flowering of the game in that beautiful country was what the International Golf Association is all about," Fred said. "And when the Japanese team of Koichi Ono and Pete Nakamura won the Cup, it was 1913 and Ouimet's historic victory all over again. They became national heroes as an entire nation started marching towards the first tee."

With the Japanese victory in 1957, Japan became a nation of golf fanatics over night, with Tokyo building twenty new golf courses and the world's first double-decker driving range that next year to accommodate the rush of hitters and players. It was a great shot in the arm for the Canada Cup, too, and the victory gave Fred an idea that led to an invitation for the Japanese players to appear on *The Ed Sullivan Show*. Ed Sullivan and Fred went back years, as Sullivan had started his career as a golf writer, before turning to organizing and acting as Master of Ceremonies at events like sports dinners, and eventually, to his iconic Sunday night television show.

"Just introduce them in the audience," Fred said like a missionary of the game and the great PR guy he was. "Have them stand up and do one of their Japanese bows. Think what it will do for international relations."

CHAPTER 30

BACK IN THE STATES AFTER THE CANADA CUP, FRED CONTINUED TO travel to the big tournaments each year, making connections, talking to sponsors, and chasing the action. Each year a fresh crop of rookie professionals lined up at Los Angeles to start battling for their spot in the limelight. "The temptation is always great to pick one of these starters and gamble on your own judgment," Fred admitted. "I've done it. I've even backed my convictions with money by underwriting all or part of two young players' expenses on the tour, hoping to see my pick vindicated. And I have yet to pick a winner."

He paused a minute, ordering another drink, and then added, "And I've misjudged a few, too. I first saw Arnold Palmer play a few years back. I took one look at his swing and passed on him. Compared to Sam Snead, Arnold's swing is choppy, angled and without rhythm. I didn't think he'd make it in the long run.

"But whatever it takes to be a champion, it's something that doesn't show up in the golf swing. All I know is that a winner is going to go out there and start winning right off the bat. The others will struggle along, just earning survival money on the tour or fading out of the picture. Offhand, I can think of a dozen youngsters who have leaped out of the collegiate and other amateur ranks in the last several years, sparkling with promise, who never quite made the top rung."

The 1958 Canada Cup traveled to Mexico City and produced another popular victory when Spain's Angel Miguel fired a 3-under-par 33 on the final nine to catch and tie Harry Bradshaw of Ireland for the individual trophy. Miguel was the local favorite as evidenced when he was carried off the course on the shoulders of cheering Mexicans. Sunday's round drew

14,000 spectators for the largest gallery in Mexican golf history. Harry Bradshaw and Christy O'Connor took home the team Cup for Ireland.

There was one sticky incident when Sam Snead, miffed by a balky putter, refused to pose for two Mexican Indian photographers who had traveled down from the mountains to record the match. That was Snead's mistake. At dinner that night, the photographers fashioned a doll out of a napkin and stuck a fork between the shoulder blades. The next day, Snead withdrew from the tournament with an aching back.

"I sweah," he said, "it feels lak somebody is sticking knives in mah back." Jockey Johnny Longden happened to be there, and he told Snead he had some horse liniment that would fix him right up.

"Oh, no," Snead said. "Ain't nobody puttin' no hoorse linament on mah back." The doctors on the trip could never quite figure out what was wrong with Sam.

In 1959, the tournament journeyed to Melbourne, Australia, at the Royal Melbourne Club, one of Fred's favorite places in the world. "I have to vote for Australia as the country that is ripest for golf promotion. With a population equal to the combined populations of New York and New Jersey, the Aussies turned out in tremendous throngs. It was the greatest tournament ever staged if you want to measure it by the I.Q. of the caddies," he said, prepping his audience.

"You see, Australia doesn't have caddies. Everyone pulls his clubs along on a little trolley. Upon realizing this, I produced 100 handbooks on the art of caddying and the Royal Melbourne hosts trained a group of university students for months before the tournament. They turned out to be excellent caddies but gave the pros big heads by calling them 'Mister,' which was a first for most of them."

Australia was a lovely spot with wonderful people, but the Melbourne tournament produced one minor discord. Peter Thomson, the Australian, came with a rush in the stretch to catch Stan Leonard of Canada and force a play-off. But Leonard protested. "You said nothing about a play-off!"

"But it's clearly spelled out in the terms of play," Fred contended.

"But this is unfair. I didn't know we would go back out, and I've now had a couple of beers." He felt this dulled the competitive edge of his game.

"Believe me, Stan, you are not the first to succumb to this problem," Fred assured him with a fatherly slap on the back. "But I'll tell you what I can do for you. If you want a little bit of time, say an hour, to freshen up and practice your game, we can all meet at the first tee then. But please, don't turn this into an 18-hole playoff."

Leonard composed himself and disposed of Thomson at the first overtime hole. Australia's Peter Thompson still went home a winner as he and Kel Nagel took home the team trophy by ten strokes over Snead and his teammate Dr. Cary Middlecoff.

But it was the two Indonesians, Salim and Sjamsudin, who stole the show in Melbourne. They arrived on the scene looking more like a couple of caddies from the Augusta National Golf Club than like working professionals. Neither had ever worn a pair of spiked shoes or heard of Sam Snead. Salim, who sent a ball through a plate glass window of the clubhouse on his first shot, carried only three woods and an iron. Sjamsudin, who used the cricket grip, had three more irons and a putter.

Fred scurried around to find them a complete set of clubs between them and fit each with a pair of shoes, and sent them off on the course, not knowing they had no idea of what to do with the wedge and fairway woods.

One of the boys came back with the highest score of the day, well up there in the low 90s. This bothered Oscar Fraley of the United Press who hunted the fellow down and asked for an explanation of his poor round.

"It was not so much worse than I usually shoot," Salim said.

"But 93," replied his partner, "you can do better than that."

The first Indonesian pro lifted his shoulders in a gesture of total despair. "Yes, a little. I just haven't had time to play," he explained. "I've been giving too many lessons!"

Their aggregate score of 726 missed the money by 163 strokes. At the presentation ceremony, they received a great cheer when they were presented with silver cigarette cases as the players who had "Tried the Hardest." The IGA sent them home with a complete set of clubs, clothes and shoes.

Middlecoff had his own story to tell. On his way to the team dinner at the start of the tournament, he stopped by Sam's room to pick him up and was astonished to find Sam shining his own shoes. Fred was one of the few people in the world who knew Sam was an artist at this. He had a way of putting his shoes on trees and holding them so he could whip that polishing cloth with the best of them. When Middlecoff witnessed this, he stopped in his tracks.

"Here's the greatest money winner in the world of golf and he's shining his own shoes!" he exclaimed incredulously.

Sam just grinned.

Ted Harris of the sponsoring Ampol Company, who was with them, had a grand sense of humor and was quick to recognize a rib. Feigning the professional interest of a dedicated do-it-yourself shoe shiner, he asked, "What kind of shoe wax is that, Sam?" Snead told him and held up the tin for inspection.

"I know a wonderful wax," Harris deadpanned. "It comes from France. It costs only thirty-five cents and does a much better job than that stuff."

Sam's shoe brush halted in mid-stroke. "What's the name of it?" he asked.

"I can't remember offhand," said Harris, waving a hand vaguely, "but I'll get some for you."

After the tournament Fred was at the Sydney airport, waving farewell as each group prepared to depart. Just before turning to enter the plane, Sam suddenly remembered something. He cupped his hands and yelled to Harris, "Don't forget to send that shoe polish!"

"And that reminds me of another great story," Fred often said as he jumped from golf to baseball, from past to present, from here to there, seamlessly connecting colorful yarns into the fabric of his experiences with his friends and around the world.

"Sam and I were staying in the same hotel, one time, and when I saw the maid, I gave her a pair of shoes and Sam's room number. I knew he had some shoe polish along, so I told her, 'Tell the man in that room that Mr. Corcoran would appreciate it if he polished these.'

"When she brought them back, I could see my face in the shoes. It was a beautiful shine. I gave her a half a buck and thanked her. Well, a few weeks later, I was back home with Ted Williams and I told Williams, 'One thing I know, that Snead is the greatest shoe shiner in the world.' Well, Williams took the bait and said, 'Give me those shoes.'

"When he brought them back they were perfect. And he says, 'All right, who does it better?'

"'They're beautiful,' I told him smiling from ear to ear, 'and I win $20. I bet a guy that before the year was out, I'd have both Sam Snead and Ted Williams shining my shoes!'"

By this time, Snead was definitely one of the richest men in golf. But oddly, the same Snead who would wrestle a cab driver for the tip, who wanted his winnings in nickels, and who hoarded golf balls, could be the most casual person in the world about investing thousands. When Fred called him to ask him if he wanted to buy into the new Ted Williams fishing tackle company in Florida, Sam had only one question: How much? The next day he sent his check for $50,000. There were no other questions. Sam didn't send an auditor down to check the books. He just mailed his money.

This was actually typical of Snead. He never blinked at laying large sums of cash on the line, but he really watched the small change. Perhaps it was the reaction of a mountain boy who developed an early and healthy regard for the value of the dollar. "I suspect that this kind of 'hard money' was the only real money to him. Checks and bank drafts were just trading stamps," Fred commented.

Sam joined Fred in another investment when Robert Trent Jones, the talented golf course architect, called Fred to say he had his eye on a tract of land near Fort Lauderdale, Florida, which would make a wonderful golf course. He wanted to form a syndicate, buy it, and one day build a course on it. "But we have to move fast," Jones said.

Fred promptly put in a call to Snead and invited him in. This time, Sam had this one question: "Are you putting up your own money?"

"Why yes, I am," Fred assured him.

The next morning's mail brought his down payment check for $10,000. Sam never bothered to go and look at the property and it sat there for years. His nephew, J.C. Snead, often suggested to Sam that they put some cows on the property to write it off as a farm, thus paying lower taxes, but Sam would just wave him off. Although the course was never built, the value of the land increased substantially before they sold it some twenty years later to become part of Lauderdale's expanding airport.

"Ty Cobb was that way with his money, too," Fred added. "He called me at home in Westchester, some forty-five minutes from Manhattan, one Sunday and said he'd like to come out and spend the day.

"Fine," Fred said, "I'll have a car pick you up at your hotel."

"Why can't I take a train out to Mamaroneck?" he protested.

"No," Fred reiterated. "It'll take you all day. I'll have a car come by for you." This was an extravagance and Cobb hated extravagance, but Fred wouldn't listen to his arguments. It was simpler to do it Fred's way.

When Cobb arrived at the house, he was carrying a briefcase and some newspaper clippings. He explained he had been in New York to set up a million-dollar foundation for the Cobb Memorial Hospital in Royston, Georgia. As they settled in, Fred noticed something on Cobb's chest.

"What's that you've got on your tie," he asked, leaning forward and squinting.

Cobb looked down and waved him off. "It's nothing."

Fred pursued his inquest. "Why, is that a paperclip?" Fred teased, reaching for Cobb's tie. "And a rusty one, at that."

"It's nothin'!" Cobb said dismissively, batting away his hand.

Fred got up and returned a minute later with a little blue box. "Here, put this on," he said, giving him a souvenir tie clasp made up in thousands by General Dynamics Corporation at the time of the launching of the Nautilus. It was a silver-plated replica of the first nuclear-powered submarine.

Cobb said thanks and put the souvenir clip and the box in his pocket.

A couple of months later, Fred had a letter from Ty asking if he had another one of those tie clasps. He had given his away to a friend who had admired it.

"Ty Cobb took tremendous pride in his own achievements, which included hitting over .400 three times and leading the American League in batting twelve times," Fred said with his insider's perspective. "Yet, he didn't lose himself in a dream world of self-admiration. He had time to develop a deep and abiding respect for others."

Fred headed to Florida with Williams at the start of the 1959 season when he bumped into Francis Stann, the *Washington Star* columnist, as they boarded the flight. He was on his way down to the Senators' spring camp. They exchanged hellos and, after a bit, Fred suggested to Francis that they swap seats so he could chat with Ted. In those days, before jets, it was a five-hour flight south. But Fred had an idea that Stann and Williams would hit it off and they did. Williams, who couldn't have been more relaxed and cordial, talked freely, and even went down the American League, team by team, analyzing their strengths and weaknesses.

For the Washington sportswriter, it was a bonanza. He extracted enough material for three or four columns which earned him a wire of congratulations from his boss. He was delighted with the interview and charmed by Williams, who after many troubled years, now had a number of friends among the newspapermen and scores of them among the ball players. Williams never refused advice to a player who sought it and often volunteered it to rivals on other clubs as well as teammates on the Red Sox. After Al Kaline won the American League batting championship in 1955, he was asked the secret of his success. "Ted Williams straightened me out," he said.

"I've heard many sportswriters—mainly those outside Boston—say they never found Ted other than thoughtful and gracious," Fred said. In fact, Ted had countless admirers from every walk of life, among them

Joe Kennedy, father of John F. Kennedy. Fred was called away from the dinner table with Ted the night before the season opener between the Red Sox and the Washington Senators at Griffith Stadium when he got a phone call. It was the senior Kennedy who got directly to the point.

"Fred," he said, "tomorrow is the opener at Griffith Stadium. My son, Jack, will be there. Do you suppose you could arrange to have Ted Williams go over and shake hands with him? It would make a good picture—for both of them." At the time Jack was the junior Senator from Massachusetts.

"Of course, I can arrange this," he assured him.

When Fred returned to the table and told Ted about the call, Ted thought he was putting him on, even though he agreed to do it. But it never happened because neither John F. Kennedy nor Ted ever reached the ball park. Kennedy injured his hand when he caught it in the door of his car and didn't get to the game, and Williams ate some bad seafood at that dinner and spent that day in bed. President Eisenhower had the photographers all to himself.

CHAPTER 31

IF FRED HAD TO PIN A BOUQUET ON ANY COUNTRY FOR DOING A GRAND job of hosting the Canada Cup, it would have to be Ireland in 1960. The Irish hosts, led by Professor Pierce Purcell, the 82-year-old bellwether of the Irish golfing flock, put on a magnificent show. All Fred had to do was meet with the Portmarnock group and rave over the way the English had conducted the 1956 event.

Fred explained further. "Every time I described the way they handled something so well in England, you could see a dozen Irish jaws square and a dozen pairs of Irish eyes flash angrily. You could almost hear their Irish minds snapping, 'Ah, did they now? Well, we'll show you a thing or two about hospitality and how to run a golf tournament, laddie.'"

And they did, too. The Portmarnock affair was a memorable one, drawing a gallery of 60,000 for the week. There was a new kid on the block, named Arnold Palmer, and Fred was delighted to pair him with Sam Snead for the first time. And it was an explosive event if you consider Palmer's failure to stick to the fairways. Young Arnie would ask the caddie where the hole was, and scorning the fairway, would go cross-country straight at the green.

On the 11th hole, Arnold hooked his tee shot into the high grass on the edge of a bunker, and Snead hurried over to help him find the ball.

"Now whatcha gonna do?" Sam asked when they found it.

"I'm going to go for it," Arnie said.

"Listen," Sam snorted, "you wedge that s.o.b. back in the fairway or we'll never get out of here."

With that, Sam turned his back and stalked out to the fairway, stopping en route when he heard a cheer from the crowd. Arnold had hit a 3-wood, squarely onto the green.

Fred later asked Sam what he had said to Arnold, and whether he had congratulated him. "Hell no," Sam snapped. "I didn't say nothing 'cause I didn't want to encourage him.'"

Fred went back to Portmarnock several years later and was told that after a few drinks, some Irishmen went out to where Palmer hit his shot to see if they could duplicate it. None of them did and one guy even broke his leg trying—on a practice swing! Dave Anderson captured that scene's sense of lore when he wrote years later in a piece in *The New York Times*, "That shot has lived in history and Irish Whisky ever since."

Palmer and Snead took home the team trophy while Flory Van Donck from Belgium captured the international honors.

"We were and we weren't surprised when more than 30,000 Irish golf fans stampeded across the course for the Sunday climax," Fred said. "And they made a mess of the place, leaving litter everywhere. The next day I went back to the course and stopped at the Lost and Found office where a club official was sorting out sunglasses, women's shoes and other articles that had been left behind. Then a bushel basket of rosary beads caught my eye."

Jokingly Fred said, "I'll bet you found them at the ninth hole." That's where Christy O'Connor of the Irish team took a seven and blew himself out of the championship.

The attendant looked at him quizzically. "Indaid," he said, "and that's where we found them...all around the big hill behind the hole."

Bouncing between golf and baseball in 1960, Fred attended a party the night before the All-Star Game at Yankee Stadium where both Stan Musial and Ted Williams were invited. Williams begged off to spend the evening with his daughter, which left Musial on center stage, where he began to criticize the All-Star team managers who never started him or Williams.

"Let's be honest," Musial said. "The people who come to this game come to see us hit. But we aren't sent in until the sixth or seventh inning, and we have to go in there cold against a pitcher who is warmed up and throwing his best." Then he said a strange thing—for him. "I'll tell you this, and you've never heard me say this before: If I get in there tomorrow, I'll hit a home run."

Musial didn't quite have the electricity that Cobb and Williams had, yet he had everything else, including the ability to call his shot—with this difference: When Babe Ruth waved his bat toward the distant stands and hit that home run in the 1932 World Series, he did it before a packed

Wrigley Field in Chicago. Musial had only the small audience of a dinner party in New York when he called his shot.

And, sure enough, he called it right. In the seventh inning, he parked a fast ball in the second deck. Williams followed in the next inning with a long ball to the fence. "I don't know whether Musial really believed it when he said he would hit a home run, but I suspect he was playing some kind of a hunch," Fred said.

1960 brought along with it the last season for Ted Williams as a player. Despite the time Ted Williams lost from baseball, he was behind only Babe Ruth and Jimmy Foxx in lifetime home runs, and with a lifetime batting average of .344, he was behind only Ty Cobb, Rogers Hornsby, Joe Jackson and Lefty O'Doul when he retired that year.

The Yankees tried to hire Ted to play one more year in 1961. Fred got a call from Dan Topping, the Yankee's owner, and they met at the Savoy Plaza bar. "We want Williams to play next year, strictly pinch-hit for us for what he's now making, $125,000." Topping asked.

"You'll need to talk to Tom Yawkey first," Fred told him, "because Ted has a deferred payment set up with the Red Sox."

"I don't want to call Yawkey!" Topping said. "I want to sign him as a free agent. Can you get his release?"

Fred called Ted and told him about the offer but he wasn't interested. "What does New York have to offer me?" Ted said on the phone. "It's a lot of bad air and traffic jams."

"There's a lot of money involved, just for pinch-hitting," Fred pointed out. "It's like they're paying you to suit up and swing once every few games."

"Nah," he shouted. "Forget it! I'm not interested. I'm never going to hit another ball in a big league park." And that was that. The Splendid Splinter, in a climatic ending to his career, played his last game for Boston on September 28, 1960, blasting a home run out of the park.

Soon after, Fred had dinner with Ty Cobb, whose health and hard-core lifestyle were closing in on him at the age of 73.

"Cobb was, far and away, the most dynamic player in the history of baseball—and perhaps the best of them all," Fred told many. "That tough spirit never left him entirely, although he did mellow a little in his later years. He never lost his interest in the game as some old ball players do. He had a great curiosity about the new generation of players, and as a result, he was more knowledgeable than you would expect of one who had stepped out of the passing parade in 1928. His judgments seemed to be unfailingly sharp and always serious, reflecting the one great drawback in his personality—an almost total lack of humor. He was friendly, but without any warmth. And whatever Ty had on his mind stayed there. He didn't speculate for the benefit of others. In his playing days, he was a lone wolf who roamed alone off the field, and if he decided to use his spikes, the first you knew of it was when you got jabbed, maybe in the Adam's apple."

Fred added, "During a night of it, when confidences were being exchanged, I asked Ty about that Durocher story, where Leo Durocher, then a rookie shortstop for the Yankees, supposedly slapped a hard tag on Cobb coming into second base and remarked, 'That's just to warn you. If you try to cut me, I'll stick this ball up your ear.' Cobb, the story goes, replied, 'Then brace yourself because the next time I come down, I'm going to put some spikes in your belly.'

"It never happened," Cobb asserted, "and neither did a lot of other stories you've heard. But, if they did, it wasn't a one-way street. Look at this!" He pulled up a pant leg to his knee, displaying a lacework of old wounds.

As dinner lingered on, Cobb confided in Fred. "You don't warn a man and you don't complain," he said, reminiscing about the days when he fought catcher Buck Herzog in a hotel room and Umpire Billy Evans under the stands, chased a newspaper man out of the park, caused a player strike, and finally was forced by Commissioner Landis to leave Detroit and play out the string in 1927 and 1928 in Philadelphia exile. Because a former ballplayer had charged Cobb and others with having connived and gambled in several instances, Cobb was banished from the only major-league team he had ever been with. And at the age of 42, in his 24th and final year in the majors, Cobb hit .323 for a never-to-be-equaled lifetime average of .367.

Fred, of course, spoke of his dinner to Grantland Rice, a hardy pioneer of the major league press box as well as the golf course, who added that Cobb was the most combative baseball player he had ever seen, and probably the shrewdest. Granny had known him from his early days in the old Southeastern and Sally leagues, when Rice was starting up the journalistic ladder as a sportswriter. Even then, he said, Cobb was a man apart, on his way to becoming a Detroit Tiger at the age of 19. After his first year, when he got into only a few games, he hit above .300 in every one of his remaining twenty-three major league seasons.

A few months later, Cobb went back to his native Georgia for the hunting season as he had done throughout his life, not just because he liked hunting, but because walking for hours behind his dogs was good for his legs. Cobb was a crank on physical fitness, and spoke of the time he lined his baseball shoes with lead for the spring workouts, to build up speed. Writers on the Grapefruit Circuit soberly reported that he seemed to be slowing down. "That was 1915, the year I stole 96 bases!" he chuckled.

With Cobb's passing in 1961, another immortal figure dropped out of the endless sports parade. "There will never be another quite like him," Fred spoke upon his death, toasting to his memory and mourning the loss of his long-time hero.

CHAPTER 32

FRED'S LIFE, FOR SOME REASON, NEVER SAILED SMOOTHLY. "WHEN I THINK back to my career with the PGA, there was always some sort of drama. I don't know why I am surprised about that now."

After seven years with the International Golf Association, his relationship with the PGA still had its moments. This latest ripple came when the PGA gave him trouble about the 1961 Canada Cup, scheduled for the same time as the Memphis Open. In a sense, it was the same old problem he had faced twenty-five years ago when the top pros wanted to skip a local tournament. Only this time, he was the one taking them away.

With the conflict in schedule, the PGA voted to uphold the sponsors who demanded that the PGA Champions from the past twelve years play in the tournament and threatened to fine Arnold Palmer, Gary Player of South Africa, and Stan Leonard of Canada $500 each and suspend them from the PGA Tour for six months if they skipped Memphis in favor of the Canada Cup. Snead was exempt because his PGA win had been more than twelve years ago.

Bob Rosburg, chairman of the PGA Tournament Committee, contended that the Canada Cup was not a true international competition. He added, "This is a competition set up by individuals for what we feel is individual gain. The individuals are Frank Pace and Fred Corcoran. They have never tried to schedule the event in cooperation with the PGA or tried to select players with any formula. The men who compete for them are paid handsomely to go to the competition. It's not like the Ryder Cup matches, where the player actually is representing the country, where you receive $250 expense money for ten days of playing."

Rosburg went on to say, "A guy like Gary Player comes to this country from South Africa. He thinks it's great winning $48,000 in four months. Now all of a sudden he doesn't think he should go by all the rules." He also accused Fred of switching the dates to accommodate Snead's schedule.

Fred called for some honesty and horse sense. "The whole situation has developed as a result of a complete misunderstanding," he told the press. "In the first place, our tournament was announced May 19, 1960, and the Memphis tournament was not signed until one month later, on June 17. This certainly gives us prior claims on the services of players who made personal commitments with us."

He went on to say that Bob Rosburg was a good friend but he had his facts slightly twisted when he said Fred had changed the dates to accommodate Snead. "Our dates were released long before any such move would have been possible. After all, we have sixty-six players from thirty-three nations to advise. This championship is not run for any one country, any one player, or anyone person's gain. It is a tournament for international goodwill. And it's quite unfair for him to say that the players competing in the international golf championship are rewarded handsomely. All players, including Snead and Palmer, receive $500 expenses and compete for what they can of the posted $7,500 in prize money," Fred said publicly.

With Snead in Fred's camp, they ended up inviting Jimmy Demaret and played the 1961 Canada Cup at Puerto Rico's lush Dorado Beach Golf Club without Palmer, Player or Leonard. Snead fired a record 272 while playing with Demaret to successfully defend the title and crush the competition by twelve strokes. Sam took the singles honors, as well.

A young man named Roone Arledge came up to Fred at that event. He was working on a new show called *ABC's Wide World of Sports* and was scouting out interesting international sporting events and this one had caught his eye. Fred, of course, had a tale to tell about his idea of broadcasting golf on television, as well as a thousand other tales. Also an idea man, Arledge was a student of golf's legend and lore, and he and Fred became instant and life-long friends. Fred would go on to introduce Roone to golf's top players, both on the course and behind the scenes, that would help build golf's television viewing audience everywhere. Roone would soon gain fame for sports broadcasting innovations like putting microphones on the playing field and using slow motion in instant replays, as well as expanding coverage of the Olympic Games and, of course, broadcasting in color.

The squabble with the PGA settled down the next year and, in 1962, the Canada Cup went to the Jockey Club in Buenos Aires, Argentina, with Arnold Palmer and Sam Snead paired together and on top again. The cheers for Argentina's own Roberto De Vicenzo, who came from behind in the final round to win the International Trophy, were only a shade more boisterous.

Dick Taylor, the editor of *Golf World* at the time, was along on that trip and recalled an incident on the bus with Mohamed Said Moussa, who was representing Egypt. With desegregation at the forefront of political news in America, Taylor wanted to talk to him.

"I saw the handsome Egyptian sitting alone on a full bus transporting players to the club from the hotel and decided to sit next to him. Not knowing any Arabic, I slowly spoke English to him. To my surprise he replied in faultless English with a British accent."

Said Moussa told Taylor he grew up in Cairo and was a caddie and professional at the Cairo Golf Club, where most of the members were British. "Part of my early green fees at the club," he said, "was a bucket of water."

Taylor went on to partner with him in the Pro Am, where he improved his game with a few lessons from "the greatest sand player ever."

The press picked up on the tournament's goodwill. Peter Stone wrote in *The Age*, "At a time when hemispheric relations have been strained, Sam Snead and Arnold Palmer were cheered long and thunderously by thousands of Argentineans as they won the Canada Cup, doing more for international and inter-hemispheric friendliness than six goodwill missions."

"Each tournament always touched me in a personal way," Fred said. "At this one, Johnny Martin of the Irish team hunted me down to ask if he could get an autograph of Arnold Palmer and Sam Snead. I told him, 'I'll do better than that. You'll play with them!'"

During another rainy-day bull session at another tournament in 1963, Fred posed a question to a leading professional and former PGA and Masters champion. "If you had to pick the ten most promising young golf professionals, who would you name?" He said he'd give it some thought and, later, he handed Fred his list.

Fred was busy with an emergency of the moment so he stashed it in his coat pocket. It was a few weeks later, at the Doral Open in Miami, that he found it and showed it to Chick Harbert, one of the most articulate and tough-minded men in the business. Chick skimmed the names quickly and handed back the list. "It's a good list," he said crisply, "but there's one name missing. I'll take him and you can have the other ten."

"Who's that?" Fred asked.

"Tony Lema," Harbert replied. "He's got 'winner' written all over him. He's got every shot in the bag and I think he's got the temperament to win, and that's important. Why don't you go out and take a look at him?"

Fred took Chick at his word and trailed the blithe spirit from San Leandro, California, through the last four holes. And he liked what he saw. The young man was good. But more than that, there was something there that struck sparks. Lema was a maverick type, and Fred liked that. In a strange way, he reminded Fred vaguely of Ted Williams—in the way he handled himself, the way he stood off and surveyed the crowd with quiet amusement, in his loose-gaited walk. Prospectors must get the same charge when they see a yellow glint in the face of a canyon wall.

"I wasn't asking questions and ranging the Doral Blue Course out of idle curiosity. In my own way, I was prospecting without really being aware of it. My business had been making money for and through sports headliners. But I had become so preoccupied with other things—and especially with the promotion of international golf tournaments—that I was literally out of business. I had used up my inventory. So now I was on the prowl at Doral and Harbert was my native guide. He pointed me toward Lema and then flushed the young tiger my way."

Lema had been burned by a personal sponsor who had financed his time on the tour in return for a share of his earnings. After five years on the road, the sponsor had turned a profit of $60,000 and Lema had nothing to show for it. He was, however, looking for an agent and business manager, and when Fred told him he would only take fifteen percent of any business he brought to him, and that he would have nothing to do with his prize money, Lema shook hands. He liked that idea.

A few weeks later at the 1963 Masters, Lema finished second, one stroke behind Jack Nicklaus, and a few weeks after that, he missed the playoff for the U.S. Open by two shots, bogeying the last two holes while thinking he needed birdies. He was now dogged by reporters and considered a favorite at every tournament. And Fred's phone was ringing off the hook again.

Also on Fred's plate in 1963 was the Thunderbird Classic. Fred was hired by to organize and run the tournament by Bill Jennings, who was also head of the New York Rangers and Madison Square Garden, and the Tri-State Ford Dealers. The first thing they did was move it to Westchester Country Club in Rye, New York, from Upper Montclair County Club in Clifton, New Jersey. The Classic was the richest tournament on the tour with the largest prize package in golf, $100,000 to be split among the leaders. It was a huge money-maker for Jennings' personal charity, United Hospital in Portchester, New York.

The tournament was successful on all fronts. With Arnold Palmer taking home the $25,000 first prize in a sudden-death playoff against Paul Harney, the gallery was huge, as Arnold had become a star. Many came out to see Ben Hogan play, after an absence of eighteen months, and Snead, each of whom placed eight and nine strokes respectively behind Palmer. Tony Lema played also, but didn't do very well that week, much to Fred's home-court disappointment.

By now, Fred had brought to the Canada Cup some pretty big corporate sponsors—Time Inc. with its iconic *Sports Illustrated*, American Express, National Cash Register, Rothman's cigarettes, Pan American Airlines and later International Telephone and Telegraph and Colgate-Palmolive. In fact, Fred had put golf on the map, taking it from the space below the racing results to the front page of the sports section and the cover of *Sports Illustrated*. And he had, in fact, become the go-to guy for golf around the world.

The 1963 Canada Cup took the players to a beautiful spot near Paris, at the Saint-Nomla-Breteche, once a grazing meadow for Louis XIV's cows. The weather, however, stole the show and the tournament was cut short, to 63 holes, due to fog. But it provided a large stage for Arnold Palmer and first-time representative Jack Nicklaus.

On the first day at the Pro-Am, former Vice President Richard M. Nixon played in a foursome with International Golf Association Directors Jim Linen, President of Time Inc., Howard Clark, IGA President and President of the American Express Company, and Hawaiian sugar magnate C. Hutton Smith. Halfway down the first fairway, Nixon discovered he didn't have a caddie. With some thirty caddies waiting around the first tee, each, in turn, was polled to determine who was caddying for Nixon. And each, in turn, shook his head. So the former Vice President of the United States, whose proximity to the presidency everyone knew, had to go back 200 yards to the tee and paw his way through the stacked golf bags until he found his. Then he had to locate a caddie and trudge back to his ball.

Fred watched with tournament host Prince Michael de Bourbon, Parme of France and a descendant of the last Louis and an OSS hero of the French underground. He finally turned to him and said, "Just think, if he had carried New York State, six Secret Service men would be toting the bag."

On Sunday, the fog arrived. You couldn't see twenty-five yards from the tee, so Fred postponed the round until Monday, which was even foggier. "We talked for a while," Fred said, "and decided we should try to get nine holes in, so we rounded up all the cars we could find and drove them out on the course and parked them behind the greens. We then had them turn on their headlights, and we sent out fore caddies to spot the balls. And we made it through."

"I remember I was in a bunker," said Jack Nicklaus, "and didn't have an easy shot but I holed it for a birdie. Then I heard all this commotion and had no idea what it was. Well, the Prince of Wales was in the gallery and when the ball fell in the cup, he got very excited and tumbled over backwards. He just fell off his shooting stick!"

The team of Palmer and Nicklaus did not disappoint as they rallied from behind to overtake the Spanish team of Ramon Sota and Sebastian Miguel on the 63rd hole. But Jack was pleased when he took home the Individual Trophy in his first time at bat. He and Palmer, at this time, were fierce rivals, especially since Jack had signed on with Arnie's long-time manager, Mark McCormack, who had also just signed Gary Player to form the "Big Three."

The tournament was another eye-opening event, because in 1963, nobody cared about golf in France. As Oscar Fraley, the UPI sports reporter who went on to write *The Untouchables*, put it, "Even the French Open couldn't draw flies in July. Now, suddenly, there were 10,000 of the proletariat stampeding across royalties' hallowed acres."

There were some sour grapes at this tournament, sometimes expressed and sometimes implied, that the American players got better treatment with special financial inducements, special arrangements and accommodations. This wasn't true, of course. They played for the purse just like the other thirty-two teams, and they got the same expense money as the others. However, it was true that the American players were sought after by resident Americans whenever they played overseas. They were often wined and dined and chauffeured in grand style.

"This happens because they're winners," Fred argued. "When you win a tournament, people shove and elbow for the privilege of driving you back to town. But if you finish second, you'd better call a cab. If you win, they hold planes for you, which I've never heard anyone do for a loser. I've said this before and I've seen it happen, time and again. It's a sorry comment on the persistent immaturity of the human animal. But there it is. That's how it is in life."

Chapter 33

Tony Lema was not riding high when he invited Fred to handle his business dealings, but it didn't take him long to prove his ability. He kicked off 1964 by winning the Crosby Pro-Am, an event that was special to Fred because of his long friendship with Bing Crosby. He always started the season with a trip to Pebble Beach, and now, with his new "star" on his arm, he was ecstatic.

Both Fred and Tony were on cloud nine as they walked to the Press Room after Tony signed his card. Fred was telling him what to highlight when talking to the press when he stopped mid-sentence and asked, "Tony, do you want champagne for the press?" Tony had taunted the press on the eve of his first official tournament win in 1962, saying if he won, he'd buy everyone a glass of champagne to celebrate.

Fred grabbed the arm of a passing waiter, not really giving Tony time to answer. "Bring us a few bottles of your best champagne," Fred said to the waiter, "and a lot of glasses." And with that, Tony Lema became "Champagne Tony," lighting a light on the tour that had been dim for some time.

"Better make it a case," Fred called to the waiter, "and hurry back." While he knew he couldn't impress the press with champagne, Fred didn't mind tempting a few of them to root for Lema to win another tournament.

Word got out about this time that Fred was thinking about "committing autobiography." It touched off a wave of popular indignation where he was asked more than once: Why would anyone be interested in reading about Fred Corcoran?

"You'd be surprised to know this struck me as a sensible question," Fred laughed as he teamed with Bud Harvey to get his stories on paper. He spent the next year on the phone, meeting with his friends, telling stories, taking notes, speaking into a tape recorder, watching Nancy type, and listening to Bud play the piano as he worked his magic into *Unplayable Lies*, which was published in 1965.

To get Sam Snead's side of Fred's stories, Fred invited him to meet in Miami. Nancy and the girls had flown in to join Fred at the Shamrock Isle in Miami Beach, and Fred promised Sam a ride back to Palm Beach as the family shifted camp to the Breakers. Sam arrived for lunch and in the late afternoon, while Fred was wrapping up some business on the phone, his ten-year-old daughter Judy engaged Sam in a friendly card game. Before Fred or Nancy realized it, Sam had taught her how to play gin rummy. And perhaps to wrap up the session, Sam, with the dexterity only a ten-year-old could follow, switched cards on her.

"That's cheating!" she shouted.

"Sam," Nancy scolded, immediately taking her child's side, "you shouldn't be teaching kids how to cheat!"

"Ah, I'm sorry, Mis' Mama," he said to her, "I was just teaching her how to spot a cheater. It's important when you play cards to know how to slip 'em, and that's all I was showing her. It works like this." He showed Judy how his sleight of hand was done, and after a few tries, she had mastered his technique. She was now her Uncle Sam's number one fan and follower.

"Now, remember," Sam added, "there's cheating and then there's playing. I just taught you how to play, not to cheat."

"Maybe you should teach her how to chip out of a sand trap next," Fred weighed in.

Prior to the trip, the girls had mentioned that they wanted to see *The Ed Sullivan Show* that night on television. In fact, it was all they talked about all day as it was the second appearance of the Beatles on the show. Fred didn't pay much attention to them until they refused to get in the car unless he promised to stop somewhere at seven p.m. When Sam got wind of the problem, he admitted that he, too, wanted to see the "mop tops," and jumped on board with the girls, further endearing him to them.

They hit the road toward Palm Beach and as the hour neared, the girls became more anxious and vocal. Fred finally told Nancy to pull off the highway and drive to the Boca Raton Country Club. With fifteen minutes to spare, they headed for the barber shop. Fred knew the manager, Louie DeBoca, and figured he would help them out.

As the girls settled in the barber's chairs to watch the small television set that hung in the corner of the salon, Fred decided to get a haircut. "Sam, why don't you get one, too," he egged him on.

"I could use a trim," Sam said, moving to an empty chair. "But don't touch the top," he instructed Louie, pushing down his straw hat atop his head. "Just clip the sides."

Fred knew a publicity shot when he saw one and quickly summoned a photographer to take the picture of Sam, with his hat on, getting a haircut. It made the papers the next day.

Judy didn't quite understand the fuss when the photographer arrived and Fred started working his magic, telling everyone where to stand and how to pose. "Never stand on the edge of a group photo," he whispered to her as everyone took their places. "It's too easy to cut you out of the picture." With that, he positioned her in between Sam and himself for one last shot.

Sam had a lot of television exposure around this time through a commercial for Alka Seltzer. It showed him at a banquet table, after a big dinner, listless, downcast and out of sorts. Then he sloshed down an Alka Seltzer and cut to the next day, showing a smiling Snead, galloping around the course on his way to a new record. As the announcer touted the product, Sam agreed, saying, "You ain't just whistlin' 'Dixie'!"

Fred and Sam were at a little party at the Savoy Plaza around that time when Nicky Hilton joined them. He was with Zsa-Zsa Gabor, the beautiful Hungarian film star, who was married to Nicky's father Conrad. When he introduced Sam to her, she leaned over to Fred and asked, "Vat does he do?"

"He's a great TV star," Fred teased with a straight face.

Zsa-Zsa brightened. "Uff course," she exclaimed. "Now I know him. He's the man on the Alka Seltzer program!"

As April and 1964 Masters arrived, Tony Lema was in the news again, finishing second by one stroke to Jack Nicklaus. And by June, he was as hot as they come. Fred invited Tony and his wife Betty to stay at his house in Mamaroneck during the 1964 Thunderbird, played again at Westchester Country Club, and they arrived two days before the start of the tournament. Fred's daughter, Judy, was ordered to clean her room and bunk with her sister, so Tony and his wife Betty could stay there.

After the Lemas settled in, Tony pulled Fred aside. "Is Judy upset about us being here?" he asked, out of earshot of her.

"Why?" Fred wondered. "Is something wrong?" Her bedroom was often used as the guest room in their small house. Ted Williams, Sam Snead, Gene Sarazen, Jack Sharkey and others had all slept in her bed.

"Well, it's just that all the wooden hangers in the closet have 'Corcoran Hilton' written on them in red marker."

As put out as 11-year-old Judy was prior to meeting Lema, she was immediately taken by him, as was her 12-year-old sister, Peggy. With Fred and Nancy's many social obligations during the tournament that week, they left the girls home under the Lemas' watchful eye. The couple quickly adapted to suburban life, grilling steaks on Fred's patio that faced the 15th fairway at Winged Foot. Tony showed the girls how to tame the flames on the charcoal when he instructed them to fill their water pistols and douse on sight. They dutifully put out any flame that shot up between rare and well-done.

Lema then challenged the girls to a fly-swatting contest, awarding ten cents per fly to the winner. Upon pulling ahead by two, he declared himself the winner and the contest over. Judy went and found twenty cents to give him but he declined.

"You only owe me seventeen cents," he said, waving her off. "Your father gets fifteen percent of anything I do."

Lema took the lead at the Thunderbird but was pitted against Arnold Palmer who drew a huge gallery, called "Arnie's Army" by TV commentators. Judy was outraged at this one-sided media attention. With that same red marker and a white poster board, she and her sister made signs calling for "Lema's Legions" and "Tony's Troops" to gather round.

Tony loved the signs. "You're lucky she likes you," said Fred. "She calls Ted Williams 'Old Yeller.'"

With a custom-made cheering section led by two little girls, Lema beat Billy Casper, Mike Souchak and Ken Venturi to win the Thunderbird. He returned to the Corcoran house and joined the family for breakfast early the next morning.

"Whoa, whoa, where are you going," Tony said to Judy who was running upstairs just as he was coming down.

"I'm late," she called only to return a minute later, having fetched something from her room.

"Isn't school over?" Lema asked.

"Yes," she answered as she scurried around. "I'm late for the golf clinic," she called as she ran out the door, stopping only to pick up Marlene Bauer's set of junior clubs from the front closet. "Mr. Isokane, the golf teacher, will be upset if we're late."

She had signed up weeks before for a golf clinic at the local public school and didn't seem to care that golf's most revered player was just sitting down at her breakfast table. To Fred, this was another story for the press, one that brought a personal visit from Mr. Isokane the next day, hoping to meet Mr. Lema.

Chapter 34

It's interesting to consider that both Tony Lema and another great player of this time, Ken Venturi, began their climb up the tournament ladder as neighborhood kids in the San Francisco Bay area. In fact, Lema's first pair of golf spikes was a gift from Venturi's mother after she saw him playing in a tournament in tennis shoes. That both men should knock off the twin Open championships of the world in the same year is a heartwarming sports story. "That both should become professional clients of mine is even more heartwarming—to me. That's a quinella that's hard to match!" Fred cheered.

The 1964 Thunderbird brought Ken Venturi to the front page in early June of this year. His story with Fred started on the eve of the tournament, when Fred received a phone call from Bill Jennings, the tournament's General Chairman, who asked if Venturi could bypass the qualifying round and secure a spot in the pairings.

Fred had met Ken Venturi in 1961 but it was only a handshake and a hello. On his tournament record, Ken failed to qualify for consideration. But at the time of Jennings' call, there was still an unfilled place in the sponsors' group, so they agreed to give it to the troubled Venturi. It was almost a gesture of sympathy as Venturi had traveled a rough road, after nearly winning the Masters in 1960 and suffering injuries in a car accident in 1961.

Ken played very well and ended up tied for third, winning $6,400 of the prize money. While his comeback was unexpected, it was most welcome and proved to be a turning point for him, providing a tremendous psychological lift.

"Right now," Venturi told a reporter, "I just feel good." It was only a short time ago that Venturi had suffered from walking pneumonia, swollen hands, a bad back, tendonitis in his thumb, and the car accident. But he was now filled with confidence, which he admitted was the key to his success. "The reason is not so much physical as mental," he said. "Actually, the whole thing is confidence. You never know what confidence is until you lose it."

Fred took Venturi under his wing at the Thunderbird, not knowing that he would go on to win the U.S. Open that next week. And what a win that was! Traditionally, the field played 36 holes on the Saturday of the U.S. Open week and on this day in June, the temperature on the sun-baked course at Congressional in Washington, D.C. soared to a dangerous level. Suffering from heat stroke during the second round, Ken walked the next day with a doctor close by, who carried ice, salt tablets, iced tea and towels for him. After this, the USGA changed its rules and never scheduled a 36-hole final again, although Ken later stated that the schedule was changed because of television revenues, not because of his ordeal.

But he made it all the way, winning the U.S. Open championship in a three-way battle with the heat, a tough course, and his own head. "I played on instinct," Ken later told Fred. "I was so weak, I didn't feel the pressure."

Hopefully, he felt the glory. Winning the U.S. Open was the crowning achievement of his career. "When you win a PGA Tour event, you get your name in the paper and a clip of your best putt on television," Fred said. "But when you win the Open, you get a new last name. He is now, 'Ken Venturi who won the 1964 U.S. Open.'"

"And to think," Ken added, "I had to qualify to get into the 1964 Open." Ken had failed to qualify for that year's British Open, scheduled a few weeks later, and by now, the entry deadline had passed. But he proved that his win at Congressional was no fluke by winning the Insurance City Open and the American Golf Classic shortly afterwards. He ended the year as *Sports Illustrated*'s Sportsman of the Year.

The Ken Venturi story is another dramatic saga. It doesn't have the crackling dialogue of Champagne Tony's musical comedy, but it's strong on plot and moral. Some stars become big men by winning. Venturi became an even greater man while losing.

Venturi was a boy who graduated cum laude from the whizbang California junior golf circuit with all kinds of promising credentials. He was runner-up in the first USGA Junior championship in 1948 at the age of 17. Then Byron Nelson adopted him as a protégé and fitted him with a carbon copy of the beautiful Nelson swing.

Tony Lema, his long-time friend, wrote about Ken's balanced swing in his book, *Golfer's Gold*. He said that Nelson taught Venturi to hit the ball straight with the perfect balance of a gymnast. "One can admire Hogan's swing for its efficiency and Snead's swing for its natural beauty and perfection, but Venturi's swing seemed like an ideal blend of the two. Ken stood up to the ball as if he, the golf club, the ball and the golf course were all part of a beautiful piece of sculpture. He looked like a great boxer, someone like Sugar Ray Robinson, ready to dance in on an opponent."

In 1956 Ken Venturi had an opportunity to become the first amateur winner of the Masters championship. He led the field by four strokes going into the Sunday final, and then proceeded to commit fairway hara-kiri by blowing himself to an 80. It was probably one of the most catastrophic attacks of nerves ever seen on a golf course.

"There's a story there too," Fred added, "in that Venturi should have been paired with Byron Nelson for the final round, but since Nelson was Venturi's mentor, the powers at Augusta felt it would be better to pair Venturi with Sam Snead, who was a serious competitor. Ken was perhaps bothered more by the wind than by the tenor of the match, but he nonetheless succumbed to his nerves."

Snead agreed about the wind. "Ken didn't blow the tournament. He just had a lot of trouble trying to figure out those real slick greens. The wind was bad and after he'd miss the green with his approach shot, it made it awful hard to get a par because the little short putts he needed never seemed to break the way he thought they would." The record shows that a lot of other players had that same trouble on the last day. Even Byron Nelson shot an 80 that day.

Yet, Venturi turned pro that same year and was an instant success, winning nearly $150,000 in the next five years. Then, quite suddenly, the lights went out. First, he lost his wonderful touch. Then he lost his poise, and finally, he lost all confidence in himself. In 1962 he finished among the top five only once and won less than $7,000. The following year was even worse. Ken was never close and won less than $4,000 in prize money.

When the pros gathered at Los Angeles for the start of the 1964 winter tour, Ken Venturi appeared on the scene almost from habit. Playing without hope and without inspiration, he was at the point of putting his clubs away and turning to some other field to support his family. But at his darkest hour, he met a devoted priest in San Francisco who turned him around. Father Francis Murray patiently set about rebuilding the young man's faith in himself.

"Father Francis reminded me of something I should never have forgotten…that a poor shot isn't the end of the tournament or the end of the world. For that matter, I learned that winning and losing a golf tournament isn't of too much consequence, really…that there are other values in life which are a lot more significant. The second and third steps were easy. I learned to accept the breaks, good and bad, philosophically," Venturi said.

"Once I learned to step away from myself and take a long look at things, something started to happen to my golf game. As I began to take the good with the bad in stride, I found myself playing fewer bad shots. I began to enjoy the game again for the first time in two years," Ken wrote in his book, *Getting Up & Down*.

Ken made some other important discoveries, too. He found who his friends were.

"One friend was Tony Lema," Fred said, "and no two persons could be more dissimilar than Lema and Venturi. Champagne Tony bristled with that indefinable thing called color while Ken always attracted a great personal following of loyal fans who would storm over the course at his heels. Both of these former caddies who came out of the San Francisco greenhouse of golf were solid bets at this time to wind up in golf's Hall of Fame. One radiated with success and already had established himself as the dashing cavalier of golf while the other had triumphed over adversity."

CHAPTER 35

By July, Lema had three more titles under his belt. After winning the Thunderbird, he went on to win the Buick Open and the Cleveland Open in a playoff with Palmer. Lema had qualified for the British Open, but he couldn't decide whether to play. Even his wife Betty complained. "First he is going and then he isn't," she told John Lovesey at *Sports Illustrated*. "I don't know and believe me, neither does he. Tell me, are other golfers like normal people?"

Lema didn't want to go to the British Open, but Arnold Palmer, who was a friend to nearly everyone on the tour, convinced Lema at the last minute to go. After all, he was on a roll, having just beaten Arnold in a playoff at Cleveland for his third victory in four starts. Palmer, feeling exhausted, had decided to sit out the tournament so he also suggested Tony use his Scottish caddie, Tip Anderson. And he gave Tony his favorite putter to use.

That Sunday night, when he finished the Whitemarsh Open in Philadelphia, Lema announced that he would play at St. Andrews. He told the press, "I've won tournaments and I've won money. Now I want to win a major championship!"

When he called Fred to tell him he'd be on a plane to Scotland the next day, they argued. "Tony, you don't go to St. Andrews the night before the tournament!" Fred repeated several times.

Regardless, Fred met him at the airport and during the ride to the course, he tried to prep him as best he could. They sat together for the next few hours while Fred described the demons that lie in wait on the windswept Scottish links.

"There's a special mischief of the wind that whirls and dances around the course, switching direction abruptly and erratically and changing the entire nature of the course with it," Fred said.

Lema jackknifed in his seat, turning those keen eyes on Fred. "I don't want to hear any more about it," he interrupted. "Just let me tee up the ball out there, that's all I ask. I don't build the courses. I just play 'em."

His statement was characteristic. It closed the discussion with a flat assertion of self-assurance. There was no false bravado about it. It was just the nature of the man who approached the game with a world of confidence.

"Lema had a jauntiness without cockiness that led many to compare him with Walter Hagen," Fred said. "But I think this comparison is unfair to both of them. True, both had a sparkling zest for living and a tremendous flair for moving to the center of the stage. But you can't fit one personality into a mold shaped by another. Lema, in his own right, was a fresh and dramatic sports personality and his gesture of cracking a case of Moët for the writers when he won a tournament was just a natural impulse that recalls the princely extravagance of Sir Walter."

With only enough time to play ten holes at St. Andrews before he began his first round, Lema arrived at the first tee in great spirits. Maybe luck was with him. As he waited to tee off, he spotted a coin in the grass. He picked it up and turned to the crowd.

"'See,' he said with his effervescent smile and contagious laughter, 'I'm already the leading money-winner in the British Open,'" Dave Anderson wrote in *The New York Times* in a tribute to Lema years later.

In his first round, Tony shot a 68. At a press conference afterwards, he described the course as an old grandmother that he was visiting. "She's crotchety and eccentric but also elegant, and anyone who doesn't fall in love with her has no imagination. The 68 I shot today was one of the finest rounds of golf I've ever shot, but I still don't feel confident. This is the most challenging golf course I've ever been on. You don't dare go to sleep for one moment. And to finish second won't mean a thing. In the year 2064, when people pick up that record book, this is the kind of championship they will look up. You'll be remembered only if you win."

Tony was later caught off guard when he agreed to collaborate on an article for a Scottish newspaper. When it appeared, it carried the headline, "I'll Win the Open." He chased Fred down, a bit angry, telling him, "I never said that!"

Fred had approved the article but hadn't seen the headline. So he offered his best advice. "Well, you have now, so go out and win it."

With Jack Nicklaus nipping at his heels, Lema took the lead after the first two rounds. In the press room afterwards, he ordered champagne for everyone.

"What's the party for," one reporter asked. "I'm the 36-hole leader," Tony shot back.

In his third round, he went four over par on the first five holes. As he was walking up the sixth hole, he passed Nicklaus, who was coming down the 13th. He then saw that Nicklaus was burning up the course, with four birdies. Jack had picked up eight strokes on him and was within one stroke of the lead. They both stared at each other in a moment of disbelief, and then Tony turned it on, shooting three birdies in a row. Lema came to the 18th and holed a 20-foot putt for a third-round score of 68, seven strokes ahead of Nicklaus.

On the final day, Fred couldn't bear to watch the match. He and Tony had argued off and on about everything, especially about using the small British ball. Fred thought he should play the American ball because that was what he was used to but Tony wanted to try the British ball. As Tony teed off, Fred headed out of the hotel and jumped in a taxi.

"Take me anywhere," he told the driver, passing him some cash.

"Anywhere, sir?" he asked, as he revved the engine.

"Yes, let's go visit your mother. Where does she live?"

"She's not with us anymore, sir," the cabbie replied.

"Well, then, just head north and let me know when an hour is up," Fred said as he buried his mind in his thoughts.

Lema played easily on the final round and came to the last hole with a comfortable lead, where he sank a birdie putt to win over Nicklaus by five strokes and in front of Roberto De Vicenzo by six. With a swift movement, he picked the ball out of the hole and threw it high into a cheering crowd.

Fred pulled into the golf club as the corks were popping. Tony grabbed him by the shoulder and as they walked together to the press room, he chided him. "You didn't think I could do it," he said as he gripped Fred's shoulder. Then he loosened his grip and laughed. "Well, let's just chalk this up and go on from here."

"He was angry with me, and I deserved it," Fred later recounted.

This was the fourth tournament Lema won in six successive weeks, and it was his first British Open, the first tournament he ever played with the smaller ball. Tony gave all the credit to his caddie, for proposing he use the small ball, and for steering him clear of the consuming bunkers. "It amazed me the way he kept putting the right club in my hand." And he also thanked Arnold Palmer for lending his caddie and his putter.

Fred and Tony were in the press room when Lema got a call from Ken Venturi, congratulating him. Tony, in an aside to the British golf writers, cracked, "It's from the lad who won that other Open championship!" This, of course, endeared him to the British. To them, there is but one Open championship—the annual tournament governed by the Royal & Ancient Golf Club of St. Andrews.

With the bubbly flowing, Fred immediately called a contact at Moët et Chandon and he and Lema headed to Paris for Tony to sign on as a representative. From then on, the only champagne that would be poured in the press room when Lema won a tournament was Moët. And all Tony had to do was order it, whether at a press party or a casual dinner, and sign for it. The bill would then go back directly to Moët's office.

Lema was blessed with a wry sense of humor which served as a counterweight for a sometimes volatile disposition. Returning to New York in triumph from the British Open, Tony received a telephone call from a young lady who handled the assignment of lining up guest stars for the television show *What's My Line*. She invited Lema to be the mystery guest on the show for the following week and Tony agreed, although measuring the fee against the inconvenience involved, it was hardly worth his while.

Meanwhile, the PGA championship was being played that week in Columbus and it was won subsequently by Bobby Nichols. Then Lema had another call from the young lady at the network. "You know, Mr. Lema," she said haltingly, "we try to keep very current on our show." She fiddled some more with her grip and took a few more practice swings before Tony cut in on her.

"What you're coming to," he said helpfully, "is that you don't want me on the show after all. Isn't that it?"

"Well," said the young lady gratefully, "we do try to be current, you know, and after all, you didn't win this week."

"Gee, I'm sorry," exclaimed Tony, his eyes lighting up mischievously. "But you didn't tell me I had to win this week. I won four of the last six tournaments, then I won the British Open, but I slipped up last week. So now I suppose you've got Nichols?"

The girl confessed this was the case. She explained again that they like to be current on the show. "Maybe we can have you on some other time," she said in a mollifying tone, "after you win another tournament."

"Well that sounds like a square deal if I've ever heard one. Tell you what," he said suddenly. "Why don't you set it up for a time that will be convenient for your people. Then let me know and I'll arrange to win the tournament that week for you. Or, better still…I'll win three in a row. How would that be?"

There was a stunned silence at the other end of the line. Then the girl gushed, "Oh, Mr. Lema! Would you really?"

In Tony, the imp lay just beneath the surface, its bright eyes darting around, looking for a fat target. Typically, when he returned to the States with the British Open title, one of the first things he did was to telephone Arnold Palmer whose gift of a putter had started Lema's chain of victories.

"Arnie," he said, "first I borrowed your putter and won three tournaments, and last week I borrowed your caddie at St. Andrews and won the Open. What else have you got I can borrow?" Then, while Arnold was thinking it over, he went on, "…like, maybe, your bank book?"

For a guy who dispensed dollars as if he were a bank, Tony was kidding, of course. But his classic comment had a strong Hagenesque flavor to it. He often said of himself, "I don't want to be a millionaire; I just want to live like one."

Chapter 36

During the summer of 1964, Sam Snead was invited to Israel for the dedication of the first golf course in that country. Fred went along as a traveling gallery with a few writers, who admitted to having just a little bit of fun. Fred had found that inviting writers along, whether it was to the Canada Cup or to a promotional match, created a working environment that was enjoyable as well as beneficial. "Don't be an editor without a tan," he used to tell them. "Come play a round with us."

On the way home, Fred and Sam stopped off in Rome for what Sam called an "audition" with the late Pope John XXIII.

"Why don't you bring along your putter," Fred suggested facetiously to Sam. "Have him bless it. It might help steer in some of those six-foot sidehill putts into the hole."

Sam's eyes widened and he put his clubs in the trunk of the car.

When they arrived in the vestry of St. Peter's, a monsignor offered to put Sam's clubs in his office. Recognizing Sam, this 100-shooter immediately confessed to Sam about his putting problems. Sam sighed, picked up his clubs, and headed back to the car.

"If he's this close to the Pope and he can't putt," he drawled over his shoulder, "the Pope ain't gonna do anything for me!"

Still battling the PGA but working to avoid scheduling problems, Fred was forced to play the 1964 Canada Cup in December, to assure that the big U.S. players could and would attend. This was fine, except that it limited him to warm climates, as weather was his life-long nemesis. But Fred was riding high that fall. Slowly, he was building his inventory again, and along with Lema and Venturi, he signed Bobby Nichols, the

1964 PGA Champion.

He took off for the Canada Cup, which was played at the Royal Kaanapali course on Maui in Hawaii that December. "The fact that we were able to play there at all was an achievement," Fred said. "I had visited there two months prior to the tournament to give the course a final inspection and found most of the greens and two of the fairways completely unplayable. I learned that there had been a change in green-keepers, and the new one was using too much water. I called Robert Trent Jones in New York, and he hurried to Hawaii with an agronomist, who prescribed some emergency actions. I started looking for alternate venues, but by the time I arrived in late November, a miracle had happened. The course was good."

The PGA and the weather weren't the only things that gave Fred headaches. With a new war brewing in Southeast Asia, global politics were in play, and golf's own competitive tensions were high. Nicklaus and Palmer, who were teamed together, had just come from a duel at the Cajun Classic in Louisiana, which would determine the year-end official money winner. It turned out to be Jack, who edged out Arnold by $81.13. "And it pissed me off," Arnold said publicly.

In addition, Palmer arrived in Hawaii with a sore thumb and he was concerned whether or not he'd be able to play well. "I can't keep it on the club," he told a worried Fred.

Palmer also mentioned it to Jack Nicklaus' father, a pharmacist, who had joined the entourage. The senior Nicklaus said, "Here, take these," and gave Arnie some pills, which delivered almost instant relief. Arnie played three great rounds but then the pain in his thumb returned. He called Jack's father and if he could give him that medicine again.

"Oh, you can't take it again this soon," Jack's father said, much to Arnie's dismay. On that last day, he shot 76 and Jack beat him to win the individual trophy.

Nicklaus, with his second International Trophy, and Palmer gave the U.S. its fifth-straight Canada Cup. Ted Makalena, who played on a local team from Hawaii, thrilled fellow Hawaiians by finishing in a tie for third, and Gary Player finished a stroke behind Palmer.

Palmer, still telling his story about his sore thumb, remarked on the team aspect of the tournament. "This is a great, great event and it should go on for a long time," Arnold said, "but something should be done. Here I am rooting for Jack all the way through and if he knocks one in the water, I'm sore at him. But then, we're all even with two holes to go, and I'm hope he knocks one in the water."

"And I did," said Nicklaus.

Fred took Nancy and the girls with him to Hawaii, and the girls made friends at the outset with the Venezuelan team of Francisco Gonzalez and Teobaldo Perez. The local gallery for this pair was limited to say the least, and the girls were indignant when their heroes and the Scottish pair of John Panton and Bobby Walker set out on their first round accompanied only by their caddies and a scorer. Loyally, the girls went off as a gallery of two, but in an hour, they were back.

"What happened," Fred asked them.

"Daddy," Judy said, "we followed them for three holes and they were never inside the ropes. We quit!"

"Maybe they need one of your signs," he said.

"Or a lesson from Uncle Tony," she snapped.

The Senior PGA Tournament relocated in 1964 to the sparkling new $1.5 million PGA course in Palm Beach Gardens, Florida, with Snead winning before a gallery that swirled and eddied around a small army of marshals. Fred again discussed the merits of a Senior Tour to anyone who would listen, but like golf on television, his ideas were a few years ahead of their time.

In the spring of 1965, Sam Snead became the oldest winner of a PGA Tour event when he won the Greater Greensboro Open for the eighth time at age 52. Fresh off that win, Fred met up with him and joined Ben Hogan as they teed up in Houston before the cameras for an historic head-to-head duel for *Shell's Wonderful World of Golf* television series. The show's producers had hired Fred as a consultant, knowing he knew the players and the courses from the far outposts of the world. Joining his friends, Gene Sarazen as host and Herbert Warren Wind as writer, Fred was charged with getting the big-name players on board the blockbuster and award-winning series.

The match went well and Fred was credited with signing Hogan for his one and only made-for-television appearance. It was reported that Hogan received a fee about ten times higher than most for his appearance, while the others were lured by the idea of an all-expense paid vacation along with a staged match. Pretty soon, however, the pros all realized what this show could do for their popularity and presence.

After the historic match, Sam and Fred headed to the airport where one of Shell's company jets waited to shuttle Sam back East for a tournament commitment. Fred couldn't help thinking back to that day in 1937 when Sam and he took their first plane ride together in an airborne jalopy from Greensboro to Augusta—with the pilot tracing his route on a Shell road map held between his feet.

No literary snapshot of Sam Snead would be complete without a footnote on one of the most remarkable competitive records in the annals of the sport. Here's a guy who won his first PGA tournament at the age of 23 in 1937—and was still winning at 52, an age span of twenty-nine years! Yet, he'll probably go down in the folklore of American golf as the perennial runner-up who blew more U.S. Open championships than anyone would believe possible. He finished second four times and was within striking distance as many more times only to stagger in the home stretch.

"I always thought that Sam, if he could have won that 1937 Open title on his first shot at it, might have gone on to win it four or five times," Fred believed. "That was the year he actually held the crown in his hands for nearly two hours. He finished early with a 283, then went out on the course and followed Ralph Guldahl around the last nine. He saw Guldahl close at a gallop to set a new tournament record of 281 and snatch the championship right out of his hands."

As time wore on, Snead's futile pursuit of the Open crown became something of an annual sports charade without any real meaning. He would enter and the sportswriters would make him a sentimental favorite to win. But a tribal superstition built up about Sam and the Open. It just seemed that every time they ran up the USGA flag on the golf course, that sacred ground became taboo for Sam Snead and everybody came to acknowledge it—including Sam.

Fred had an interesting call from Ken Venturi around this time. Mark McCormack, who started the International Management Group with Arnold Palmer as his first client, now managed the affairs of Jack Nicklaus and Gary Player, among others. He was promoting them as the "Big Three" at tournaments and in television matches, much to the annoyance of the rest of the players. Ken called Fred in early 1965, totally convinced that he and Lema had enough game to take on the three of them in a special match. Fred went to McCormack with the idea and told him he could set up five matches, including one at Winged Foot, near New York City.

"You think I'm crazy?" McCormack said. "I've been building the Big Three all year. If your two guys beat my three guys, I have no case."

McCormack, twenty-five years younger and a brilliant lawyer and negotiator, did business differently than Fred. When he signed a client, he took a large percentage of their winnings along with a percentage of any endorsements he would sign them to. McCormack went on to become one of the most powerful men in all sports with his International Management Group (IMG), which handled everyone from the Pope to, years later, Tiger Woods. He approached Sam Snead to jump ship at one point, but Sam was loyal to Fred and didn't like the aggressive terms of the deal.

Fred, through McCormack, started to see the business he had designed get away from him. Handshakes were no longer considered binding. Meetings moved from the locker rooms to the board rooms. Contracts had to be reviewed. Papers had to be filed. Fred often longed for the old days, except for push-button phones. He loved those, as his affair with the telephone continued.

"I once walked from the gate of the plane to the luggage area with Fred," said John Ross, then editor of *Golf* magazine, "and he peeled off five times to make five different phone calls. There was no one like him."

Venturi did get his chance to take on one-third of the Big Three when he played Gary Player in the Piccadilly World Match Play championship at the Wentworth Club in England in late October of 1966. He was looking forward to the challenge and they were having a good match until Ken started having trouble with his hands. He finished the match but lost to Player.

Within a year, Venturi would lose his touch, literally. In 1965, he had begun to suffer from a loss of feeling in his hands, at first diagnosed as Raynaud's Phenomenon. A doctor put him a massive dosages of cortisone which affected him adversely. He had a terrible time at the Los Angeles Open and at the Crosby, both in January of 1965, as his hands felt worse in the cold, damp weather. Finally, he went to the Mayo Clinic where his problem was diagnosed as carpal tunnel syndrome, possibly from twenty years of hitting thousands of balls on the practice tee.

After an unsuccessful attempt to defend his U.S. Open title in June of 1965, Ken underwent surgery on his hands. He never really played after that. A few years later, he began a 30-year television career with CBS as one of golf's most beloved commentators. This in itself was quite a feat for someone who as a child had quite a stammer. "I hit golf balls alone in those years," Venturi once said, "while teaching myself to speak."

Fred also signed Tom Weiskopf in 1965, his first year on the tour. Weiskopf told Fred he wasn't interested in making a lot of money. "I just want $30,000 a year," he said. He went on to tell Fred that he had become interested in golf when he was 15. Both parents played—his father was a fine college player able to break 70 and his mother, when she was 16, reached the quarter finals of the National Amateur, losing to Patty Berg on an extra hole. He said she could outdrive Babe Zaharias, and Babe told her she had the greatest potential of all the women golfers. They both wanted to go on the tour, but the war was on and they didn't have the money to support and risk it. So they stayed home and started a family.

Even without knowing of his genes, Fred knew Tom was someone to watch. Tony Lema and others on the tour agreed, adding that Tom, armed with a temper, only had one guy to beat—himself. And at age 30, Tom burst on the scene, winning five out of eight tournaments before arriving in Rye for the $250,000 Westchester Classic, where Fred again was the Tournament Director. Having just won the British Open, Canadian Open, Colonial Invitational, the Kemper Open and Philadelphia Classic, and finishing second in the Atlanta Classic, third in the U.S. Open, and fifth in the American Golf Classic, Weiskopf's yearly total so far was $260,000.

Dave Anderson in *The New York Times* reported, "Over 32 rounds, his average score has been a spectacular 68.9, a total of 77 strokes under par. In only four of those rounds did he finish over par. In none did he misplace his maturity."

Tom even kept his cool during a difficult shot in the U.S. Open, when on a par 5, he pushed his drive into a concession stand near the green. Somehow, the ball landed on a wooden counter next to a few loaves of bread. He was awarded a free drop outside the temporary obstruction and waited for workers to clear the area of empty beer and soda cans that littered the way to the green. Once he dropped his ball, he chipped on to the green, landing five feet from the pin where he made a birdie. He didn't beat Johnny Miller that week, but three weeks later, at the British Open at Troon, he did.

CHAPTER 37

TONY LEMA WAS SELECTED TO PLAY IN THE 1965 CANADA CUP IN Marbella, Spain. Fred invited him to stop by the Corcoran Hilton so they could travel together. Lema graciously accepted, always preferring Fred's informal yet comfortable house to a hotel.

The night Lema arrived called for cocktails, steaks and water pistols. Fred, on the phone all day, invited a few friends and sportswriters to stop by for one of his impromptu parties. Tony started telling a story about how he had thrown a party in a hotel in St. Paul in 1963, and before long, everyone was hitting golf balls from the coffee table out the hotel window. Fred told about a soiree on the roof of Boston's Ritz with Byron Nelson. Before he knew it, Tony had a driver in his hand and a pocket full of golf balls and was up to old tricks, like bouncing a ball off the head of the driver and striking it before it hit the ground. He was also betting Guido Cribari, the sports editor of the Westchester Newspapers, that he could clear the trees across the fairway on Winged Foot's 15th fairway from Fred's patio.

As Fred saw him lining up balls on the naked slate patio, he grabbed him. "Tony! For Chrissake, you could break your wrist!"

"There you go again, Fred. You never trust me," came his response. As he addressed the first ball, Fred closed my eyes.

"Wow!" shouted Guido. "Did you see the sparks?" Tony placed another ball in front of his club and drew it back. As the club grazed the slate ever so slightly right as it met the ball, sparks again bounced around their feet like a sparkler, hitting the ground.

Fred begged him again to stop, but he went on to hit three more balls, each one clearing the trees on the far side of the fairway, just beyond a hedge. As Guido lost his bet, Tony didn't offer Fred his fifteen percent.

The next day, they took off for Spain for the 1965 Canada Cup at Club de Campo in Madrid. On the day when most of the players arrived, Jack Nicklaus didn't. Jack had gone home to Columbus, Ohio, prior to the tournament to nurse a sore throat. Fred was expecting him on Monday before the tournament and finally got word that he would be there Tuesday. He arranged to meet all the flights on Tuesday but there was no Nicklaus that day either. Jack finally arrived on Wednesday morning, barely in time for a single practice round.

When Fred finally caught up with him, he thanked him for making the trip but let it be known that he was worried. "After all," Fred said, "you are fifty percent of my headline act."

"Well, it was touch-and-go there for a while," Nicklaus replied.

"Touch-and-go?" Fred repeated. "For me, it was touch-and-jump if you hadn't made it!"

The Spanish crowd grew to 9,000 on the final day, as thirty-seven teams participated with the addition of Czechoslovakia. This was the first time a competitor from behind the Iron Curtain had participated in the West. The Czech amateur team posted scores of 88-93 and 95-97 on a course that was not that difficult. They played to applause for just showing up and finishing, which was the attitude the tournament always hoped to impart.

But this was a tournament of maladies. Nicklaus, who had his sore throat and appeared to be playing in low gear, found a few hazards on the course, including at least two bees that stung him. Lema had a bad elbow and low spirits, due partly to his performance on the course, and Gary Player, a self-proclaimed exercise nut who had been playing superbly, awoke on Saturday morning with a stiff neck. It seemed he had been standing on his head the night before and as a result, injured his neck. He spent the rest of the night taking hot showers and pills, which must have worked because he loosened up on the practice tee and went on to birdie two of the first four holes.

Player later recalled, "I'll never forget 1965 with my partner, Harold Henning. We were leading going into the last round, but that morning, my neck was very, very sore. I couldn't swing. So I told Harold I didn't think I could play. He came right back, saying, 'Don't tell me that; tell my lawyer. Here I have a chance to win the Canada Cup for the first time and you tell me you can't play? Go out there and find a way!'"

After a few more aspirin and hot showers, Player loosened up enough to join with Henning and lead the South African team to the to the team title. Player even took home the individual trophy over Nicklaus. Spain's Ramon Sota and Angel Miguel delighted their countrymen with a second-place finish, beating Tony Lema and Jack Nicklaus.

But this tournament truly belonged to Gary Player as he stole the show, commenting at the award ceremonies, "Believe me, it is something to sit there and realize you have helped to raise your country's flag and to hear you national anthem played. It puts goose bumps right here." He pointed to his heart, not his wallet. His check was $1,000 for the individual trophy and $1,000 for his share of the team title.

"There's another thing, too," Player added, "about a tournament like this. It brings golf to so many countries that never had much feeling for it. You sense that you have done something for your game. Just think what these matches did for golf in France in 1963, and then look at all the people who were out there. You just watch if golf doesn't start booming in Spain."

Czechoslovakia finished 36th, next to last, in team play. At the reception following the final day of play, the International Golf Association and the Spanish Golf Federation presented Jiri Dvorak and his teammate, M. Plodak, each with a new set of clubs. As they walked through the reception line carrying their gifts, both burst unashamedly in to tears, overcome by the gesture. Back in Czechoslovakia, explained Dvorak, golf clubs are shared by all members of the club.

After the tournament, Fred accompanied Lema to Greece, for the filming of *Shell's Wonderful World of Golf*. When they arrived, the course was brown, due to the dry weather, and the producer rented a small plane to spray the course with green paint for their aerial shots. In a practice round the day before, Fred missed two short putts on the eighteenth green, in front of everyone. A bit embarrassed, he quipped, "Now I have three-putted in eighteen countries."

Snead won another tournament in 1965, bringing his total to 84. Lema went back to the Buick Open and won it again, along with the Carling World Open, and he finished second in money to Jack Nicklaus for the year.

And toward year end, Fred got a call from Ted Williams. "There's a kid in Boston I think you should sign," Williams said. "His name is Tony Conigliaro." In his second year, at the age of 20, Conigliaro hit 32 home runs. Ted arranged the meeting and Tony came on board. Fred immediately called his old friend Sy Berger at Topps Bubble Gum and signed Tony to his first baseball card contract.

Then Fred got a call from a Charlie Gogolak, the Princeton football field goal kicker. He was a friend of a Princeton alum who knew someone Fred knew, and he was graduating soon. He was currently on track to be the number one draft choice of the Washington Redskins, and he needed help with his contract negotiations and didn't know where to turn.

"Are you a lawyer?" Charlie asked on the phone.

"No, and let me just tell you about lawyers," Fred started. "I use them when I have to, but to me, they're useless. I just shake on my deals. I give you my word."

"But you do use lawyers?" he continued, the Ivy League sounding through his voice.

"When the time comes," Fred said. "I can get more done in thirty minutes at Toots Shor's bar with an owner than in thirty hours in an office with his lawyer—who will bill you for sixty hours. And these lawyers bill you whether they make a deal or not!"

Fred's outburst continued. "The lawyers all travel with briefcases, mind you, and what we used to agree on, they need to write down in six-page contracts and put in briefcases that make a loud snap when you push the latch."

Fred wanted no part of the "Briefcase Boys" or with people sitting around a mahogany conference table. "Let me get them out on the golf course and I'll talk to them," Fred would say. "You can say hello to the President of the United States on a golf course. But you'd never get past the guards and secretaries to wave at him across the lawn of the White House. And it's the same with the man who poses as the 'Great American Tycoon.' You can share his miseries in a sand trap, but go to his office and you wind up sparring with a private school-type who gives his scalp a dozen scuffs with the military brushes every morning and spends the rest of the day with his feet on a desk, paring his fingernails at people."

"So let's just go to dinner at Toots Shor's on Wednesday," he said to Charlie. "I have tickets for the hockey game and if you want to go, we can talk there." Fred had signed on to consult for the National Hockey League and make recommendations to increase attendance. After a winter of games, he said they should cut their season and move the Stanley Cup to March, while it was still cold out. He had a point.

Charlie was intrigued with this ranting Irishman and agreed to meet him, and on the way to the game, Fred agreed to represent him. During the walk to the Garden, Charlie mentioned he had a brother, Peter, who played for the Buffalo Bills. The Bills were one game away from winning the AFL championship and Peter, also a soccer-style place kicker, was setting all sorts of records. Only two years out of Cornell, he was having contract issues, too.

Peter Gogolak called Fred the next day and told him that the New York Giants had been his heroes ever since he arrived in this country from

Hungary at age 12. The Gogolak brothers, along with their parents, had crawled across the Hungarian border into Austria one dark night in October of 1956. Fred agreed to look after his interests, too, but only when the time came. "And that will be after May first," Fred said.

Both he and Peter knew that there would be big trouble if Peter approached an NFL team. At the time, the American Football League was challenging the National Football League on all fronts. "With all this merger talk, there's more wheeling and dealing and long-distance phone calls and what's-the-latest-rumor going on in football than I've ever heard before in all my life," Fred told him. "All you have do is make one fancy little mistake and you'll be such deep in trouble that you'll never get out of it."

Peter took Fred's advice and laid low for the next few months, continuing with his degree at Cornell in hotel management.

"I knew I played through a war in the 1942, but I had no idea of the war I was about to enter on May 3, 1966, when I called Peter, telling him that Wellington Mara, the owner of the New York Giants, wanted to meet him," Fred said. "I emphasized that this would be 'private' meeting and suggested that Peter fly to New York under a different name. There were a few stories in the paper already that Mara and I were meeting to secretly work out a deal. The two leagues, the NFL and AFL, had agreed in talks to merge, but not until June and so far, neither league had signed a free agent from the other league. We all knew that if and when Mara signed Gogolak, all hell would break loose."

Peter met Fred in New York City and they rode to Winged Foot Golf Club where both Mara and he were members. To dispel any rumors, Fred loudly introduced Peter as George Smith as they settled down for dinner. It was clear that Mara wanted to sign Peter, but he needed to wait for all the coaches to agree and some were still on vacation.

When the conversation came around to money, Mara nixed a bonus. "We can't give him a signing bonus," Mara said. "That would look like we're bribing him to jump leagues.

"Then you can make it up to him in salary," Fred said, who went into a long story about how valuable Peter was, both as point scorer and as a promotional tool for the team. As a rookie with the Bills, Peter had kicked a record-breaking 50-yard field goal against the Jets.

"How much?" Mara asked.

"How about three times what he's getting at Buffalo?"

They didn't settle the deal right then and there but Peter got just about that much a few weeks later when the Giants announced the signing. Peter ended up with the highest salary ever paid to anyone for just kicking a football. And everything that Mara told them would happen did happen. The next two weeks were all about the "grid war," and how Gogolak had started it. He was the first top-ranked player in football history to jump leagues.

In *The New York Times*, William Wallace wrote that the signing of Gogolak to the New York Giants dealt the American Football League a blow while endowing the Giants with a first-class field goal kicker they desperately needed. Gogolak, in the year before, kicked 28 field goals, a record, in 46 attempts and he had kicked a record-breaking, unofficial 57-yard field goal in an exhibition game. He also kicked 77 of 78 extra points in two seasons.

Arthur Daley, also at the *Times,* wrote it up as if a shot had been fired from Fort Sumter, triggering a gridiron war. But the rules called for a player to play for one year past his contract at a reduction of ten percent in pay in order to become a free agent. Gogolak had done that.

When the hubbub in the press began, Wellington Mara issued a statement, passing the ball back into Fred's court, saying he was assured by Fred Corcoran and Mike Mooney, Gogolak's agent and lawyer, that Gogolak was a free agent, and he had no qualms about signing him. "We honor contracts of other organizations," Wellington Mara said, "just as we honor the ones in our own league."

If Fred had a dime for every phone call that came his way over the next few weeks, he'd be a rich man. According to which side you were on, Peter was either a self-centered ingrate who was only interested in his own financial gain and didn't care about the game of football, or he was an independent Hungarian immigrant who was following the American dream by making his own way in the world, a hero for not bowing to the powers that be.

And a war of sorts did start. The AFL owners, in turn, announced that they were interested in all top NFL players and would pay the highest rates. Charges of "tampering" flew back and forth. But by early June, the NFL owners "capitulated," as the papers put it. Their agreement called for the retention of the present teams and a common schedule, along with some other terms that had been in negotiations for months.

At the same time, Charlie Gogolak signed with the Washington Redskins, making it the first time that a placekicker was signed on the first round of the NFL Draft.

As the weeks passed, the football noise lessened and Fred went on to his duties at the Thunderbird golf tournament. It had moved back to New Jersey in 1966 and had lost its luster. Fred resigned after this uneventful event.

CHAPTER 38

Tony Lema and Fred had drifted apart and had not spoken during the spring of 1966. Tony had hinted that he was unhappy with their business arrangement, even confessing he preferred another brand of champagne to Moët, and he had not responded to some offers Fred had for him. Fred, of course, wanted him to stay in his fold. Over the past four years, Lema had won twelve official PGA events, finished second in eleven, and third in four. Fred had just gotten Tony a deal with Izod shirts to make the Lema brand, with a little champagne glass rather than an alligator on the front. He invited Tony to his house one evening to talk about it.

Lema wrote about Fred in his book, *Golfer's Gold*, recalling an average day. "Fred rings me shortly after nine o'clock in the morning. He is short and round and sometimes jolly, but he also tends to be overanxious about things. Fred wants to know how I feel, how I played the day before, and how I will play today. Maybe from my answers he gets an idea of my mood and what items of business it is safe to discuss now, what items to hold for tomorrow. Then we talk business: a bid for our endorsement from the manufacturer of a practice club that clicks when you swing it correctly (no); the offer of a tie-in with a high-quality, well-known clothing manufacturer (yes); an invitation to play on a filmed TV golf match (yes, I'll call the producer). Our telephone discussion lasts twenty minutes."

On this evening, after dinner, Fred and Tony took a walk out to a hill alongside the 15th green of Winged Foot and sat down for a discussion that lasted hours. They talked about business and golf, and trust and love, and what it took for each of them to do their jobs. After several hours, they decided to work out their differences and stay together. They shook hands on it.

A few weeks later, in May of 1966, Lema ordered champagne again, after winning in Oklahoma City. He was particularly pleased about winning there because his wife Betty came from Oklahoma City and they had just found out that she was pregnant. He was 32 and she was 30.

Fred saw Tony a few weeks later at the 1966 PGA at Firestone in Akron, Ohio. He didn't play that well but was in good spirits. Fred left the tournament that Sunday morning, as he often did at the majors, just to beat the crowd out, and headed home. The last thing Tony said, as they parted, was to say hello to Peggy and Judy for him. He wanted a fly-swatting rematch.

That evening, Tony Lema begged off from a dinner planned for him and Ken Venturi by the local Italian-American Club. Venturi and he had words about it.

"I'm not going because they're giving me two thousand dollars for a one-day outing in Illinois and they're flying Betty and me there in a private plane that leaves in an hour," Tony boasted.

"You're letting those people down," Ken said, angry about Lema's attitude. "You're Italian. I'm Italian. They're Italian. You don't just cancel out on them. They've got the whole dinner set up, with flowers and a program, and all sorts of people wanting to meet us."

Lema waved him off. "I'm going where the money is."

"You'll live to regret those words," Ken called out as they parted.

An hour later, on July 24, 1966, Tony and Betty Lema climbed aboard a small, twin-engine plane. They, along with a pilot who allegedly was drinking, were killed in the crash while trying to make an emergency landing on the golf course he was to play the next day, near Chicago. He and Betty were wearing matching necklaces.

Venturi went to the dinner and when he returned, the hotel clerk said to him, "It's too bad about the golfer who got killed today." Ken said she didn't mention the name and didn't need to. Somehow he knew.

Needless to say, Fred was crushed. Tony's untimely death brought back memories of Babe and others who were robbed of their crowning achievements, their stars extinguished way too early in their record-breaking careers. But he also felt the loss of a person he cared about tremendously.

CHAPTER 39

THE CANADA CUP RETURNED TO TOKYO IN 1966 WHERE GOLF WAS bigger than ever. Even though the Los Angeles Dodgers had toured Japan that year, all the shop windows had Arnold Palmer's picture in them, heralding his arrival. He was "Mr. Pa-ma-san" and all the talk was about golf.

The team of Palmer and Nicklaus compiled an all-time record-breaking score of 548 and dominated the tournament, forcing the defending South African team to settle for second. George Knudson of Canada took home the International Trophy by winning in a playoff over local favorite, Hideyo Sugimoto. Nicklaus, trying for his third International Trophy, finished a stroke back, despite a blazing final round of 65.

In December of 1966, Fred signed on as Tournament Director for the Westchester Classic, to be played at Westchester Country Club with many of the same people who had put on the Thunderbird. This tournament, with Eastern Airlines as a sponsor, would take the lead as the nation's richest tournament with a first prize set at an astounding $50,000 and a total purse of $250,000.

"I pointed out that thirty years before, in 1936, the year before I took over at the PGA, the prize money for the entire year was $125,000," Fred said. "That year, Paul Runyan was the top money winner with $6,300. Now some pros pay out close to that in caddie fees."

Fred's phone rang in January of 1967. As he went to pick it up, he thought quickly about all the times one phone call had changed his or someone's life. Good new or bad news was always a ring away.

On the phone was Peter Gogolak with news Fred didn't want to hear.

At age 24, Peter had been inducted into the Army on the spot, despite three prior deferments for health reasons. Many people suspected this was a political move as a Michigan Congressman had recently charged that professional athletes were getting special consideration while regular boys were being shipped off to Viet Nam. And even though the Giants had a totally forgettable '66 season, Peter Gogolak was at the top of his career, having made 29 out of 31 extra points and 16 of 28 field goals, which led the team with 77 points that season.

Peter would go on to spend most of his military service split between New Jersey and Germany. Fred, however, wasn't able to do much for him after he returned to the Giants two years later. Peter Gogolak would retire from the Giants at the end of the 1976 season with many franchise records, one being the all-time leading scorer with 268 of 277 extra points and a better than fifty percent average for field goals made.

On both a personal and business level, Fred felt his losses and wondered if the Corcoran Curse had returned. With Lema gone and Venturi ailing, Fred's Big Three was down to a Big One, Tom Weiskopf. And now with Peter shipping off in a controversial war effort, Fred relived the anguish he had felt in 1953, when Ted Williams had been called to serve the country a second time and headed off to Korea, also at the height of his career.

A phone call in February, 1967, turned the page when another King asked for a meeting with "Mr. Golf." Through an interpreter at the Plaza Hotel, King Hassan II of Morocco wanted to talk about golf and the Canada Cup. Fred had visited Morocco in 1963, only to find the golf facilities unsuitable for an international tournament, but still, the King persisted.

Fred gave him an informal putting lesson on the hotel's carpet and the King knocked a 6-footer into a wooden cup on his first attempt. Over a discussion of croquet-style putting, which this amateur preferred, Fred extended an invitation to him to send a team from Morocco to the next Canada Cup in Mexico. But the King asked for more.

"Please tell your committee that we want them to have the tournament in Morocco," the King said to Linc Werden of *The New York Times*. "We'd like you to send over an architect to inspect our courses." An aide pointed out that there was a perfect course some twenty miles from Casablanca.

Seeing how serious the King was about playing golf, Fred quickly called one of his good friends, Claude Harmon, who had two of those special last names—the Masters, which he had won in 1948, and Winged Foot, where he was the pro. Claude, the father of four young champions including Butch Harmon, was one of the country's best teaching pros. He went on to become the King's personal and frequent teacher, as did Butch, before gaining fame as Tiger Wood's teacher and coach.

And then another phone call brought more bad news. Tony Conigliaro was headed for the All-Star Game that year, and at the age of 22, he had just become the youngest player to reach a career total of 100 home runs. He was already up to 104. But in August of 1967, while the Red Sox were playing the Angels at Fenway, Tony was hit in the head by a fast ball. It broke is cheekbone and damaged the retina in his left eye. As he was carried off the field on a stretcher, Fred saw a future star go down the drain. The helmets batters wore in those days did not have the protective ear-flaps that have since become standard.

Fred felt the weight of the Corcoran Curse again.

Chapter 40

The Canada Cup changed its name to the World Cup in 1967 while playing a return engagement in Mexico. Palmer and Nicklaus won the new Cup, with Arnold taking home his first International Trophy. New Zealand placed second and an enthusiastic crowd of thousands of Mexican fans carried the third-place Mexican team of Antonio Cerda and Ricardo Cazares away on their shoulders, bestowing hero status on the home team.

Fred's rivalry with Mark McCormack at this time was starting to grow into an obsession. McCormack was signing players right and left, adding associates to his business and attracting away Fred's clients. Fred was introduced to Jean-Claude Killy, the French downhill skier with the movie-star looks who would go on to win the 1968 Olympic triple crown, and during their business courtship, Killy signed with McCormack's IMG. Fred, who worked on handshakes and his word, just couldn't compete against a bullpen full of lawyers, secretaries and agents.

On to the 1968 Masters in April, Fred was particularly pleased when one of his World Cup players, Argentinean Roberto De Vicenzo, took the lead. Having won the first Canada Cup in 1953, Roberto had played in most of them, scoring near the top each time, and winning the Individual Trophy in 1962.

Fred, having been an old hand at the scorer's table, unfortunately knew what was about to unfold when he heard the furor around the 18th green. He knew Rule 38, Section 3 all too well. "No alteration may be made on a card after the competitor has returned it to the committee. If the competitor returns a score for any hole lower than actually played, he shall be disqualified. A score higher than actually played must stand as returned."

While the nation of television viewers watched as De Vicenzo took a birdie "3" on the 17th hole, no one saw De Vicenzo's marker and pairing partner, Tommy Aaron, write a "4" on his card. De Vicenzo, thrust into a tie for one of the world's major crowns, did not spot the mistake and signed his erroneous score card, making the four, not the three, the official score. There would be no playoff. Bob Golby took the title.

Roberto had signed the card and had already left the scorer's tent when Aaron told the officials about the mistake. Through an interpreter, Roberto was called back and the situation was explained. It was also his 45th birthday.

"I can't begin to tell you what De Vicenzo lost that day," Fred said. "It was a lot more than that special last name. It was his legacy. But you gotta hand it to him. Roberto was very gracious about it."

"It's my fault," Roberto told the press. "Tommy feels like I feel, very bad. I think the rule is hard."

When someone asked him how the situation would be handled in Argentina, he responded, "We play friendly golf there." What was remarkable, too, was that he shot a 65 at Augusta. He started the round with an eagle two and followed it with two birdies, and then birdied 13, 15 and 17. Not only did he lose the $20,000 first prize, but he lost the $15,000 second prize and countless dollars in what a Masters win means for anyone.

But Fred was still able to help. With his friend Dick Ryan, a New York lawyer, they marched with Roberto up Park Avenue where he signed on to represent Coca-Cola for all of South America. "If he hadn't signed the wrong card, he could have represented the world," Fred lamented.

Fred continued to spread world-class tournament golf and infuse some muscle into the European Tour when he signed on to produce several American Express Pro-Amateur events in Europe, kicking off at the Golf Club Crans-sur-Sierre, in Crans-Montana, Switzerland. The family made the trip that summer, with teenage daughters in tow, who much to Fred's concern, attracted 20-year-old golf pros, who tagged along through Germany all the way to Amsterdam. As Fred walked the course Zandvoort, discovering World War II bunkers hidden beneath the greens' gentle slopes, the girls discovered head shops, discos and Budweiser as an "imported" beer. He decided then not to include them on his next European trip.

Rome's Circolo Golf Olgiata was the host club for the 1968 World Cup a few months later, and Fred assembled a bawdy group of writers and players, led by the U.S. team of Lee Trevino and Julius Boros. Despite their fun, Trevino earned a lot of respect as a great player and ambassador for the World Cup. He worked his galleries with his mix of Mexican-American and golf humor and demonstrated how to play, as a champion who used his hands better than anyone since Jimmy Demaret.

Charlie Price in *Golf* magazine wrote, "Trevino was sitting next to his partner on a bus from Circolo Golf Olgiata to downtown Rome and said in a voice just loud enough to be heard from the last seat in the bus to the first, 'This is a hell of a tournament. Spain sends over two Spaniards. France sends over a couple of Frenchies, and Italy uses two Eye-talians. So who plays for the United States? Julius Boros and Lee Trevino. A Lithuanian and a Mexican!'"

The Romanian Paul Tomita arrived in Rome a day late due to visa problems. Fred sent him out on a token nine holes. He shot a 39 and said, "I just wanted to see the Romanian flag raised with all the others." But they had to send a search party out for him when it got dark and he and his partner still hadn't finished the course.

"Run out and tell them there's a prize if they finish," Fred yelled to a caddie. "It may have taken them thirty-one years to get out of their country, but they should be able to get off the course in fifteen minutes."

At the winner's ceremonies, the band struck up, "The Maple Leaf Forever," as Canada's Al Balding and George Knudson took home the team cup and Balding won the International Trophy. It also meant the end of a great stand by Italy's host professionals, Roberto Bernardini and Alfonso Angelini, and the Republic of China's Lu Lian Huan and Hsieh Yung-Yo, who finished third and fourth, after the second-place U.S. team of Boros and Trevino.

When asked about his win, George Knudson of Canada replied, "You treat the World Cup like a vacation. You don't get uptight like when you got the bread going for you. And you benefit. You get respect—from the people of Canada."

By this time, the press loved going to the World Cup, especially when the inducements included group airfare and hotel. It was much like a junket, where the reporters were treated royally and as part of the party. And this year, Fred had told the press that he would arrange an audience with the Pope on Tuesday of Cup Week. "If truth be known," said Renton Laidlaw, Scotland's most popular golf writer, "some members of the press were encouraged to go that year for that reason alone."

Well, Tuesday came and went. Obviously, the Pope had something else to do. The meeting, Fred told them, would take place on Wednesday—maybe Thursday or Friday.

"The fact was we never did see the Pope," said Laidlaw, "and maybe, dare I suggest, we were never going to, but that year Fred had one of the largest press turnouts in years. He was a shrewd showman."

The following year, Fred took the 1969 World Cup to Singapore, where Orville Moody and Lee Trevino took home the Cup for the U.S., followed by Japan and Argentina. Moody had noted that the course was ideally suited for Trevino's style of play and that he would "murder" it and he did. Both he and Roberto De Vicenzo shot course-record 65s in the final round, and Trevino took the individual trophy with a course record of 275.

Of his loss to Trevino, De Vicenzo said, "Sometimes it is better to make friends than to win tournaments. Me play here for country. Me no play for money. Do I enjoy? YES! Meet good friends from other countries."

Charlie Price got the sentiment of the World Cup perfectly as he wrote in *Golf* magazine, "After the day's play, you go back to the hotel and have tea or cocktails in the lobby, European style, with Ben Hogan or Sam Snead or Peter Thomson or Gary Player or Orville Moody. Over there at another table is Suchin Suwanapnog of Thailand sharing an aperitif with Ramon Sota of Spain and Flory Van Donck of Belgium. Next to them is Alfonso Angelina of Italy with Mohamed Said Moussa of Egypt and Ossie Gartenmaier of Austria. Choo Kwan Conng of Malaysia is chatting with John Sotiropoulis of Greece, and Jiri Dvorak of Czechoslovakia. If this scene isn't goodwill internationalism at its finest, the U.N. ought to be torn down to make way for a parking lot."

Will Grimsley at the Associated Press had similar words. "The Czechs hired a defector to serve as an interpreter. The Uruguayans had trouble communicating with each other—they spoke different dialects. Christy O'Connor of Ireland teamed with Hugh Jackson of Ulster. There was never an incident. The United Nations would do well to adjourn to a golf course."

When April of 1970 arrived, Fred traveled to Augusta for the Masters. He had no official capacity at the any of the major tournaments but he always attended the April event and roomed in a private house near the course with his good friend, Gene Sarazen. The two men would spend their days on the course, renewing acquaintances, and in their evenings in the clubhouse, spinning tales and telling stories.

Fred was on a roll one night when he turned to Gene and proclaimed, in front of a handful of golf writers, "Did you realize that you are one of four men who have won all four of the world's major titles – the Masters, the U.S. Open, the British Open, and the PGA."

Gene scratched his head trying to figure out who the other three were before anyone else and named Hogan and Nicklaus. "And Palmer?" he added.

"Player," one of the golf writers called out, as if he were a student in a class.

Fred nodded, with a satisfying smile. He now had an idea. He had been thinking all week of ways to get some extra publicity at the Westchester Classic. The tour at that time was lacking a superhero. The Big Three—Palmer, Nicklaus and Player—were no longer dominating the game and the year before delivered twenty-seven different winners for thirty-five events. Frank Beard, who was the leading money winner, looked more like a banker than an athlete, and many on the tour considered tournament golf a job rather than a sport. Sarazen and Hagen had made way for Hogan and Snead who had made way for Palmer and Nicklaus, but no American had the necessary crowd appeal or yet shown any real "color."

Now, Fred had his hook for the Classic. He would invite Sarazen, Nicklaus, Player and Hogan to attend a dinner that honored the "Four Who Had Won the Four."

That next month, Fred hired Bill O'Hara, a law student and the son of a Winged Foot buddy, to work for him over the summer. Bill, along with the Harmon boys, Butch, Craig, Dick and Bill, was one of the best golfers in the New York area. When Fred asked Bill if he wanted to tag along for the summer, Bill couldn't say "yes" fast enough.

First stop on the Corcoran Tour was the 1970 U.S. Open at the Hazeltine National in Chaska, Minnesota, a new course designed by Robert Trent Jones. It was a tough course and the weather on the morning of the first round was raw and windy. "At least this bad weather in not my problem, this time," Fred said, breathing a sigh of relief as they took refuge in the clubhouse.

When the scores came in, only one player cracked par. Tony Jacklin, the 25-year-old from England and current British Open champion, smiled when he heard that his 71, one under par, was the only sub-par round. Fred smiled, too, because Tony had already accepted the invitation to play for England in the 1970 World Cup.

As Nicklaus turned in an 81, Player an 80, Trevino a 77 and Palmer a 79, Jacklin could only laugh at Mother Nature. "I quite enjoy this type of golf," Jacklin told Linc Werden of *The New York Times*. "I grew up in this kind of weather. I try not to fight the wind but use it. By that I mean when it blows right to left, I hit right and let the wind carry the ball."

The winds diminished the next day but the drama didn't. Jacklin went on to win, the first Brit to do so in fifty years, and Dave Hill, who had won three tournaments the year before and had the lowest average on the tour, spoke out about the course, even though he came in with a 69 that day.

"The man who designed the course had the blueprints upside down," Hill said. "All the greens slope away." When asked what the course "lacked," he answered, "Some eighty acres of corn and a few cows."

With Fred all excited about the Four Who Had Won the Four tournaments, he called Ben Hogan and told him that he was throwing a dinner in his honor, and with Sarazen on board, he'd invite Player and Nicklaus and honor them during the Westchester Classic. And since this would include an expense-paid trip to New York, perhaps he'd want to play in the Classic. Fred had invited Snead to play as well.

Hogan agreed and arrived in Westchester in time for a practice round. Fred sent Bill O'Hara out to play with Hogan and as they teed off, they picked up about 100 spectators per hole until a gallery of 1,000 was walking the course. Hogan went around in 69 and O'Hara in 72.

"After the match, Ben wanted to go and hit some balls, so I followed along," O'Hara said. "At the practice tee were Tom Weiskopf, Jack Nicklaus, Arnold Palmer and few others pounding out drives. Ben and I walked down to the far side of them and started hitting a few balls. I stopped at one point to get something from my bag and realized that everyone was now down at our end, including Nicklaus and Palmer, just standing there, watching Ben swing. It was an incredible moment for me."

The dinner was held that night and, in typical fashion, a good time was had by all and money was raised for charity. The next day, Fred asked O'Hara to drive Sam Snead from Westchester to Riverdale, about thirty minutes away, so Snead could shoot a Burger King commercial.

"There was a twenty-five-cent toll on the Saw Mill Parkway at the time, and all I had was a twenty-dollar bill," O'Hara recalled. "I turned to Sam and explained that I only had a twenty and asked if he had a quarter."

"Fred said all my expenses would be paid," Sam drawled, and then went on. "Why don't you go ahead and break that twenty."

"Later that day, all hell broke loose," Fred said, "when Ben Hogan received his starting time from the PGA. Two weeks shy of his 58th birthday, they gave the greatest golfer in the world, who was playing in his first tournament in years, a 7:24 a.m. starting time. I just couldn't believe it."

"At 7:24 a.m. the only spectators will be the official scorers and some birds," Ben said to Fred. "And that means I have to get up at 5:30 to get my knees in shape for that hilly course. I don't get up at that time to shut the window!"

Fred went to bat for Hogan. This wasn't his first battle with the tour officials nor the first time he dealt with the issues of starting times.

"I used to cringe every time I looked a clock in the face. You don't know what grief is until you assign players starting times. They usually want to go out early when the greens are smooth and fresh, free of foot prints and scuffs. That, of course, is impossible. I always tried to be fair but at the same time, the name stars were the ones who drew the crowds, and we needed to send them out later to give the galleries time to assemble. Why on the nights when starting times were posted, I used to lock myself in my hotel room and take the phone off the hook!"

And now, twenty years after his near-fatal and crippling car accident, Hogan, who still used a brace on leg, was being asked to tackle the hilly Westchester course at dawn when a later starting time would have benefited the gate, the sponsors, the charities, and Hogan.

"You might be surprised at the gallery, even at that hour," Fred told Ben. "You're a legend. People will show up."

And sure enough they did. Hogan teed off in front of about five hundred people, and as the morning wore on, his gallery grew to over a thousand. Ben was very pleased with the reception and tipped his hat throughout the round, but he wasn't happy and he withdrew after a disappointing round of 78. Fred wasn't too happy either.

CHAPTER 41

THE FOLLOWING YEAR, THE 1970 WORLD CUP RETURNED TO THE JOCKEY Club in Buenos Aires, where Australia's Bruce Devlin and David Graham led all the way to win a third time with a tournament team record 544—32 shots under par—for 72 holes. Roberto De Vicenzo broke the individual record with a 269 and thrilled the home crowd, who turned out en masse to cheer their national hero. This World Cup was dedicated to him because of his outstanding contribution through the years to "international goodwill through golf."

David Graham's win was especially sweet to him. He had failed by one stroke to qualify for the U.S. Tour in the PGA school only a few weeks earlier. He showed a lot of confidence and skill on this course with his 65-67-65-73. And Bruce Devlin's win was especially gratifying, as well. The Australians traveled the farthest, clocking a 55-hour trip from Sydney to Fiji to Honolulu to Los Angeles to Mexico City to Bogata to Lima to Buenos Aires. "If that isn't goodwill, I don't know what is," Bruce Devlin said.

There was quite an entourage of press at this event. Nancy and the girls had joined Fred on the trip, as did some other wives, who all seemed to enjoy the shopping and fine dining in Buenos Aires. Dinner was typically served at 10 p.m., which was just about the time everyone arrived back from the course. The elegant Jockey Club was harrowing 45-minute drive out of Buenos Aires and one thing everyone talked about was the crazy driving and traffic jams. Three of the World Cup courtesy cars crashed the first day and everyone stopped counting after that.

Dan Jenkins, in *Sports Illustrated* wrote, "Golfers of good will and unintentioned trick shots traveled 20, 30, 40 and 50 hours to reach

Buenos Aires last week so they could see America's Lee Trevino crowned 'Idiot of the Year,' discover the real steak sandwich, learn that durable old Roberto De Vicenzo plays as well in his home town as he does everywhere else, witness the emergence of a new star from Australia named David Graham, and satisfy themselves that Hitler could not have been alive in Argentina for very long because he would have been killed in a traffic accident."

Jenkins went on to say, "As a tournament, the Copa del Mundo is never going to crowd its way into the Big Four any more than the Azalea Open is, but it is always going to be a lot more worthwhile than a number of events on the U.S. tour because it does bring folks together—two-man teams from forty-three nations last week, in fact—and it stands as one of those increasingly rare things in life: a sports event where the money is irrelevant."

Dick Taylor wrote in *Golf World*, "An important custom in Argentina is reciprocating cordiality. And the gallery expected its plaudits to be acknowledged each and every time by a tip of a hat of some indication that the player and gallery were in this together. Gary Player was one who apparently understood, for he showed pleased emotions to the applause, and by the final day, he had been dubbed, 'the little darling,' of the fans. 'Find out what they're calling me, won't you,' he asked me. 'I don't know if they're being friendly or not.'"

The American team of Dave Stockton and Lee Trevino didn't fare all that well and Stockton gave Trevino the "Idiot of the Year" title. It seems Lee left all his best clubs at home and bought a new set of clubs in Australia on his way here. "I thought I'd try them out here," Trevino said. "I can't hit 'em a lick."

Stockton felt proud of his performance until he finished his round. "I walked off the 18th green and an Argentine newsman asked me how it felt to be on the worst U.S. team ever. At first I thought it was a crummy question, but then I realized he was right. It's a team, not an individual tournament."

Tony Jacklin, the 1970 reigning U.S. Open champ represented England, but didn't play that well either. He had refused to play in a previous World Cup and it was considered an open insult to his country. He never missed again. Fred signed him on his team and represented him for a short time, but he preferred to play in England and, consequently, Fred wasn't able to do much for him.

By 1971, the Westchester Classic was a "classic." It became the world's most charitable tournament because it had raised $1 million for four

Westchester hospitals. It was once the world's richest tournament, with its $250,000 in prize money, but Liggett & Myers had recently usurped that title with its $260,000 Professional Match Play Championship. "Now," Fred told a reporter for *The New York Times*, "the name of the game is money. It used to be that I'd sell a tournament to a local junior chamber of commerce for what it could do for their city. I'd tell them that the pros would leave $10,000 in their city if they put up $5,000 to host. Now, corporations can sponsor many aspects of the tournaments, from the name of it to the television rights to the incidentals. Times had changed."

And the playing field was definitely changing as far as marketing for a golf tournament. Fred now had to consider whether a corporate sponsor would drive away volunteers who worked for a competitor. He had to negotiate rights and terms, and he had to deal with lawyers, accountants, ad agencies, Harvard MBAs and women executives—none of which he particularly liked.

At home for the 19th World Cup in 1971 at the PGA National in Palm Beach Gardens, Florida, Jack Nicklaus burned up the course with a record 63 on the third round. Nicklaus and Lee Trevino won the Cup and Nicklaus set another course record with a 271 for the International Trophy.

A fifth place finish by the Korean golfers provided the tournament with another memorable moment when Fred went off to find Hahn Chang Sang of Korea to tell him the news. "You beat the Japanese team," he said, congratulating him through an interpreter.

A smile lit up Sang's face. "Good," he said, "very good!" Back through the interpreter, he said, "The Japanese and Korean people don't always hit it off, to say the least, and we Koreans didn't come here figuring to beat Nicklaus and Trevino, but we did want to beat Japan."

Nicklaus, a few years back, had agreed that the United States team should be comprised of the winners of the PGA and the U.S. Open. That was about the time he quit winning major championships and he missed the subsequent tips to Singapore and Buenos Aires. And then recently, he won the PGA and immediately became eligible for the World Cup, to be played, of all places, at the PGA National Golf Club, in Palm Beach, about five miles from his home in Lost Tree Village. "Some trip!" commented Nicklaus.

Dan Jenkins was on hand, covering the tournament again for *Sports Illustrated*. He called it one of the most fascinating, if not the most necessary, tournaments in professional golf.

"In a sport and world where money—big gobs of it—has come to mean so much, it seems sort of nice to have this one week out of the year when Nicklaus can pound out a nine-under-par 63 for the sheer pleasure of it, and when Nicklaus and Lee Trevino, our two best players of the hour, can go out and try to defend the honor of the flag against forty-five other countries with little other reward than the simple satisfaction of proving they really are the best," Jenkins wrote.

Jack, however, had his answer. "I bought $700 worth of tickets and a $300 sponsorship, so I had to win it to break even."

At first, no one wanted this tournament except the major corporations that came to sponsor it, but now at least fifteen countries a year begged to be the host. "It's the only event I know of where guys shake hands on the first tee and wish each other luck instead of asking what number ball they're playing," Fred told Dan Jenkins. "In fact, it's probably the only opportunity for the player from Singapore, who tallied an 18 on one single hole, to post his score on the same board as Jack Nicklaus."

"If I am invited next year," Trevino said, "I'll play even if I have to pay my own way. That's what I think of this tournament. Sure I could make a lot more money back home but this is something special, an honor, a chance to play for my country and meet lots of nice foreign folks."

But not everyone felt the love of this special tournament. Mark McCormack, whose huge IMG was now involved in nearly every sport and who had upped the ante on endorsements and big-dollar deals, made a public comment about the World Cup and what he thought it needed. This, of course, started a war of words between Corcoran and McCormack, and caused Fred to consider restructuring the tournament, which often balanced delicately between goodwill and small budgets.

Al Balding, of Canada, who won both the team and individual title at the World Cup in 1968, stepped up to defend the tournament's current structure and wrote this letter to the Editor of *Golf Canada* magazine.

"Mark McCormack said that the World Cup needs more prize money to make it a great event, and Fred Corcoran, the organizer, said that the players are proud to play for their countries. I would like to say that I agree completely with Mr. Corcoran. Having competed several times in the World Cup, I know of the feeling I had representing Canada. The money meant nothing. If the purse had been a great deal larger, that would not have been significant. Competing for your country is the real objective. I can honestly say that I have been proud to play for Canada, and I cannot describe how proud I was the year our team was able to win the title."

Having survived this first attack, Fred and the International Golf Association then dodged some bullets from the PGA. It had stepped in and asked the World Cup to invite the U.S. team according to their formula. It started with the winners of both the PGA and the U.S. Open, and then deferred to the previous World Cup Individual Trophy winner (if American), the leading money winner, the Masters Champion and so on. Gary Player, who was already playing for South Africa, had won the PGA and Jack Nicklaus, in an odd stroke of luck, owned all of these other titles and he opted to be excused this year.

"Because of my opportunity to play in Australia," Nicklaus wrote, "I am forced to decline playing in the Kaiser International Open and the Sahara Invitation—tour tournaments which are the backbone of the fall tour here. I feel I have an obligation to play in these two tournaments this year, as I don't think it would be fair to those here in the American tournaments nor to my family to continue on to Australia."

This letter left Fred without any players so he invited the top Americans on the money list, starting at the top and working down. He called Trevino, but his manager, Don Whittington, told Fred that Lee was out hitting balls but that after four years in the World Cup, Lee didn't want to play this year. If he had won the PGA, it would've been different.

Next on the list was Jerry Heard, the young Californian. "When I asked him, I could hear him yawning on the phone," Fred said. "He told me to ask his manager, Ed Barner, who later explained that Heard would be in Australia for two tournaments before retuning here for the Kaiser and the Sahara, and it didn't makes sense to come home for them and then go back to Australia 'again' for the World Cup in November."

George Archer was next and he also refused, with his manager citing prize money as one reason. Both Weiskopf and Jamieson had made more than $100,000 in 1972, with Weiskopf taking the $50,000 first prize in the $300,000 Jackie Gleason Inverrary Classic, and Jamieson winning the Western Open, incidentally, using a mis-matched set of clubs. Both graciously accepted Fred's invitation.

"I consider it the highlight of my career to play for my country in this tournament," said Jim Jamieson.

"If I hadn't been picked," said Weiskopf, "I would never have learned about this part of the world, and more importantly, never learned what nice people the Australians are. That's what I'll remember most—the people." You can bet that Fred was praying that Weiskopf and Jamieson would with the Open and PGA in 1973.

The tournament's return to Australia for the 1972 World Cup, played again on Royal Melbourne's famous "composite course," was indeed, a long trip. For some, the trip was even longer. Jim Kinsella of Ireland traveled fifty hours to get to Melbourne, spending ten hours stalled on the ground in a exotic port in Kuala Lumpur due to fog, a few hours flying and finally, at his hotel, with a hot bath and warm bed ahead, he got stuck alone in the elevator between floors.

Play was slow and the rounds on the first day took over six hours to complete, which brought criticism from many. The second round was abandoned due to rain that saturated all but two holes. At that point, Fred shortened the tournament to 54 holes, which brought another round of criticism. There were times when Fred felt that he just couldn't win, no matter what he did.

But the team from Taiwan, Hsieh Min Nan and Lu Liang Huan, produced the win and took the Cup for the Republic of China. The strong Japanese team of Takaaki Kono and Takashi Murakami finished second. Jim Jamieson and Tom Weiskopf finished fourth for the U.S. and Roberto De Vicenzo was in with the pack as well.

"I bet they will be dancing in the streets of Taiwan and they will declare a national holiday in our country when they hear we won the World Cup," said Lu Liang Huan. "This is the happiest day of my life. The Republic of China has done it. Our first triumph is in the World Cup. Maybe they make me president now." And they later found out, via cable, that there was indeed a big party at the Taipei Golf Club, thousands of miles away, celebrating their win.

Chapter 42

When the World Cup returned to Marbella, Spain, in 1973 and the dazzling setting at the Nueva Andalucia Club, golf was booming. Spain's own Valentin Barrios, a tall, handsome man, played well for the first two rounds, before he got "too much nerves." He told Fred that winning the World Cup would mean more to Spain than if he were to win the Masters.

"The Spanish understand something called the World," Barrios said. "The Masters they don't know about. I know about the Masters, and I would swim there to play just once, but when you call something the World, the Spanish people think it's more important."

Jack Nicklaus and Johnny Miller went on to recapture the 1973 World Cup for the U.S. with a 588, eighteen under par. Miller won the International Trophy with a score of 177, eleven under par, beating Gary Player by three strokes.

Miller admitted that he was ready for the win. "I got darned near as up for this as I do for any major championship. I didn't want to go home and hear that the good ole' USA would have won if Nicklaus had not been teamed with that dog, Miller." That dog broke the course record with a 65 on Saturday and a 67 on Sunday.

"I think when you're playing, they'll remember you for the major titles you won. I think any time you're representing your country, it's a major thing," said Miller.

When asked if he had any trouble getting excited for the event, Miller replied, "Are you kidding? My first World Cup? I want to do the very best I can for my country."

Dan Jenkins was again on the scene for *Sports Illustrated* and opened his article saying, "Once a year, the sport of golf sneaks away to some exotic place and attempts to prove that all the ills on the globe could be cured if more people hung around country club grill rooms. This ritual is known as the World Cup."

The local officials complicated this ritual a bit by distributing enormous plastic badges to be worn around the neck and placing multi-colored armbands on everyone to restrict access to various areas of the grounds and clubhouse. The attending press had a field day with that.

Jenkins wrote, "The way a World Cup manages to run itself is often more fascinating than the golf. Such was the case when I glanced out at the 18th green before the final round began and noticed that the pin was practically off the green. It seems that the Spanish television team had moved the cup from where it belonged because a tree blocked the shot between the pin and the camera. After some discussion in both English, Spanish and a four-letter word language, the pin was replaced."

The U.S. team was usually the big draw at any of these tournaments, and Fred did his best to accommodate them. So when Jack Nicklaus, as the leading scorer, complained that his starting time at the end of the field was too late, Fred moved the U.S. team to the middle. Nicklaus loved that these types of rules could be changed for his convenience and comfort.

But Fred had decided, after dealing with tournament rules for thirty-five years, and especially at the international level, that it was easier to keep it simple and please whomever he could. That's why he made it a point at the World Cup to use officials to keep score and count clubs on the first tee. He thought it was best this way because of the different customs and languages of the players. "The World Cup is not about eliminating players through mistakes but including them through goodwill," he told many. He ruled "unconventionally" on a few other incidents as well.

"What makes this tournament so different," Nicklaus said with a smile, "is that you keep your own score and then hand it to someone who doesn't speak or read your language, and he's supposed to verify it."

Sam Snead grabbed a headline in 1974, when he placed third in the PGA Championship at age 62. He had placed fourth two years before age 60. "At this rate," Fred predicted with pleasure and pride, "You'll win it in 1978 at age 66."

"Desire is the most important thing in sports," Sam once said. "I have it. Jeez, no one has more than I've got."

The 1974 World Cup was played in South America, at Lagunita Country Club in Caracas, Venezuela, a course that sat 4,000 feet in the Cordillero de Caracas Mountains and 1,000 feet up above the bustling city of Caracas. It was the custom at the World Cup that the defending champion, in this case the U.S., be paired with the host country for the first round on opening day. Fred went to the Venezuelan committee and told its members that the onus of playing with Trevino and Hale Irwin could work against the Venezuelan team of Noel Machado and Ramon Munoz. He offered to pair them with a less powerful team, but the committee thanked him and said Machado and Munoz were looking forward to playing with the U.S. team and in fact, had been practicing on the course religiously for six months. The next day, the headlines rang, "Munoz Supere a Trevino," after Munoz beat Trevino by two strokes.

Bobby Cole and Dale Hayes, representing South Africa, beat the Japanese team of Masashi Ozakoi and Isao Aoki to win the team competition. The U.S. team of Lee Trevino and Hale Irwin placed third. Cole won the International Trophy, five strokes ahead of Ozaki, with Hale Irwin placing third.

"Coming from South Africa," Dale Hayes said, "this tournament really means a lot to me. This is one of the few world sporting events we're still allowed to play in. All sporting events should be like this." South Africa still practiced apartheid in those days and many athletic events boycotted South African athletes due to increased civil-rights awareness.

Then he added, "It's more important that we win the team trophy than I win the Individual. Gary Player had played in this cup for fifteen years and he decided this year, it was time to give us younger fellows a chance. We don't want to muff it."

Fred continued to befriend the golf press, and as spring approached, Fred asked Dave Anderson from *The New York Times* and Nick Seitz, the editor at *Golf Digest*, to join him and a friend for a match at Winged Foot. Anderson and Seitz were leading by two strokes after the 15th hole when Fred invited them to stop by Club 15, his patio near the green. After insisting that his guests have two drinks each, Anderson and Seitz wobbled back to the course and lost the last three holes and the match. When Anderson wrote about that in the *Times*—without mentioning who the two players were—he received calls from twenty people, asking if he was writing about them.

Anderson wasn't sure whether Fred invented "Media Day" at the tournaments, but he confessed to enjoying a few of them. He recalled playing at the Westchester Classic where he had two birdies on two par-three holes. And even though he didn't play that well, he was awarded a prize that evening.

"I've never had two deuces in a round before or since," Anderson said, "so I guess it was worthy of a prize."

That was Fred, adhering to his favorite rule of publicity: Salute "the first, last, oldest, youngest or only" of any category and build a story around it for the press. The "best" could be argued, but the "first" or the "only" could be proved—especially with Fred as the source and keeper of the facts.

Chapter 43

In September of 1975, Fred received the top honor of his life when he was inducted into the World Golf Hall of Fame. The Hall of Fame, which he first proposed in 1940, had recently found a home in Pinehurst, and this was the second induction ceremony there. Fred, along with Joe Dey, who had served as the director of the USGA and the Commissioner of the PGA Tour, were the first non-playing members to be honored.

As Fred took his place behind the podium at the black-tie ceremony, he began with a story from the past. "I got a call from the Boston Chamber of Commerce many years ago," Fred said. "They wanted to honor me as Man of the Year at a big dinner they were planning. When they asked if I could attend, they also asked if I could bring some people with me to the big event. And I asked them, who do you have in mind?"

"'Well, the organizer said, if you could have Ted Williams on your right that would be great. And Sam Snead on your left would be fantastic. And if you could bring Babe Zaharias with you. And if Bing Crosby and Bob Hope could sit on the dais, that would be terrific." Fred paused and laughed at himself. "Well, by the time they were finished, I said, I'm going to be the only 'who's he?' at the head table!"

Appreciating his audience, Fred continued. "Golf is my game, and to it, I owe everything. It made it possible for me to go just about everywhere, do just about everything, and see just about all any man could hope to. It's been a life filled with laughter and tears, triumphs and frustrations, lights and shadows. But it's never been a bore and never really a chore. Thanks to golf, I've met kings and ex-kings, pros and con artists, old masters and young kids, those that have it, and those who never knew what 'it' was.

"But I cannot help but remember the putt that hangs, the tee shot that strays, the calculated fade that doesn't quite come off. These are all part of the game. Golf is a mirror that reflects all the flaws of human nature. Just as in life, perfection exists as a distant ideal that can be approached but never attained. A man's golf game, like his life, is a serial story of little triumphs and fumbled opportunities. The perfect game of golf would require only eighteen strokes for eighteen holes. And this is impossible. Anything short of it has to be an exercise in frustration. All that remains when the first ball is struck from the tee is to determine the degree of the frustration.

"Failure, I'm convinced, is the very essence of the game. To err is human, and far more golf championships have been lost than have been won. It's a game of retrieval, of scrambling to victory over a fairway littered with the wreckage of somebody else's dreams.

"For every tournament that was won by a bold stroke or a wild gamble that paid off, I can give you three dozen that were lost when an apparent winner took a pratfall as he was reaching out for the trophy. But that's golf, an endless story of man's failure against the unchanging and unyielding conditions of nature, punctuated by rare and thrilling instances when man, inspired and unconquerable, actually takes the game by the lapels and shakes it into submission.

"This profound discussion brings us to our starting point: Somebody wins and somebody loses—and nobody leads the cheers for the loser. I sometimes wonder if it might not be a good idea to build an annex to the Golf Hall of Fame and reserve it just for the guys like Roland Hancock and Jose Jurado and Lee Mackey who deserve a better fate than oblivion. But that's life, I guess. One guy takes three deep breaths and accepts the trophy and the other guy takes three putts and pays the caddie."

Fred was honored that year during the Westchester Classic with an on-air interview by CBS's Jack Whitaker. "Fred has a smidge of a rogue about him which keeps him eternally interesting," Jack said, adding that being with Fred was a little like being in the middle of a history book.

When Jack asked the tough question, "Who's the greatest golfer of them all?" Fred winced a little before answering.

"I'd have to say Ben Hogan," Fred said, hating to go on record like that. "And Sam Snead," he added, saying both "would have played the course." Privately, he'd add Jack Nicklaus to that short list. And of course,

Tiger Woods was due in a cradle later that year and hadn't yet made it to the first tee.

During the Whitaker interview, Fred went on to deliver a message. "I'd like to see the game speed up. We're into five-hour golf these days. The R&A and the USGA need to go back to the rule where the players don't touch the ball and putt out," he said forcefully.

Fred later explained that when tournament golf went from "open" to "invitational" golf, the intention was to get the field in before dark, not to keep people out of the competition. "But this business of pacing off the distance, taking three practice swings, and taking forever to putt should stop. The game needs to speed up."

At the age of 70, Fred was starting to slow down a little bit and reflect on his life. He recited Walter Hagen's favorite slogan many times. "Never hurry, never worry. You're here for a short visit. Be sure to stop and smell the flowers." Fred asked Nancy, who was always by his side, traveling with him, typing for him, loyally defending him at every turn, to plant more flowers at their house that summer.

By fall, it was on to the Navatanee Golf Club in Bangkok, Thailand for the 23rd World Cup in 1975. Only a year before, the course was a rice paddy, and only a week before, concrete was still being poured at the clubhouse. Players from forty-seven countries competed in the largest World Cup to date, which met on the 6,900-yard course that was receiving praises from all sides. The U.S. team of Johnny Miller and Lou Graham achieved top honors, finishing with a 554. Miller also won the International Trophy.

"I feel it's one of the greatest honors you have in golf to compete for your country," Miller said. "I was on cloud nine two years ago after helping win the cup, when we started our next tour at the Crosby. The momentum carried me through the first three tournaments." He won all three.

There's another special thing, Miller said, about playing in the World Cup for the pros. "All year round you are competing against a fellow. Then suddenly, when you're selected to play for your country, you find yourself out there, spurring him on, helping him line up the putts or discussing the best shot on the fairway. You even find yourself—for once—hoping like hell he'll drop that 50-foot birdie putt."

"After Miller won in Bangkok, the crowds went wild," Fred said. "I swear, I had never seen anything to equal this—never! I was literally swept along with them toward the official score tent in a big crush of fans. Boy Scouts formed a human chain to hold back the crowds and tournament marshals for the Thailand Golf Association eventually got everyone settled down, but it was five minutes of cheering, happy pandemonium and no one, including the players, seemed to mind when they all had to settle for par fives."

The World Cup returned to the United States in 1976 World Cup, to Mission Hills in Palm Springs, California. Jerry Pate reported that he was "tickled to death" to be representing the U.S. and said he wasn't even thinking about the individual title because this was a team competition.

"All you have to do is walk through the hotel where all the golfers are staying this week to know what this tournament is all about. Those guys from all those countries are as thrilled as they can be representing their countries. That's a feeling Americans don't get. We jump for the money," Pate admitted.

Dave Stockton told others that he felt the pressure. "The pressure is worse when you play for your country. This is a prestige event and you do not want to not only let yourself down, but you have to think about your country and partner as well."

This tournament introduced several young men to the golf world, especially one 20-year-old from Spain—Severiano Ballesteros. Also on their first trip to the U.S. were Greg Norman from Australia and Bernhard Langer from Germany. Nick Faldo would join the lineup the next year.

Ballesteros and his partner, Manuel Pinero, took home the Cup for Spain, and Ernesto Perez Acosta took home the Trophy for Mexico, marking his fifth successive win in his most successful year. The U.S. team placed second.

Winning the World Cup was always more important around the world than it was in the U.S. Seve Ballesteros, who was second to Johnny Miller in the British Open, skipped the PGA qualifying school for the 1978 tour because the dates conflicted with the World Cup.

"I play in the World Cup," he explained to Dave Anderson in the press room, "because if I play in the school, in Spain, the people don't like it."

Fred signed Ballesteros on the spot in Palm Springs and arranged for a special press conference to introduce him. He was then the Arnold Palmer of Europe, and he went on to win six tournaments in 1978, on three different continents, and then to win the British Open in 1979, 1984 and 1988, along with the Masters in 1980 and 1983. He won the World Cup in 1975, 1976 and 1977 with Manuel Pinero, and took home the International Trophy in 1976 and 1977.

The team from Brazil admitted to their own goal. They were hoping to better any previous score posted by a team from Brazil, so they could become the "lowest scorers from Brazil in any World Cup competition."

Barry Mandel, a 19-year-old amateur from Israel did his part for international relations. "I went out of my way to shake hands with the Egyptian players and the Moroccan players," Mandel said. Mandel was given a week off from his duties as an Army soldier to play in the World Cup. "This is the purpose of this tournament—international goodwill. But on the golf course, I want to beat them more than any other nation."

Dave Anderson from the *Times* played with Mandel in the Pro-Am and noticed two big guys following them on the course. He caught up to Fred later and asked who they were. "Security," Fred said plainly. "You know, it's only been a few years since Munich and I don't want anything happening on my watch, so I hired some guards."

Mandel went on to say, "For me, it's not so much playing well here but just being able to play at all. It's being able to participate in something when Israel isn't left out, as we are in so many other sports."

Arnold Palmer was the guest speaker at the Meet the Teams dinner. He admonished the players, sponsors and press to keep the tournament going upwards, to maintain its spirit, its goals.

"It's very important not only to golf but to the world," he said. It was ironic that he was speaking on Dec. 7, and nodding to the table of Japanese players, officials and guests and declaring, "Some of my good friends are here and I have many more in Japan through golf."

To Fred's surprise, some of the players dressed up for the dinner, wearing blazers, shirts and slacks of matching designs but varying with each country. The Japanese brought along sixteen changes of clothes and had the name "Japan" embroidered on the sleeves of their shirts. The Nigerians came to dinner in their flowing robes and the Scots in their kilts. The Philippine players challenged the ladies with the frills and lace of their national dress shirts.

One of Fred's favorite tributes to the World Cup came from Jim Murray of the *Los Angeles Times*, who wrote a great piece about "his" kind of golfer. It began, "Are you as sick as I am of guys shooting 68s? Had a belly full of birdies? Ever wonder how any human being anywhere in the world can ever hit a 1-iron? Had it up to here with Johnny Miller's 61s and 62s? Want to cut your throat when you see Ben Crenshaw running down those 80-foot putts?"

He continued, "Have I got a tournament for you! Guys do a little dance on the green when they are still away after they take two putts. They leave balls in the traps. Their caddies are giving them playing lessons."

Howard Clark, then Chairman of American Express, which funded the World Cup along with Time Inc., Colgate, IT&T and Pan American Airlines, paid Fred a great compliment that year when asked, of all of the World Cups, of all of the players and officials, who has he admired most?

"Freddie Corcoran! What a marvelous human being," he exclaimed without hesitation. "Business types, golfers, all were wonderful, but Freddie is one of a kind—like the Statue of Liberty."

"It's always fun to be with him," he continued. "He's a great storyteller, wonderful with the players, the media, everyone. And he's so agreeable and so successful in his way. And geez, he never has any money and is living off whatever we can scrounge for him, which isn't a hell of a lot. Oh, sure, he did well with Snead and the other players he managed, I think, but God, Freddie is nervous. He's always afraid he's going to lose his job, and this, from the man who takes care of everybody else."

CHAPTER 44

FRED WAS IN THE MIDST OF PREPARING TO TAKE THE WORLD CUP TO Manila, Philippines, with Ferdinand Marcos as the Honorary Chairman, when he fell ill that winter. It was nothing more than an episode of depression due mainly to the fact that he was getting older and many of his friends were passing away. Plus, he rarely took stock of his own accomplishments and often re-played the battles he had fought. He had millions of supporters, yet he couldn't let go of the old feuds, his own insecurities, and the shots he had missed along the way.

Plus, in the mid-1970s, there was a changing of the guard going on. Fred was getting older while the players were getting younger, and women were coming to power in business. He claimed he never understood women and often had a hard time relating to them, and he honestly couldn't figure out why any woman would want to join the "Augusta Boys' Club."

Fred was also taunted by the "agencies" like McCormack's IMG and others now on the scene. Fred was still a one-man shop, with Doris Sims still in his office and Nancy helping at home. On top of that, the World Cup was staged on a political minefield, and the PGA rarely offered its support, placing new requirements on it every few years. And Fred, now over 70, was working as hard as ever at a time when many of his friends were retiring—to play golf.

"I'm at an age where I want to talk and have people listen," he told Nancy, which was quite funny coming from the man who always had a story to tell. But perhaps, it was his audience that was changing and this new audience was looking forward, not back.

Fred checked himself into a hospital near Boston for a physical and they told him he should stay for a few weeks. Nancy was never clear as to what was going on there, and after a week, Fred called home, very despondent, saying that no one there played golf and they didn't know who he was. In fact, no one there knew who Ted Williams was.

Nancy rose to the occasion and told him to get the hell out of there. She booked a room at the Copley Plaza and invited Sarazen, Snead, Williams, Sharkey, his brothers, anyone she could get a hold of, to meet them there for a weekend party. It snapped Fred out of it and before long, it was golf season again and he was up to his old tricks.

One sunny afternoon that spring, Fred's son-in-law, Bob Mead, arrived at their home to find Fred sprawled in the grass in the back yard with a golf ball balanced carefully on his head.

"Fred! Are you okay," Bob called as he ran toward him.

Fred waved him off, trying to keep the ball in place. "Go away," he said. "My friend just hit his second shot into the yard and he's walking up the fairway now. Go in the house."

From inside, Bob heard the rowdy laughter as he saw Fred getting up and ushering the foursome to the patio for drinks at Club 15.

Fred continued his work on the World Cup and went to the U.S. Open in Oklahoma in late June. He returned home early on that Sunday, as he usually did at a major tournament, but also, because he wasn't feeling well.

After an early dinner with Nancy, he went upstairs to make some phone calls. Kings, presidents, chairmen, directors, editors, legends and superstars would have taken his call but he couldn't decide which number to dial. Something was going on in his head that he didn't quite understand. It had been 64 years since he had first picked up a golf club and now he felt like he needed to leave the locker room and go pay his caddie. But as he looked across the fairway at Winged Foot, he saw Hagen and Lema and Cobb and Babe waiting. In fact, they were holding the plane for him—the way they do only for champions. That night, Fred passed away peacefully when he suffered a stroke.

Dave Anderson of *The New York Times* happened to call the Corcoran home about an hour later. "There had been a death threat against Hubert Green who won the Open and I wondered if there had ever been another death threat at a golf tournament. If anyone would know something like that, it would be Fred," he said. "But Nancy seemed a little flustered on the phone so I let it go."

The news hit the next day. "Fred Corcoran Dies at 72" read the headline in the *New York Post* on June 23, 1977. As his friend and lawyer,

Dick Ryan, pointed out, "He died at even par."

Accolades and condolences from around the world poured in. Bob Hope and Bing Crosby called. Red Smith of *The New York Times* gave the eulogy to a packed church and Nancy gave Fred a superb send-off. So many people arrived or sent flowers to the funeral home that the staff paused to ask his daughter, "Who was this guy?"

"He's the guy who taught the world how to put on golf tournaments," Judy said, "and he was the first, last, youngest, oldest and only man to promote golf the way he did."

With a permanent home in the World Golf Hall of Fame and as a winner of every golf award invented by 1977, Fred Corcoran will be remembered most as the man who sold the world on golf, taking tournament golf from a minor curiosity to a major business, and putting it on the international stage and the front page of the sports section.

"Fred was a salesman, alright," said Nick Seitz, the long-time editor of *Golf Digest.* "But he was not a hard-sell guy. He'd lead you delightfully into a story and before you knew it, you'd run head on into whatever he wanted you to know. And you didn't mind, because he was so entertaining and his stories were always true."

When Fred Corcoran left golf that day, with him went a style of doing business that blossomed from creative minds on a rainy day, meeting in the locker room and at the bar. Today's writers, players and agents all have places to go and work to catch up on. Few people have time to hang around listening to the stories of a master seanachie and the ideas of a promotional champion.

Fred's wife Nancy remained loyal to him for another twenty years at their home bordering on Winged Foot until she joined him "wherever Walter Hagen went."

BIBLIOGRAPHY

Arledge, Roone. Roone: A Memoir (New York: Harper Collins, 2003).

Barkow, Al and Sarazen, Mary Ann. Gene Sarazen and Shell's Wonderful World of Golf (Ann Arbor: Clock Tower Press, 2003).

Barkow, Al. Gettin' to the Dance Floor: An Oral History of American Golf (New York: Atheneum, 1986).

Barkow, Al. Sam: The One and Only (Ann Arbor: The Sports Media Group, 2005).

Cataneo, David. I Remember Ted Williams: Anecdotes and Memories of Baseball's Splendid Splinter by the Players and People Who Knew Him (Nashville: Cumberland House Publishing, 2002).

Cayleff, Susan E. Babe Didrikson: The Greatest All-Sport Athlete of All Time (Berkeley: Conari Press, 1995).

Cayleff, Susan E. Babe: The Life and Legend of Babe Didrikson Zaharias (Urbana: University of Illinois Press, 1996).

Chambers, Marcia. The Unplayable Lie: The Untold Story of Women and Discrimination in American Golf (New York: Pocket Books, 1995).

Clavin, Tom. Sir Walter: Walter Hagen and the Invention of Professional Golf (New York: Simon & Schuster, 2005).

Corcoran, Fred with Harvey Bud. Unplayable Lies: The Story of Golf's Most Successful Impresario (New York: Duell, Sloan and Pearce, 1965).

Dawidoff, Nicholas. The Catcher Was a Spy: The Mysterious Life of Moe Berg (New York: Vintage, 1995).

Diaz, Jaime, Rosaforte, Tim, and Davis, Martin. The World Golf Hall of Fame 1998 (Greenwich: The American Golfer, Inc. 1998).

Dodson, James. Ben Hogan, An American Life (New York: Random House, 2004).

Frost, Mark. The Greatest Game Ever Played: Harry Vardon, Francis Ouimet, and the Birth of Modern Golf (New York: Hyperion, 2002).

Frost, Mark. The Match: The Day the Game of Golf Changed Forever (New York: Hyperion, 2007).

Gogolak, Peter with Carter, Joseph. Nothing to Kick About: The Autobiography of a Modern Immigrant (New York: Dodd, Mead & Company, 1973).

BIBLIOGRAPHY

Hagen, Walter. The Walter Hagen Story: I Never Wanted to Be a Millionaire –
I Just Wanted to Live Like One (New York: Simon and Schuster, 1956).

Halberstram, David. The Summer of '49 (New York: HarperCollins, 1989).

Harmon, Claude "Butch" Harmon, Jr. The Pro: Lessons About Golf and Life
from My Father, Claude Harmon, Sr. (New York: Three Rivers Press, 2006).

Hope, Bob. I Never Left Home (New York: Simon And Schuster, 1944).

Jerris, Rand. Golf Golden Age: Robert T. Jones, Jr. and the Legendary Players
of the'10s, '20s, and '30s (National Geographic for the USGA).

Lema, Tony with Brown, Gwilym S. Golfer's Gold: An Inside View of the Pro
Tour (New York: Little Brown, 1964).

Lema, Tony with Harvey, Bud. Champagne Tony's Golf Tips (New York:
McGraw-Hill, 1966).

McDonald Mark and Milne, George. Cases in Sports Marketing (Sudbury:
Jones and Bartlett Publishers, 1999).

McGrath, Charles, McCormic, David and Garrity, John. The Ultimate Golf
Book: A History and a Celebration of the World's Greatest Game (New York:
Houghton Mifflin, 2002).

McKay, Jim. My Wide World (New York: MacMillan, 1973).

O'Connor, Ian. Arnie & Jack: Palmer, Nicklaus, and Golf's Greatest Rivalry
(New York: Houghton Mifflin, 2008).

Pepper, George and the Editors of Golf Magazine. Golf in America: The First
100 Years (New York: Abradale Press Harry N. Abrams Inc., 1988).

Sarazen, Gene with Wind, Herbert Warren. Thirty Years of Championship Golf
(Unknown: Ailsa, Inc. 1987).

Snead, Sam with Pirozzolo, Fran. The Game I Love: Wisdom, Insight, and
Instruction From Golf's Greatest Player (New York: Ballentine Books, 1997).

Stanton, Tom. Ty and the Babe: Baseball's Fiercest Rivals: A Surprising Friendship
and the 1941 Has-Beens Golf Championship (New York: Thomas Dunne
Books, 2007).

Strege, John. When the War Played Through: Golf During World War II
(New York: Gotham, 2005).

Various. 20th Century Golf Chronicle (Lincolonwood: Publications International, 1998)

Venturi, Ken. Getting Up & Down: My 60 Years in Golf (Chicago: Triumph
Books, 2004).

Williams, Ted with Underwood, John. My Turn at Bat. The Story of My Life
(New York: Simon & Schuster Fireside, 1969, 1988).

Zaharias, Babe Didrikson with Paxton, Harry. This Life I've Led: My Autobiography
(New York: Dell, 1955).

INDEX

INDEX

Index

INDEX